The Truths of Monsters

CRITICAL EXPLORATIONS IN SCIENCE FICTION AND FANTASY
(a series edited by Donald E. Palumbo and C.W. Sullivan III)

Earlier Works: www.mcfarlandpub.com

Recent Works: 55 *Gender and the Quest in British Science Fiction Television: An Analysis of* Doctor Who, Blake's 7, Red Dwarf *and* Torchwood (Tom Powers, 2016)

56 *Saving the World Through Science Fiction: James Gunn, Writer, Teacher and Scholar* (Michael R. Page, 2017)

57 *Wells Meets Deleuze: The Scientific Romances Reconsidered* (Michael Starr, 2017)

58 *Science Fiction and Futurism: Their Terms and Ideas* (Ace G. Pilkington, 2017)

59 *Science Fiction in Classic Rock: Musical Explorations of Space, Technology and the Imagination, 1967–1982* (Robert McParland, 2017)

60 *Patricia A. McKillip and the Art of Fantasy World-Building* (Audrey Isabel Taylor, 2017)

61 *The Fabulous Journeys of Alice and Pinocchio: Exploring Their Parallel Worlds* (Laura Tosi with Peter Hunt, 2018)

62 *A* Dune *Companion: Characters, Places and Terms in Frank Herbert's Original Six Novels* (Donald E. Palumbo, 2018)

63 *Fantasy Literature and Christianity: A Study of the Mistborn, Coldfire, Fionavar Tapestry and Chronicles of Thomas Covenant Series* (Weronika Łaszkiewicz, 2018)

64 *The British Comic Invasion: Alan Moore, Warren Ellis, Grant Morrison and the Evolution of the American Style* (Jochen Ecke, 2019)

65 *The Archive Incarnate: The Embodiment and Transmission of Knowledge in Science Fiction* (Joseph Hurtgen, 2018)

66 *Women's Space: Essays on Female Characters in the 21st Century Science Fiction Western* (ed. Melanie A. Marotta, 2019)

67 *"Hailing frequencies open": Communication in* Star Trek: The Next Generation (Thomas D. Parham III, 2019)

68 *The Global Vampire: Essays on the Undead in Popular Culture Around the World* (ed. Cait Coker, 2019)

69 *Philip K. Dick: Essays of the Here and Now* (ed. David Sandner, 2019)

70 *Michael Bishop and the Persistence of Wonder: A Critical Study of the Writings* (Joe Sanders, 2020)

71 *Caitlín R. Kiernan: A Critical Study of Her Dark Fiction* (James Goho, 2020)

72 *In* Frankenstein's *Wake: Mary Shelley, Morality and Science Fiction* (Alison Bedford, 2020)

73 *The Fortean Influence on Science Fiction: Charles Fort and the Evolution of the Genre* (Tanner F. Boyle, 2020)

74 *Arab and Muslim Science Fiction* (Hosan Elzembely and Emad El-Din Aysha, 2020)

75 *The Mythopoeic Code of Tolkien: A Christian Platonic Reading of the Legendarium* (Jyrki Korpua, 2021)

76 *The Truth of Monsters: Coming of Age with Fantastic Media* (Ildikó Limpár, 2021)

The Truths of Monsters
Coming of Age with Fantastic Media

Ildikó Limpár

Critical Explorations in
Science Fiction and Fantasy, 76
Series Editors Donald E. Palumbo *and* C.W. Sullivan III

McFarland & Company, Inc., Publishers
Jefferson, North Carolina

This book has undergone peer review.

ISBN (print) 978-1-4766-8348-5
ISBN (ebook) 978-1-4766-4374-8

LIBRARY OF CONGRESS AND BRITISH LIBRARY
CATALOGUING DATA ARE AVAILABLE

Library of Congress Control Number 2021005783

© 2021 Ildikó Limpár. All rights reserved

No part of this book may be reproduced or transmitted in any form or by any means, electronic or mechanical, including photocopying or recording, or by any information storage and retrieval system, without permission in writing from the publisher.

Front cover illustration by Tithi Luadthong (Shutterstock)

Printed in the United States of America

*McFarland & Company, Inc., Publishers
Box 611, Jefferson, North Carolina 28640
www.mcfarlandpub.com*

Table of Contents

Acknowledgments vi

Introduction: Monsters Roaming the Space of Coming of Age 1

Part I—Monstrous Family Matters

1. The Monstrous Friend and Lover: *Buffy the Vampire Slayer* and Stephenie Meyer's *Twilight* Saga — 16
2. Apocalyptic Monsters in Need of a Family: Daryl Gregory's *Raising Stony Mayhall* and M.R. Carey's *The Girl with All the Gifts* — 36
3. The Rebellious Child: Jon Skovron's *Man Made Boy* and Sarah Maria Griffin's *Spare and Found Parts* — 58
4. Oppressed Daughters and Oppressing Fathers: Theodora Goss's *The Extraordinary Adventures of the Athena Club* Series — 81

Part II—The Monstrous Wilderness of the Teenage Mind

5. Dangerous and Safe Spaces: Neil Gaiman's *The Graveyard Book* and *Coraline* — 100
6. Destructive and Healing Psychic Landscape: Siobhan Dowd and Patrick Ness's *A Monster Calls* — 121

7. Spaces of Escape for the Abused: Seanan McGuire's *Wayward Children* Series   140

Part III—Inhuman(e) Frontiers of Growing Up

8. Alien New World Wilderness: Patrick Ness's *Chaos Walking* Trilogy   160

9. "Muttated" New World Garden: *The Hunger Games* Trilogy   181

10. Frankensteinian Wild West for Adults Growing Up: HBO's *Westworld*   197

Conclusion   219

Chapter Notes   225

Works Cited   235

Index   247

Acknowledgments

I would like to thank Pázmány Péter Catholic University for granting me a sabbatical semester in the fall of 2018, during which I could write most chapters of this book, as well as providing me the opportunity to teach several of the novels I write about. Discussing these texts on a regular basis helped me crystallize what interests me the most about monsters and prompted me to turn my research into a focused academic project. I am also thankful for my university's financial support for the various international conferences that allowed me to discuss and improve my chapters based on the feedback and the knowledge I received.

Heartfelt thanks to Donald E. Morse at the University of Debrecen, who encouraged me to write this book, and Ibis Gómez-Vega at Northern Illinois University, who not only gave me emotional support during writing, but also generously volunteered to read through my manuscript and provide suggestions. I am equally indebted to fantasy writer and Monster Studies scholar Theodora Goss at Boston University, who was very kind to discuss my research on various monsters with me, and who is always ready for a friendly and scholarly chat about the fantastic in the arts.

I work in a very supportive academic environment, and thus I would like to express my great thanks to my colleagues in our Research Group for Popular Culture and the Fantastic in English Speaking Countries: Károly Pintér, Vera Benczik, Anikó Sohár and Kinga Földváry, all learned scholars and great friends, who continuously inspire me to venture beyond borders guarded by the most fascinating monsters.

Last, but not least, great thanks to my family for being patient with me and making my life less monstrous.

Introduction
Monsters Roaming the Space of Coming of Age

Although literary monsters have occupied the space of fiction ever since we have been writing and reading literature, only a few decades ago did scholars start to focus on the specific issue of monsters and monstrosity, feeling the need to provide a theoretical framework that would allow systematic study in the field. Research in the Gothic and, relatedly, in psychoanalysis is the foundation for modern monster theory. As a result, early interpretations of the literary monster focused primarily on the psychoanalytical aspects of the monster as metaphor, making use of especially Sigmund Freud's concept of the uncanny, Carl Gustav Jung's theory of archetypes and the notion of the abject as explained by Julia Kristeva. This psychoanalytical approach was completed and turned into a more comprehensive theory in 1996, when Jeffrey Jerome Cohen looked into the cultural signification of monsters, extending Foucault's idea that each age has its "privileged forms of monsters" (*Abnormal* 66), since monstrosity is constructed by society's norms defined by its laws. With Cohen's openly Foucauldian "Monster Culture (Seven Theses)," the study of monsters received a new boost: Cohen gave a name to the discipline (Weinstock, "Introduction" 29) and provided a firm reference point for scholars in the field. Due to the impact of this concise essay on the defining characteristics of monsters, the cultural-historical interpretations of the monstrous have come into the foreground. This approach has prompted the work of important scholars, such as Stephen T. Asma, who in his monograph *On Monsters: An Unnatural History of Our Worst Fears* (2009) mapped how the concept of monster has evolved in the Western imagination; and this is also the approach Marina Levina and Diem-My T. Bui embrace in their Introduction to *Monster Culture in the 21st Century* (2013), where the authors offer a theoretical framework combining three approaches that may effectively be used in monster scholarship: the psychoanalytical, the representational, which is "historically conditioned" (5), and the ontological. Levina and Bui's claim that "monster narratives ... offer a space where society can safely represent and address anxieties of its time" (1) clearly echoes Cohen's first thesis on monsters, which considers the monster's body as the "embodiment of a certain cultural moment—of a time, a feeling, and a place," that is, a "cultural body" ("Monster" 4).

In the past two and half decades, Monster Studies has established itself as a very diverse and dynamically developing branch of literary scholarship that fruitfully aligns with various disciplines from Social Sciences through Gothic Studies to Film Studies, as, for instance, the recently published *The Monster Theory Reader* (2020), edited by Jeffrey Andrew Weinstock, demonstrates. Researchers of the Gothic and Horror have long been examining the relationship between child characters and the monstrous, but their focus has mostly been on the representation of the evil and thus monstrous child,[1] or innocent children as the antithesis to and ultimate victims of the monstrous, while they have paid little attention to the ubiquitous presence of the monstrous and the specific roles of monsters in fantasies intended for adolescent readership. The present book, therefore, aims to start filling this gap in the study of the monstrous. Monsters seem to be perfect tools for writing about various aspects of coming of age, which is a major theme of adolescent literature. The reason for this connection between metaphorical monstrosity and youth literature, which discusses the problematics of growing up, lies in the common and related characteristics of the two concepts.

First of all, several of the monster's functions, as Cohen argues, link with understanding culture ("Monster" 4), and teenagers, in their years of maturation into adulthood, need first and foremost to acquire knowledge about the culture and society they are required to integrate into. This process is characterized by the inseparable coexistence of the desire to explore adulthood and the anxiety of meeting the unknown and leaving childhood safety. Between these familiar and unfamiliar territories lie the borders that mark the end of the safe zone, and these borders, in monster literature, are embodied by the monster itself.

Border crossings—however personal they might seem from the characters' perspective—are culturally embedded endeavors. As the monster is a *"cultural category"* (Asma 13; italics in the original), it communicates the specific fears and desires emerging from cultural context: the monstrous body exhibits the borders that are not to be crossed (even if there exists a dark desire to transgress) (Cohen, "Monster" 17). Due to this function, the monster provides knowledge concerning the culture to which it belongs: it unveils what that culture holds normative and different, what it considers as possible and safe as opposed to unacceptable and therefore dangerous (12). And since the monster's body is the marker of this very borderline, the monster belongs to at least two spheres whereas it does not fully belong to any; it is a hybrid creature, or, as Noël Carroll explains, an impure entity that is "categorically interstitial, categorically contradictory, categorically incomplete, or formless" (55).

From a mythical and cultural perspective, the monster constitutes a specific borderline: "the imaginary region that lies between being and non-being, presence and absence" (Boon, "Ontological" 33), but this liminal space is defined from a perspective that privileges human existence over any kind of life form.[2] The monster, derived from the Latin base word *monstrare* ("to demonstrate") and *monēre* (to warn) is created to demonstrate—or, differently put, embody—the perceivable difference between being human and being Other. By doing so, the monster warns us against what is uncategorizable and thus labeled as Other. Yet otherness is a theme that calls to teenagers in intricate manners. Adolescents feel other than children and other than adults; they often feel that they are simply Others in an environment that they do not fit into. Their coming of age is a process of leaving this kind of disturbing otherness, and by doing so, joining human society with a full membership. In order to do so, they must confront their monsters, and through understanding differences they must fight whatever constitutes their otherness. The monster indicates an "other" form of existence and shows the anxieties that belong to the nevertheless desired form of existence.

Adolescents occupy a liminal space between childhood and adulthood, experiencing, actually, a fluid state in which they are drawn back to childhood while already halfway into adulthood; accordingly, the novels marketed for them apply the strategy of confronting this hybridity. Young Adult fiction addresses the young and the adult, and purposefully inquires about the borderline between these two phases of identity development. But whatever the narrow focus within the coming of age theme is, the conflicts that the protagonists need to win (or lose) are all concerned with power relations, as Roberta Seelinger Trites claims (*Disturbing* x). The promise of metamorphosis from a powerless identity (a child) into an individual who has been bestowed with power by society (an adult) is the grand narrative of all youth fiction even if many of the novels present only a partial transformation, a process that leads to moments of revelation or a turning point in one's character development. This is the context in which I use the contested term coming of age narrative, aligning my position with Kenneth Millard's, who argues that "the specific age of a fictional character is ... perhaps not the best guide to that teleological process which is the proper focus of the coming-of-age narrative" (5). Agreeing with this observation and that adulthood is also a culture-related term (5), I prefer using coming of age in the broad sense of the word,[3] focusing on turning points in the examined characters' stories of growth and occasionally looking beyond the corpus we may conveniently label as Young Adult literature.

Youth literature, as a literature of power relations, is deeply embedded in the psychological process of abjecting, as Karen Coats explains (*Looking* 138). Her observations are based on Kristeva's ideas on social abjection—the process whereby society purifies itself of what it deems unclean—as well as the notion that group identity is a defining experience for adolescents and therefore socially abject figures are of central importance in fiction written for young readers (138). As the monster is a manifestation of abjection, it naturally fits in these discourses and thus may effectively demonstrate (as it should) various challenges in coming-of-age narratives.

Maturation, or coming of age, then, is an omnipresent topic in youth literature; there has been, however, a paradigm shift in how fiction for adolescents presents this process. The part of this corpus that we label now as Young Adult fiction,[4] a product of postmodernism, as Seelinger Trites claims, disposed of the notion that the individual may be treated independently of the social environment that (s)he is part of (*Disturbing* 16). As a result, while modernism linked the idea of maturation with the revelation that society launches an attack on the individual, and thus rejecting society is the sure sign of coming of age, "the narrative of growth in postmodernism … becomes constituted as an acceptance of one's cultural habitat" (18). This change in the evaluation of maturity has brought about a fundamental paradox of Young Adult fiction: however much Young Adult literature seems to be about rebellion and transgression (as the period of adolescence itself is about trying to cross prohibited borderlines), the novels fulfill the role of educating the reader about the social order that (s)he will have to accept as a mature, adult person (34).[5] How monsters in contemporary fantasy may accentuate this dimension of coming of age and provide insight into this amorphous state of existence that we call adolescence is the focus of this book.

The Truths of Monsters, naturally, mostly examines stories—novels and films—of the fantastic that we put under the rubric of Young Adult, but it does not exclusively rely on that material. The chapters focus on the theme, and not on the genre; and while the theme of coming of age indeed dominates fiction for Young Adults, occasional divergence from that corpus when selecting works for case studies has proven useful, as this branching out underscores the connection between coming-of-age literature written for adolescents and stories of coming of age targeting an adult audience through their use of the monstrous, while providing variations by emphasizing alternative sub-themes.

As monsters reflect culture, I aimed at selecting recent texts to be examined: all the narratives that I have included come from the 21st century, and most of them come from the 2010s. The notable exception is *Buffy, the Vampire Slayer*, which premiered a few years before the millennium, in 1997, but ran until 2003. This highly acclaimed TV show quickly achieved cult status and has prompted the renaissance of vampire romance narratives as well as supernatural mystery narratives for a teen audience. *Buffy* has influenced popular culture to a great extent by its complex, thought-provoking approach to monstrosity and heroism; therefore, I found it an apt starting point for my research and my manuscript. About half of the corpus I analyze in detail come from the widely-known works of popular culture that often find a way into college or university curriculum; the other half consists of even more recent works that are highly revealing concerning how we think about monstrosity and their promises at the moment (in 2021) and thus may easily be incorporated into higher education curricula. These works give us a glimpse into the multitude of monster narratives that utilize various concepts of the monstrous to reflect on our need to better understand the world—a key component in one's individual process of coming of age as well as in the grand narrative of mankind's coming of age.

Monster narratives now flood the market, and it is beyond the limitations of one book to give an all-encompassing guide to the varieties that they represent; therefore, I limited my focus in a manner that allowed me to accentuate trends yet go into details and write of nuances and differences in the approaches that the narratives apply. My strategy in selecting texts for analysis was prompted by the desire to map three big categories in which the strong presence of monstrosity opens doors to reconsidering our contemporary attitudes to otherness and their implications. The first section includes narratives in which well-known, classical revenants, such as vampires, zombies and Frankensteinian monsters, try to make themselves at home in our contemporary world or in a not too distant future. These monsters are considered in relation to their classic predecessors and were chosen because of their family context without which they are impossible to interpret. In these chapters the protagonists are monsters or/and characters that feel aligned with the monsters they encounter or create; as a result, these works all tackle the problems of maturation where growing up manifests as a process in which understanding one's relation to monstrosity defines the future for the character—and sometimes for the whole world. The other two sections apply a somewhat broader approach to the terms monstrous and monstrosity, as they focus on how monsters have an influence on the space they inhabit and how that space becomes, as a result, symbolic in terms of coming of age. Part II is the most reliant on the psychoanalytical approach, as it includes the analyses of works where the focus is on the mental landscape, whose monsters are indicative of the phase of maturation that the character who encounters the monsters goes through. Both Part I and Part II comment on the importance of the family providing a safe home for the adolescent protagonist. While most of the examined texts seem to adhere to the idea promoted by children's literature that home (provided by adults) is a safe haven to return to after facing various perils (Nodelman 224), youth literature in which the protagonists are adolescents often questions the idea that a safe home is indeed provided by adults/parents and at times explores one's home as a specifically dangerous place. The last section (Part III) reinterprets the concept of home as a New World that mankind strives to make his home. The chapters scrutinize physical, if imaginary places and look at works that constitute a special category, in which growing up is linked with New World narratives and thus the space dominated by monsters is a symbolic reflection on history and future. Characters who must mature in such a monstrous space need to cope with monstrosity as an inherent quality of the world that stems from mankind's immature or evil attitude to nature; the characters' way of coping, therefore, is as much an individual survival as a contemplation concerning what humanity may or should do for survival.

Part I, "Monstrous Family Matters," is comprised of four chapters on how different types of monsters are used within family narratives to reveal the nature of the challenges coming of age holds for protagonists in terms of interpersonal relationships. This section looks at variations of three classical monster types that have gone through considerable transformation in the past few decades: the vampire, the zombie, and the man-made monster.

When we think of Young Adult fiction with monsters, the genre of supernatural romance, and specifically Stephenie Meyer's *Twilight* saga (2005–2008) surfaces usually as a prime example. The teenage romance between a human girl and the "good vampire," however, is not Meyer's invention. *Buffy the Vampire Slayer*, a television show that ran from 1997 to 2003 in the United States, explored the idea of such a relationship in depth before the Cullens appeared on the literary field. The first chapter in Part I, "The Monstrous Friend and Lover," therefore, focuses on the popular character of the humanized vampire in these two teenage romances, examining the marked differences in how the seemingly same type of monster—the sympathetic vampire—may generate distinctively different paths in the female protagonists' coming of age. While in both works the monster's body displays the borderline between the human and the monstrous, the live and the (un)dead, the temporal and the eternal, the context of the two relationships define what the responsibilities that relate to coming of age mean. Buffy's mythical context renders her coming of age as a spiritual journey tied with the fate of the universe; Bella's context, in contrast, substitutes the mythical depth with what gives power in a contemporary western reality: appearance and what assures good appearance (beauty and money, emphatically). In both fictions, the concept of the family is reinterpreted by the protagonists, both yearning for an alternative family-like company to complement their single-parent family unit. Yet, similar as the two female characters' family backgrounds are with divorced parents, the fact that Buffy has a company of friends—among them a strong father figure in the person of Giles, her Watcher who anchors her to her "job" of fighting evil forces—allows her to maintain a realistic understanding of her vampire lover Angel's complex nature. Bella, however, is on her own when she meets the supernatural in her life, and she must base her decisions on very limited information about the monstrous. Therefore, what turns out to be the deepest fear in *Buffy*—getting transformed into a vampire—becomes the utmost desire in *Twilight*, and these anxieties and desires address the question of what it means to be human and what gives power in the world these girls exist in.

After the encounter of the vampire friend and lover, the analysis turns towards the other end of the undead category of monsters, the zombie. By the nature of their existence, zombies are rarely associated with growth, maturation, or character development; in fact, they generally stand for disintegration and fall in a social context. Deeply rooted in the tradition that interprets zombies as the signifiers of the human condition bound by real or metaphorical slavery, the zombie of contemporary fiction has become one of the most expressive metaphors for the degenerative effects that consumer society has on the individual. However, similarly to the paradigm shift in the signification of the vampire, which emerged with the introduction of the sympathetic, or "I-zombie," zombie fiction has seen a new boost by the appearance of the humanized zombie. This is the type of zombie that may uncover the strange, painful, and unexpected dimension of coming of age, too. As the chapter "Apocalyptic Monsters in Need of a Family" discusses, both Daryl Gregory and M.R. Carey use the zombie for expressing a growth that is incredible and that is, nevertheless made possible by the family. In

Raising Stony Mayhall, the traditional family is extended by a zombie baby, who miraculously becomes capable of growth. His experience of maturation emphasizes a limitation that comes with his "special condition"; his growth, nevertheless, highlights the possibility of unconventional development. Zombie coming of age, in this novel, symbolizes hope for the disprivileged, but it also offers hope for society at large. Stony's existence redefines the concept of love, ableness, and family for all the other family members, and the concept of disintegration for a larger community. A similar idea is detectable in M.R. Carey's *The Girl with All the Gifts.* The dystopian setting in this fiction, too, contrasts the idea of growth and development that we associate with coming of age, but one of the underlying arguments that the novel presents is that development has to be interpreted in context, so it depends on the perspective. From the viewpoint of humanity as we know it at present, Melanie, the protagonist zombie girl, stands for the fall of the society and becomes a symbol associated with apocalypse. The story, however, argues that adaptation is the key to survival in any circumstance and that the special, humanized zombie may transform into an emblem of adaptiveness. Within the coming of age narrative, this interpretation sees the individual growth that manifests in "all the gifts" as a successful attempt at fighting the limitations that seemed to have doomed the character irreversibly. Yet as even the "I-zombie" character is inseparable from the social context, the monster is strangely presented as the character who learns to become able to educate society. The gifts that this special zombie character possesses is both the result of her origin, that is, family (of a special type, as we learn), and the cause of developing a strong sense of what family means in this dystopian environment. Coming of age is, therefore, a narrative of taking responsibility of the family that Melanie recognizes and chooses as her own, as well as of the future that she can imagine as possible and as good as it may get.

The need for taking responsibility is a well-known theme in monster literature. *Frankenstein* by Mary Shelley is the epitome of fantastic fiction that explores the hazardous consequences of hubris, and thereby the responsibility tied to the act of creation. Variations of the *Frankenstein*-theme keep the focus on the coming of age of creator and creature alike, underscoring the role of transgression during the maturation period. The chapter titled "The Rebellious Child" first discusses Jon Skovron's *Man Made Boy*, examining the titular character Boy in his role of a creator and a creature, as he is the created (that is, assembled) son of Frankenstein's Monster and his Bride, and the inventor of a rapidly evolving AI. Boy's dual position is indicated by his monstrous, cyborg-like body, a combination of the human and the machine, driven by the mixture of science and magic and also the occasional hybridity of the text that presents his speech. His existence is so hard to categorize that he is a misfit in both the community of magical creatures, where he lives, and the human world, where he wishes to belong. As he seems to exhibit the kind of hubris that his father's creator did and as his behavior betrays the kind of irresponsibility that Frankenstein's behavior exhibited, his actions appear to recreate Frankenstein's story; yet his process of maturation takes a different turn because he is aware of the original story and, in the end, he is able to better respond to his own mistaken actions not only in the context of his Frankensteinian existence but also in the context of family, community and romance. The other novel that this chapter looks at is Sarah Maria Griffin's Young Adult novel *Spare and Found Parts*, which, unconventionally, has a female protagonist and links the theme of isolation with the main character's desire to create and to prove worthy of the family heritage. As the story unfolds, we learn that the family heritage is, actually, very different from what the protagonist Nell imagined. The girl's new knowledge about how her father plagiarized his wife's research places the theme of creative work in the context of gender-biased power relations and opens up the discussion for further themes, such as the challenging relationship between scientific interest and emotional, human existence. Nell's struggles with her family and the sense of being different both in body and in soul allow us to see her as a miniature island of her own, representing the post-apocalyptic setting of the story, an island deliberately detached from the rest of the world. The novel emphasizes the need for communication through the act of creation and also highlights the necessity to learn from past mistakes to observe a clear divide between the human and the monstrous and to create a safe space for scientific and technological evolution instead of choosing the path of de-evolution or hubris-driven transgressions in the field of experimental research.

The last chapter in Part I, "Oppressed Daughters and Oppressing Fathers," looks at the Frankenstein theme from a different angle. Theodora Goss's *The Extraordinary Adventures of the Athena Club* series, set in Victorian England, expands the Frankenstein universe by giving voice to the (familiar and the previously unmentioned) daughter characters of the most famous 19th century literary ("mad") scientist characters. The group of monstrous gentlewomen form an untraditional family based on sisterhood created by their common experience: monstrosity. Coming of age for all of them is an issue of how to deal with monstrosity—how to deal with the fact of having a father whose utmost ambition was to experiment on his own daughter. Gender works as a significant factor in the girls' experiences: their otherness is the result of gender-biased science, as girls were experimented on and considered better subjects of gene manipulation than male patients; furthermore, the limitations imposed by their femaleness are often paralleled with limitations resulting from their monstrosity. The monstrous female body is thus a signifier of scientific transgression as well as a consensus of the historical period about the inferiority of women. Coming of age for these ladies, therefore, springs from a repeated transgression of not only the borderline that is imagined between the monster and the human but also the borderline set by cultural conventions between the female and the male genders. Taking responsibility to a certain extent appears as a counter-reaction to the irresponsibility of the fathers, which also affects how the story is conveyed: the genre becomes mystery adventure novel, as the need to take responsibility for the fathers' scientific and moral transgressions generates investigations; in addition, the narrative form not only reflects the central theme of hybridity, but through subversion it also points to the most important cultural convention that led to the female protagonists' traumas: that of silencing women.

Part II is comprised of three studies in which the monstrous signifies the psychic dimension of the troublesome aspects of the maturation process. The chapters in "The Monstrous Wilderness of the Teenage Mind," accordingly, heavily rely on the psychoanalytical approach in exploring manifestations of the monstrous as representations of coping mechanisms, while also utilizing the representational and the ontological approach as well. The chapters demonstrate the alterations in how the monsters in the presented mental landscapes function to expose the inner conflicts of the protagonists: Gaiman's *The Graveyard Book* and *Coraline* reflect on the "average" experience of growing up presented in very peculiar clothing; Seanan McGuire's *Wayward Children* series focuses on deviant adolescence and the traumatic dimension of otherness; and finally, Patrick Ness's *A Monster Calls* links coming of age to the trauma of losing one's parent at an early age.

"Dangerous and Safe Spaces" looks at two novels written by Neil Gaiman for a younger audience, *The Graveyard Book* and *Coraline*, which present sharp contrasts between the real world and an otherworld. An examination of the monstrous in these novels discloses the manifold signification monsters may take in the context of coming of age. In *Coraline* the monstrous pretends to be safe at first and then reveals its horrific aspects to signal the frightening adventure of the maturation process, whereas *The Graveyard Book* presents the seemingly hideous space of the cemetery inhabited by ghosts and monsters as a safe space of childhood, untouchable by reality, which, nevertheless, has to be left in the end to face life/adulthood. In both fictions the relationship with a strong parental figure stands in the center: the archetypal beldam in *Coraline* provides a monstrous double for the girl's mother, which allows the protagonist to come to terms with her altered place in the family and consequently in society, while Silas the vampire in *The Graveyard Book* is a strictly symbolic parent whose monstrous body represents various borderlines, including the ones between childhood and adulthood, as well as life and death, providing this way a philosophical dimension of what it means to grow up.

"Destructive and Healing Psychic Landscape" on Patrick Ness's *A Monster Calls* also places emphasis on the mental journey, this time as repeated encounters with the fantastic wild—a tree monster. The chapter interprets the manifestation of the monstrous as a complex image of the natural and the unnatural that comes to heal the injured, using the power of destruction and reconstruction, and enabling the teenage protagonist Conor to process trauma with the help of storytelling. The monster as the product of the psyche thereby reveals how the imagined monstrous is part of the mind's successful coping mechanisms for trauma and thus speaks of the importance of fantastic fiction, too. In Conor's experience, coming of age directly affects his concept of family, his understanding of friendship and community, but most importantly, the concept of fairness, or justice. His maturation relies on understanding that life may not be interpreted in a binary system of good and evil. To reach such a recognition, he must understand the complex and complementary relationship that exists between the monster and what or who creates the monster.

However peculiar Gaiman's metaphorical spaces of maturation seem, they correspond to a process of coming of age that may be seen as normative, or even ordinary. This is not the teenagehood that Seanan McGuire is interested in in her *Wayward Children* series. "Spaces of Escape for the Abused" therefore examines the queer experience of growing up. Surveying the manifold deviances that society does not tolerate (but in a number of cases generates) and the traumatic experiences that society does not even register, McGuire's series makes a very disturbing statement about how adolescents are often left alone to cope with what proves unbearable for them. The secret otherworlds that these troubled adolescents discover may be read as the result of their coping mechanisms, and the monstrous in these psychic landscapes appears as an ultimate response to these teenage characters' needs that the real world does not care to respond to. In this respect are Jack and Jill's "apprenticeship" years examined in more detail, focusing on the roles of the two master characters that shape their maturation process:

the mad scientist and the vampire. For Jack and Jill, otherness defines their identity in relation to what is normative in the real world, but the twins also act as each other's uncanny doubles, so they seem to stand as metaphors for brokenness (as two halves of a unit). Beside them, other major characters are also examined in the context of the monstrous that makes them feel at home and thereby provides comfort against their various anxieties. The spaces that welcome their difference mostly familiarize and occasionally beautify the monstrous to fight fears concerning queerness, physical disability, mental deviance, terminal illness and thus death, but McGuire also warns about the dangers of finding comfort in the hideous, and shows how the coping mechanism either accumulates trauma or makes it impossible for the adolescent to ever integrate into society.

The three chapters in Part III, "Inhuman(e) Frontiers of Growing Up" interpret the theme of coming of age in the context of a dystopian wilderness, utilizing the myth of the American Adam/Eve in the New World garden as primary framework. This modern myth in the western world—a variant of the Campbellian monomyth—is recurrent in SFF fiction, and several of its components naturally link with the discourse on coming of age and monstrosity. First of all, the myth relies on the dichotomy of spaces: the natural, in the works that utilize this myth, is contrasted with the civilized space, and to accentuate the difference between the two, one of them is often made to be seen as monstrous. Moreover, as the American Adam or Eve character often assumes the role of a hero(ine) who is able to (or at least tries to) reform his or her own world, this fiction has the potential to offer a basis for discussion about transformation, rebellion, as well as the role of the individual within society. These issues are of defining importance for adolescents, which partially explains the immense success of dystopia among younger readers, too.

The chapters in this section examine the monstrosity of space with a special focus on its monsters that turn the space of maturation inhumane and that teach the protagonists about humanity. As the chapter "Alien New World Wilderness" discusses, Patrick Ness's *Chaos Walking* trilogy places the American Adam in the New World garden topos on a planet that people from Earth colonize, and combines it with a narrative of coming of age, where growing up inherently links with violence. The aggressive process of becoming a man springs from the horrible aspects of the presented New World's monstrous wilderness, but the novel dismisses the easy binarism of good and evil that usually characterizes juvenile fantasy. Monstrous wilderness, on the surface, is associated with the aboriginal species of the planet, the Spackles, but this notion becomes destabilized by contrasting the apparent monstrosity of the uncivilized with the hidden monstrosity of human civilization. Maturation for the protagonist Todd lies in finding his own integrity by reevaluating what monstrous and what human(e) mean. This, however, is an especially challenging task in an environment where self-censuring is the key to survival, and where the overload of information, like a brutal monster, ceaselessly attacks one's integrity.

"'Muttated' New World Garden" provides an analysis of the Capitol culture in *The Hunger Games* trilogy as the manifestation of monstrosity, focusing on the Capitol as well as its arena as monstrous equivalents of a re-imagined, dystopian New World. The chapter centers around Panem's bipartite structure that contrasts not only poverty and wealth but also highlights the opposition between nature and civilization/technology. The latter phenomenon connects Collins's dystopian trilogy to the myth of the American Adam/Eve in the New World Garden; however, the wilderness (that is, the arena) in this case is a GMO garden, subverting the garden theme, and presenting wilderness as an extension of the Capitol's high-tech world. The chapter explores the ways the arena demonstrates specific features of the Capitol's dictatorial system. To underscore aspects of the space as Other, monstrous, and artificial, the chapter details how special components of the system, such as blood, poison, and mutts, contribute to a fuller understanding of President Snow's dictatorship that is best characterized by an inhumane attitude to others—an attitude that completely lacks compassion and empathy. In close relation to the image of the monstrous garden and its transforming power, Katniss's character is analyzed as a new type of the American Eve character whose coming of age is tightly connected with the social responsibilities that she needs to undertake in this environment.

To conclude this section, I present a final chapter that touches upon a combination of the topics previously discussed. "Frankensteinian Wild West for Adults Growing Up" further investigates issues of moral and intellectual growth in a dystopian, artificial wilderness. *Westworld* (2016-), a science fiction western thriller television series, is preoccupied with the significance and signification of space, which this chapter scrutinizes. The TV show appears to be characterized by the possible binary opposition between two types of spaces evoked by the genre definition: the western genre is linked to the wilderness and the frontier small town areas of the American Old West, artificially recreated in the future as a theme park; and the science fiction genre recalls images of a more visibly, highly technologized space, which in this case is linked to a peculiar city space limited to a subterranean building complex. The two kinds of space exhibit extreme dissimilarities on the outside, suggesting that each one may be—in fact, should be—understood and interpreted in contrast to the other. *Westworld*, however, uses a concept of space in which the seeming dichotomy reveals manifestations of how the very same idea of space is mirrored and projected to various types of spaces. Spaces in *Westworld* are connected via the concept of monstrosity, explored in terms of the inhuman and the inhumane. The monstrous theme park is inhabited by androids, and the simulated frontier space thus serves to explore the difference between humans (visitors) and robots (hosts), revolving around the issues of learning, gaming, feeling, and, most importantly, having a free will. Accordingly, the themes of childhood and adulthood, as well as the transformation between the two, are also analyzed in this chapter both in terms of character development and in terms of cultural memory, understanding the recreation of the past as the representation of U.S. nostalgia for the lost American Dream.

Monsters may take various shapes, but their fundamental role in coming of age literature is to allow the character who faces them to confront her/him with one's limitations, fears, and desires. The monsters' ability to adapt to the culture that creates them guarantees that they stay with us and return in a renewed, perhaps mutated version to offer guidance to the characters who need it. They teach characters and readers alike what it means to grow up, that is, what it takes to live as an adult in the culture that, for whatever reason, makes the character feel like an Other.

Part I
Monstrous Family Matters

1

The Monstrous Friend and Lover

Buffy the Vampire Slayer *and* Stephenie Meyer's Twilight *Saga*

Introduction

Perhaps no other type of fiction may as convincingly demonstrate that the monster reflects both our fears and our desires[1] as the vampire romance does. The genre *romance* indicates that attraction, desire, and love are central themes to the work it belongs to, while the qualifying word *vampire* expresses the warning that the desire is fueled by the fearful and the monstrous, or, in other words, the forbidden. Romances have been consumed by young adults even before the labels vampire romance and supernatural romance as marketing categories were invented because romances focus on a phase of life when the protagonist must make a decision that will determine his or her life. This genre is essentially about transformation and is often combined with the genre of the bildungsroman, not only acknowledging the transformative power of love but also highlighting the notion that entering a relationship demands people to come to terms with their own identities in relation to their closer and broader community as well as the set of values they embrace.

The vampire romance underlines what the protagonist's decision is about because, since they are "eternally alive, [the vampires] embody not fear of death, but fear of life" (Auerbach 5); accordingly, in romances, these undead promise various transgressions that are incompatible with the life the innocent youth may lead. Any kind of monstrous lover has this potential, but for a simple reason it is the vampire lover that manages to conquer the book and film markets: the vampire is the monster whose necessary hybridity is not necessarily visible (Cohen, "Monster"

6). Looking human yet possessing features of the posthuman, the vampire has evolved into the monster whose physical characteristics mirror the human ideal and whose monstrosity, nevertheless, threatens the existence of the beloved. As Bruce A. McClelland argues, "Perhaps the most dangerous form that evil takes is the visibly human, since when it is ambulatory and mimetic of the individual, it is difficult to distinguish the evil being from a fellow member of the community" (2).

Another feature of the vampire that makes it especially suitable for becoming the most emblematic monstrous lover is his or her association with sexuality. The motif of one's initiation into sexual life is a recurring component of coming-of-age stories that target male and female teenagers alike, so the vampire lover may aptly stand for the desire and the fear of the unknown or the possibly dangerous in such works. The fanged vampire poses an incessant threat of taking his or her victim, and this threat is sexual on its first metaphorical level, as "the vampire represents the productions of sexuality itself" (Judith Halberstam 100). Christopher Bentley's seminal 1972 article "The Monster in the Bedroom: Sexual Symbolism in Bram Stoker's *Dracula*" establishes a clear link between vampires and sexuality. In psychoanalytical readings, the male vampire's bite into his victim has been interpreted variedly as sexual perversion (e.g., Gelder 65–80) or rape (e.g., Lorrah 31), the fang standing for the phallus and the bite metaphorically read as sexual penetration. Vampire romances (and romances, in general) mostly target a female audience,[2] but since the fangs perform the symbolic task of turning vampires into sexual symbols, the vampire lover does not have to be a male undead with bloodsucking habits. The fangs of the female vampire are not less dangerous or sexual than those of the male monster—it was a female literary vampire, Carmilla, after all, who paved the way for Dracula, whose popularity does not seem to fade. In *Carmilla*, the female monster takes girls and the sexual transgression is homoerotic, but the female bite has been analyzed in the context of heterosexual relationships, as well. As early as 1931, Ernest Jones' Freudian reading compared the female bite to oral sex in which bloodsucking stands for sucking semen and suggests perversion. The female vampire, as Barbara Creed puts it, "threatens to bite, to draw blood and sever the penis" (Creed, *The Monstrous-Feminine* 70). Performing dangerous sex, she embodies the archetypal fear of the *vagina dentata* (Creed, "Horror" 67) that threatens with castration and thus "the feminization of the male victim" (Creed, *The Monstrous-Feminine* 70).

As I noted elsewhere,[3] in vampire fiction the bite as the signification of sexual intercourse also suggests "taking" in the context of power relation both on the level of individual relationships and on the political level. In romances featuring a female protagonist seduced by a male vampire, this taking indicates a patriarchal or masculine power over the feminine (Limpár, "Masculinity" 207). In a love-relationship, the vampire lover also embodies the threat of taking the integrity or agency of his victim—a threat that most Young Adult works (even without vampires) address. Coming-of-age stories revolve around a character who evolves through a transformation from an innocent and often safe yet mostly impotent and passive childhood to a more empowered adolescence; therefore, when that transformation can possibly result in a loss of power, the text creates a space for discussion concerning the ways through which agency may be kept or regained. This is also why vampire romances are so popular among teenagers; they offer an exciting combination of forbidden or tabooed love with a maturation narrative in which one must fight for her position in various power relationships. The female protagonist finds herself in a romance where she may not be an equal partner and in a community where she could easily become an outcast, a position that affects her chance to properly integrate into family and society.

Contrasting two different takes on how the struggle for agency and power is presented in contemporary vampire romances addressing a Young Adult audience provides a useful approach to discussing the potential inherent in these narratives. *Buffy the Vampire Slayer* (1997–2001), created by Joss Whedon, is the TV show that gave a boost to vampire romances both in the printed and the filmic medium and advocated the idea of the strong heroine in a supernatural setting, where her task is to save the world, cope with her love relationship, or deal with a combination of the two. Stephenie Meyer's *Twilight* saga (2005–2008), probably still the best known and popular of Young Adult vampire romances, is the product of the trend that started with the *Buffy* series; however, *Twilight* discarded what made *Buffy* really popular, the strong female protagonist capable of repeatedly preventing apocalypse. Nevertheless, Meyer's quadrilogy also became an instant bestseller and paved the way for the publication of other supernatural romances, many of which copied its basic formula of bringing together the very average girl and the very special lover in what is basically a very average—and definitely not apocalyptic—setting.

Meyer focuses exclusively on the romance, while Buffy is fundamentally a hero(ine) narrative that flirts with romance. The girls' choices come from character and not from genre, even if it is very tempting to hold the generic difference accountable for the diverse choices the protagonists make. The genre is important for many reasons, but in the analysis that follows I will focus on how the values the characters endorse have an impact on their choices and thus how the vampire as the monstrous friend and lover is an emblematic character that gives thrust to the character development of the female protagonist.

Otherness: Recognizing the Familiar or the Unfamiliar

Buffy and the *Twilight* series have much in common. In both universes, most people are not aware of the existence of vampires even after they have interacted with them. The protagonist is a teenage girl who moves to a new small town and needs to find her place in her new school community. Her parents are divorced, and she is an only child (until in season five Buffy is given a sister who was created by magic). The motif of moving house itself is suggestive of the change from innocence to adolescence, and the new space that the protagonist explores is emblematically marked by a strange vampire, who will fundamentally determine the nature of her maturation process. The two strange vampires— Edward Cullen in *Twilight*, Angel in *Buffy*—have a lot in common. They both belong to the category of the humanized vampire, the result of a literary evolution that started with Anne Rice's *Interview with the Vampire* (1976). Their beauty and apparent youth conceal the truth that they are past 200 years old. Not only do they appear as Byronic heroes with a secret past that torments them, but they also try to compensate for their monstrosities by acting as "good vampires," so they refrain from drinking human blood and aim to protect humanity from various attacks by evil forces. As vampires who find the female protagonists irresistible, they force their beloved ones to make important choices concerning their lives. They pose a lethal threat to the protagonists especially by loving them; therefore, in both works abstinence becomes an important motif. The vampire is a first serious love for both protagonists, who lose their innocence (virginity) by giving up abstinence and choosing to make love with the vampire lover.

The vampire lover embodies the complexity of coming of age for the two female characters. For Bella, Edward Cullen incorporates the antithesis of her own life. While she is an average, clumsy girl who lives in a broken family with a humble financial background, doomed to mortality as humans are, Edward is immortal and beautiful; he also has all the supernatural skills a vampire should have, but he has in addition the special ability of reading minds; he has an attractive family of special vampires who form a caring community and are very well-to-do. Bella's passion for Edward makes sense, and the first phase of their romance is classic in its nature; as Bella gets to know Edward better, she becomes able to associate him with all the above listed characteristics plus Edward's feelings that make Bella appear attractive, moreover, irresistible. Edward, however, poses a real threat to Bella because his suppressed but fundamentally violent nature, a feature of his own nature as a vampire, often surfaces. Bella chooses to see Edward's perilous nature as an unquestionable proof for his hardly satisfiable, supernatural desire that turns Bella into an object of desire—obviously a new experience for the girl. She learns to love herself through Edward's craving and never notices that her evolving narcissism begins to drive her when making decisions. The issue of Edward's immortality could also generate problems with which Bella cannot cope. Immortality is, in fact, what makes the vampire a monster because the vampire embodies that liminal space between life and death, belonging fully to neither, turning it into the hybrid form of the undead. As a living dead, the vampire is immortal but does not live a human life. Edward, accordingly, is stuck in time. His maturation and transformation are invisible on the outside, and he looks eternally a teenager while his character is supposed to be aging. This desirable immortality, however, hinders the possibility of a long, harmonious relationship with the human Bella. When they meet, they *look like* a perfect match, but Bella is aware that each day she spends as a human will make their age difference more apparent (and, ironically, the visible difference will suggest the reverse of the actual situation, as it is Bella who will gradually—and noticeably—grow old when, in fact, she will always be much younger than Edward[4]).

Bella's desire to become a vampire of course stems from her love for Edward, but her wish to become a vampire as soon as possible is rooted in her fear that time will change their *appearance* as a couple. However, Edward rejects turning the teenage Bella into a vampire, arguing that the girl does not understand the implications of the choice she wants to make. Edward explains his vampirehood in the context of classical demonology, making the possession of a soul the real divide between human and Other. His definition of the vampire, however, depends on his feelings and not knowledge. *Twilight*'s fundamentally secular world creates a space for the supernatural, but this narrative basically writes itself out of the cultural context in which the western vampire story has traditionally operated. In fact, when Edward explains his vampirehood to Bella, he emphasizes the difference between the stereotypical representations of vampires and his own experience. He reveals that literary representations and popular beliefs about what people think harms vampires, such as the holy cross or holy water are not true, and neither does garlic provide protection against the undead. The contrast between

1. The Monstrous Friend and Lover

Edward and Dracula, the classic literary vampire, subtly implies—although it does not prove at all—that Edward is immune to symbols of the Christian faith that work on vampires like Dracula because he is not a demon who has lost his soul and has therefore become sensitive to anything sacred in the Christian sense.

Unlike in Buffyverse, where there is confirmed knowledge about the relationship between (the lack of) souls and demons, such as vampires, in the *Twilight* saga neither the vampires nor Bella may be sure if the soul is an imaginary concept or a real entity that may be lost as a consequence of transformation. Bella is convinced that Edward's judgment about his own demonic, soulless existence is wrong because she sees an unquestionable incompatibility between beauty and soullessness. The strange beauty that reflects "a humanly unachievable ideal" (Rocha 269) marks the transformation, but with a twisted logic Bella perceives it as the proof that vampires stay unchanged concerning their spiritual existence. Her associating vampire beauty with "airbrushed pages of a fashion magazine" and her identifying the vampire face with the "face of an angel" (Meyer 10) reveal how the material and the consumerist are intertwined with the spiritual in her imagination. Bella's attitude to an Otherness that is defined by superhuman beauty comes from her cultural context, the consumer society marketing the image of a good, desirable life with beauty. Bella buys this ideology, just as people buy any other goods in this society. She admires the goods that her vampire lover and his family have and interprets them as testimonies of a beautiful life, a kind of proof that what commercials and magazines promote is true; the beautiful life is attainable, and those who are beautiful attract things of beauty, ultimately allowing them to create the beautiful, extraordinary environment for themselves that they deserve. Those photoshopped magazine images and a painted angel's face form parts of the same sentence in Bella's inner monologue, revealing an inner world in which the highest principle governing her life is beauty. In a religious framework, the angelic look signals the connection to the divine, but Bella's admiration of the vampiric beauty ties the nonhuman appearance to consumerism, overwriting any possible religious connotations and suggesting, in fact, that Bella is more interested in market superficiality than religious spirituality.

Bella's association suggests to the reader that vampires may be like commercial goods, made to look attractive on the surface, independently of the inner qualities they may have. They may or may not make a person's life more comfortable or pleasant in other ways, as most consumers who have been tricked into buying disappointing items sold by lying ads know. Bella insists that she has seen enough of Edward to know that she wants to share with him the product of eternal life that he may give her; Edward, on the other hand, argues that Bella does not know the manifold complications of the product that she is determined to buy with all the fortune she has—her human life.

One might say that Bella's naivety, stemming from growing up in a consumer society where looks suggest social position, compels her to make a clear correspondence between appearance and quality, but such a claim should also come from a much more complicated argument instead of a simple observation. Her generation is the product of the consumer society, yet it would be bold to generalize that nobody in her age group can see beyond looks. Bella's circumstances make her especially sensitive to the importance of both appearance and financial stability. Bella associates having money with having fewer worries. When she states, "Of course [her mother] had Phil now, so the bills would probably get paid, there would be food in the refrigerator, gas in her car, and someone to call when she got lost" (Meyer 2), she reveals an image of safety that comes from both money and having a person—a man—who is able to provide the financial and practical safety that she finds important. Such an image is contrasted with her everyday reality, full of cheap, second-hand items, such as the old truck Charlie gets for her or the laptop her mother gives her so that they can keep in touch.

Bella goes to Forks as a favor to her mother, but like a successful, lying advertising person, she sells her gesture as her own desire, creating a beautiful package around her decision, making it look attractive to the person who is buying it—for, of course, her mother would not like her daughter to suffer in her new place with Charlie but would like to travel with her new husband, who is always on the move because of his job. Bella's mother wants to enjoy her life without a guilty conscience. She does not examine why her daughter would want to go to Forks even though the girl had earlier stated that she hated the place. Bella loves her mother but also describes her as "harebrained" (Meyer 2) and shows how her mother is really unable to take care of herself.

Living with a "harebrained" mother and worrying about financial security shape Bella's character. She thinks of herself as an independent person who is more mature than her own mother, a woman who needs her daughter's help to find her own blouse even when Bella is hundreds of miles away. Bella's family circumstances make her mature enough to make sensible decisions concerning specific practical issues, but her upbringing does not provide her with the emotional safety that she needs, especially during her teenage years, to grow up. She does not develop into an emotionally complex, round character, and as a result, she is not close to her mother, who should have given her the emotional support that she needed as a child. She introduces herself as a girl who does not "relate well" to people (Meyer 5), which proves so true that she ends up relating well with vampires instead. Her lack of skills relating to people isolates her completely from her environment and cuts her off from the support and influence of people who have a more complex view of the world than she does.

This is the point from which Bella's and Buffy's process of coming of age significantly diverges. Buffy is conscious of fashion, and she is not likely to change her high heels or pretty clothes just because she is a slayer and needs to fight demons every day. Instead, she quickly adapts to her new circumstances and keeps fighting in pretty clothes and high heels. She finds pleasure in shopping and she does not limit herself when opportunity knocks on her door; for example, she knows that her father feels guilty that he has not spent enough time in his daughter's life, so Buffy takes advantage of this gilt and welcomes all the gifts that her dad's credit card can buy during the short vacation they spend together. However, the first episode of the show makes it clear that she does not make judgments based on appearance. She quickly makes up her mind to make friends with Willow instead of Cordelia, who has a very shallow value system and a tendency to bully those who do not conform to her idea of the popular. Buffy is established as a fashionable girl who, based on her appearance, would make an ideal member of Cordelia's plaza-girl gang; nevertheless, she demonstrates an inner maturity that contradicts the assumed system of values that Cordelia attaches to Buffy's image. Her performance of femininity in this opening episode presents her as character who "both reflects and challenges conventional feminine norms" (Jackson par. 21).

Buffy the Vampire Slayer and *Twilight* effectively recognize that a world in which choices are dictated by appearance produces a generation of young people who will have problems making their own decisions. They could by default rely on other people's interpretation of images, which could in turn lack substance. This can have tragic results, as Buffy's attempt at becoming Prom Queen in "Homecoming" (3.5) warns the viewing audience. In this episode, Buffy tries to become Prom Queen not simply as an act of vengeance directed against Cordelia but as a desperate attempt to prove to herself that she can also have a life beyond just being a slayer. Her wish to appear as a normal girl who had some good years in secondary school because she was popular generates an awful tension among her friends and then results in a life-threatening battle against the assassins who join the slayerfest, an event specifically organized to kill the slayer. (Paradoxically, the near-death experience resolves the conflict the girls have, so the girls' rivalry threatens primarily the harmony that the group of friends enjoyed before.)

Other episodes beyond this one underline how images of normativity can poison a person's life, especially concerning gender roles, which is a crucial issue in the life of adolescents. "Halloween" (2.6) investigates the dangerous or painful experience that results from gender roles that are assumed to be prescribed by one's immediate environment. Buffy thinks that she should try to appear as the 18th-century female ideal because this is what attracted Angel when he was human. Her desire to impress Angel nearly gets her killed; in addition, she learns in the end that while those women in the past looked pretty in their decorated clothes, Angel saw beyond appearance and was not entertained by the dull personalities of the women that those elegant dresses hid. In "Helpless" (3.12) he confesses that he fell in love with Buffy's heart that he could see because she "held it before [her] for everyone to see," confirming that his love does not depend on societal expectations or superficial images—it is Buffy's personality that makes Angel be in love with her.

Harmful stereotypes of masculinity also emerge as recurring issues in *Buffy*, and Buffy's friend Xander's character is regularly utilized to rethink the problematics of enforced gender role performances. Both "Halloween" (2.6) and "The Zeppo" (3.13) underscore the difference between appearance and reality in this context, and the latter episode specifically focuses on the inner development of Xander, who learns about himself that he can indeed behave heroically once it matters and there are no others around him to save the world in his stead. The episode shows that such a knowledge builds Xander's self-confidence, so he no longer has to depend on other people's opinion of him. The show investigates masculinity through the fates of other characters, as well. In "Phases" (2.15), it is compulsory heterosexuality that makes Larry Blaisdell act the role of the nasty bully, thinking that such a "macho" image will prevent people from suspecting that he is gay. In his case, there is a very positive resolution because he becomes comfortable with his sexual orientation, comes out of the closet, and starts acting as a gentleman, helping girls instead of molesting them, understanding that masculinity does not have to be linked with aggression. Less fortunate is Pete in "Beauty and the Beasts" (3.4) because he is a modern Jekyll and Hyde character who turned to scientific experiments in order to enhance his masculine image and impress his girlfriend Debbie. In accordance with the original Jekyll and Hyde story, Pete loses control over his violent self and thus he himself must die violently.

The cited examples along with many other episodes reveal the show's interest in presenting the complexity between appearance and reality and teaching a young adult audience to see beyond appearances. In fact, the romance plot line of the show is the narrative arc that most intricately discusses the puzzling relationship between seeming and reality. Angel is a cursed vampire, which makes him a good revenant whose souled character questions what is known about demons; his two faces, however, constantly remind us that he may be re-transformed any time, and he could become the wild beast known as Angelus.

In *Twilight*, Bella interprets Edward's beastly nature as a special feature that serves her protection or the survival of his family, while Buffy, in contrast, appears to be drawn to Angel despite his vampirehood and not because of it. She hesitates to accept what she feels exactly because she is aware of the demonic nature of vampires and her mission to fight them to death. She needs to convince herself that Angel is an exception, whereas Bella sees Edward not in contrast to other vampires but rather as the best manifestation of the alluring group of supernatural beings. Yet paradoxically, the attraction Buffy feels despite her being a slayer comes from the very fact that she is a slayer. It is repeatedly pointed out that the slayer's power is aligned with darkness. In this respect, Buffy shares similarities with Angel that she may not share with any other person around her. She is associated with the demonic, but serves humanity and constantly fights evil, even the evil that could drag her into a dark abyss. It is Spike—the vampire who first appears as a villain and then becomes Buffy's lover and ultimately a hero—who reveals in "Fool for Love" (5.7) that Buffy has an inherent death wish, the weakness that all slayers suffer from, which echoes Angel's desperate death wish presented in "Amends" (3.10) and comes from the slayer's desire to identify with her victims.

Buffy's desire to die, however, is very different from Bella's aspiration to get bitten quickly so that she may share an eternal existence and love with Edward. What the slayer longs for is, fundamentally, rest; she wants to stop existing in a world filled with evil and forcing her to fight relentlessly. For Buffy, to die is not to become a revenant; in fact, her deepest fear, as we learn in "Nightmares" (1.10), is to die and return as a vampire. Telling Angel "When you kiss me, I want to die" ("Reptile Boy" 2.5) foreshadows the moment when she learns about the slayer's death wish. She does not want to become a vampire but wishes to have rest from her obligations and be a person who may prioritize her private life over her duties. The context for Buffy's first expression of her death wish is Angel's warning against the danger he poses to Buffy's life: "This isn't some fairy tale. When I kiss you, you don't wake up from a deep sleep and live happily ever after" ("Reptile Boy"). Buffy's reply foreshadows that the slayer never has a narrative in which romance triumphs and that what she could end up with is the opposite of what others usually hope for. While everyday girls are more likely to dream of a prince who will kiss them and transform them by awakening them from the Sleeping Beauty moment—the moment that suggests an awakening from sleep or lack of consciousness to a life of conscious choices and a life with the prince (instead of an apparent death due to a curse)—the most Buffy can ask for is a fall from light to darkness after sharing one moment of true happiness that turns her prince into the beast as a result of the curse Angel received from the Gypsies.

The slayer, however, knows that she must not give in to the idea of embracing death in the hope of finding peace and calm because this weakness would risk the fate of humanity. Her death wish comes from the slayer's origin story that positions the slayer as a victim of men turning her into a demonic creature by forcing the spirit of a demon into her body. It is this demonic spirit, the source of her power, that manifests as a death wish. Therefore, the desire to die is a fleshless monster that attracts the slayer, who must continuously abject it from her life in order to function properly[5] as the protector of humanity.

This death wish connects Buffy to Angel in a manner that greatly differs from the way Bella is tied to Edward through her desire to get transformed. The death wish for Buffy and Angel is an acknowledgment that they want to act correctly but feel too weak to go on and do the right thing. That is why a slayer can be killed in her weak moments; and that is why Angel wants to give up his existence after he regains his soul for the second time and cannot cope with his bad consciousness. Tied to the demonic, both Angel and Buffy are attracted because of their similar positions, whereas Bella finds the Other in Edward, and her attraction stems from her admiration of the Other. To Buffy, Angel is not a redefinition of herself but a confirmation of her own otherness, while Bella wishes for a transformation that actually begins with Edward seeing her as an Other—a person whose mind he cannot read. Buffy's otherness, then, is a key to her romance and explains why she feels comfortable with Angel (and why she bonds with Spike later) and why she has a problematic relationship with Riley. As always, it is Spike who reveals the suppressed truth when he points out where the Riley-Buffy love conflict is rooted. "The girl needs some monster in her man," he says in "Into the Woods" (5.10), suggesting that this desire matches her partially monstrous nature, a dark heritage from the first slayer. This connection establishes the "underlying pattern of Buffy's relation to the night, the unconscious, the id, the shadow, or the animus. The hero must embrace this darkness to become truly strong—to save herself" (Wilcox 85). Monstrous darkness emerges as uncanny for Buffy: strangely familiar and unfamiliar, which when embraced, gives power; the explicit death wish, however, is an abject that pushes Buffy beyond the border of the I and threatens her existence.[6] Bella, in contrast, needs a monster lover primarily because she hopes to become different, which significantly colors simplified comparisons between Buffy and Bella.[7]

Becoming different, nevertheless, is very rich in meaning to Bella. It encompasses all the potential that she sees in those beautiful images that sell anything in the world. In her imagination, the Cullens' otherness is synonymous with being powerful. Her decision to belong to the beautiful aligns her with her wish to have more power, more agency.[8] When the enemies of the Cullens pose a real threat to her as well, this desired power becomes associated with physical power, the ability to defend herself and step out of her role of the damsel in distress. Looked at from this perspective, her choice may be read as feminist in nature, even though this interpretation divides *Twilight* critics. Yet instead of entering the dialogue that compares the Buffy-narrative with the Bella-narrative on the basis of how progressive the feminism they represent is, I will proceed with focusing on the theme of coming of age by looking at the girls' choices from the perspective of maturity and interpreting the characters' encounters with the monstrous as suggestive of some of the problems that contemporary adolescents face.

Friends, Foils and Faërian Drama

With few exceptions, studies on Buffy tend to agree that the title character of the show is a feminist role model for its female audience. In contrast, the interpretation of the *Twilight* series is much more dividing. Bella is often said to represent "female submission in a male dominated world" (Rocha 268),[9] but articles defending and rationalizing her central choice also abound. Several authors claim that the very idea that Bella insists on having a choice independently of her circumstances aligns her with feminism. Catherine Coker, for instance, echoes Meyer's own claim[10] when she insists that choice is choice, and Bella's choice should be respected and seen empowering even if one does not identify with the character's preferences (par. 22–23). This empowerment is underlined in Tara K. Parmiter's reading, which contends that Bella's "attitude may initially appear like a rejection of life, but in becoming a vampire she instead gains greater access to and appreciation for everything living" (228). I think that the choices these girls make constitute only one segment of what there is to explore when we aim at comparing what they represent. Bella's choice suggests immaturity not because of what she chooses but because of why and how she chooses to become a vampire and share an eternal life with Edward as wife and as the mother of their child.

The immaturity I criticize in Bella's decision-making process comes from her circumstances that push her to make an uninformed choice. The narratives that show the two girls in their love relationships fundamentally differ not simply because Buffy's romance is inserted into a hero(ine)-narrative. The difference lies in their relation to their environment: Bella completely isolates herself from other people, while Buffy's story is embedded in a story of companionship, friendship, and team work, going against the traditional hero-concept in American culture, which has a long history of lone heroes (Cochran and Edwards 146), and a somewhat shorter history of lone heroines because female superpower was not so much favored by history. Buffy, however, represents a new kind of heroism-concept in American culture; as Sharon Ross points out, the individualism that used to define hero-narratives has been challenged by two prominent TV series: *Buffy* and *Xena*, in which the female protagonists "grow as heroes because of their female friends," empowering their friends, opening up a space for them to become heroes, too (230).[11]

Male and female friends alike are part of Buffy's armory. The activity of the Scooby Gang, comprised of Buffy and her various friends fighting evil, recurrently confirms the point that triumphing over a situation that seems hopeless is made possible by joining forces. The lone hero would fail and even die (or, in Buffy's case, would stay dead) without friends' help. The first such example is provided in "Prophecy Girl" (1.12) when Buffy dies as a result of fighting with the Master, but thanks to Xander's courage and stubbornness, she can be resuscitated. Buffy needs the support of her human friends, which may be read as a reminder that while her mission might make her an outcast in human society, her special existence ties her to the human world which she protects. Her friends and family are the anchors to humanity, allowing her to perform her job from one day to another. It is therefore of emblematic importance that when she drowns, her love interest, Angel, is unable to help her with CPR, but her friend Xander is (Wilcox 75).

The most difficult confrontations with evil forces need co-operation and a division of labor, in which everyone has a task that suits his or her abilities. The mayor in season four is overcome because the whole school fights his vampires to distract their attention from Buffy, who can therefore trick the monster-mayor into the trap that was set for him. But the two most powerful demonstrations of the claim that power lies in unity may be seen in season four and season seven, as Wilcox notes

(75). In "Primeval" (4.21), Xander points out that to defeat the Frankensteinian monster Adam, they would need a "Buffy-combo," and indeed, they manage to fuse their special abilities with the help of magic to create a superior version of the slayer. In the series, the repeated cooperation is at times humorously presented, but always receives emphasis and serious treatment when a major villain is to be overcome. The grandeur of uniting power comes from sharing power and responsibility. It comes from acknowledging that the hero is more powerful when she understands that she does not have to fight all her combats alone. She has backup; she has a hinterland to rely on. The seven seasons of *Buffy the Vampire Slayer* build on this recognition and acceptance in the titular character, so the closure of the show naturally celebrates an extraordinary unity that comes from the most spectacular sharing of power, creating slayers from all potential slayers in the world.

Bella, in contrast, has no such support behind her even though Coker argues that both heroines have their chosen families

> presented as preferable to the real or blood family: these family members take you in because they want to rather than because they have to. The chosen family also offers a distinctively protective state as well, as each member is willing to—and does—defend the other members of the group with their own lives [Coker par. 13].

However, I think while at first sight the notion of the chosen family indeed links the two characters, the differences again are more revealing than the apparent similarity. First of all, neither of the protagonists' real parents loves the child because he/she has to. Bella's parents may not be the most competent ones, but this says nothing about their willingness and ability to love their child. Buffy's father is not often seen in the show, but he does appear to have a strong bond with his daughter even though they rarely see each other; also, while Buffy's mother does not always have a smooth relationship with Buffy, she proves to be a very loving mother who not only loves her daughter but is also ready to fight for her as she did, for instance, in "School Hard" (2.3). For Buffy, the chosen family is not better than her real family and is not chosen *over* her blood family; her chosen family is her extended family. As this family of hers grows, Buffy becomes surrounded by more and more supportive people; Bella's decision to join the Cullen family, in contrast, makes her even more isolated from people, and this is a very important difference between the social contexts of the two girls. Buffy's friends always offer various perspectives of conflicted phenomena, situations, and thus the slayer is forced to consider differing opinions even if she does not like them. She learns from her friends and learns to listen to other people in dire situations, while Bella is practically on her own when she most needs a best friend to both listen to her and shout at her to prevent her from making a hasty decision. She can discuss the dilemma of her wish to become a vampire only with a company of vampires, which does not allow her to see the complexity of her decision even though Edward tries his best to give Bella a more convoluted vision of what she asks for.

Both Angel and Edward warn their girlfriends that loving them is dangerous, but these warnings do not convince or frighten the girls. Buffy knows without Angel's warning that dating a vampire is a bad and dangerous idea; Bella would not understand this even if Edward tried much harder to make her see the problem. Their different attitudes come from the worlds in which they operate as well as their personal characteristics. Bella lives in a world where reliable knowledge about the supernatural powers that come to define her life is not available. She does not have a Watcher to provide her with the information she seeks; all she can find as an inadequate equivalent for a storehouse of knowledge is a "new age" bookstore, but she "refuses association with the 'fifty-year-old woman with long, gray hair worn straight down her back, clad in a dress right out of the sixties,' in order to distinguish the 'real' problems she is having with vampires from the 'fake' narratives and tools sold in the bookstore" (Kim and Anatol 199). Yet her insistence that "there had to be a *normal* bookstore in town" (85; emphasis added) reveals her naivety and her being completely lost in the new world she has discovered. She lacks the certainty of knowledge concerning vampires, and even the vampires cannot enlighten her about their existence, as they cannot comprehend their own nature, either. All they can tell Bella is what they assume or believe or have experienced, but none of this is the objective truth that could help her make a decision.

In Buffy's world moral behavior is defined by fighting against evil— mostly represented by vampires—in all circumstances. There is definite knowledge about the evilness of vampires, who are clearly tied to Hell's evil world, and as a result, there is also definite knowledge about Angel being an exception to the company of vampires who lack souls and therefore kill without guilt. The world Buffy knows includes selected people who are entitled to gain access to knowledge unavailable to most people. This rare but reliable knowledge helps Buffy to interpret the world on the axis of good and evil, and as a result, the slayer has a very clear moral compass that informs her even when she is about to make a personal choice. When she does not have information about the fact that Angel may re-assume his former evil self, Angelus, as a result of the complexity of the curse that re-installed his soul, the lack of knowledge brings tragedy and ends with Buffy killing Angel. Yet when Angel returns and takes possession of his soul again, Buffy and Angel make decisions based on the knowledge they gained before and do not risk tragedy again despite their innermost feelings.

The knowledge Buffy can rely on is indeed connected to her supernatural feature, so in this sense we may argue that the hero-narrative defines Buffy as a character making choices based upon knowledge. She is initiated into a world that average people are not allowed to see. Bella is such an average person, so her disadvantage comes from this position. However, both productions highlight the importance of character within a narrative. Bella is not an average teenager even though nearly every teenager may identify with her, because the feeling of being an outsider is a familiar feeling to most adolescents, and exaggerating that sentiment works in favor of the identification process. And Buffy is not a slayer who works in an automated slayer-mode that characterizes each and every slayer; in fact, we have several foil characters to point out what other paths could have been walked by Buffy had she had a different character. Her most important foil, Faith, is a slayer who fails to reject the darkness in her and becomes a tool in the hands of evil. Faith's fate in *Buffy* repeatedly reminds the audience of the thin borderline that is easy for a slayer to cross; it takes not only knowledge and education but also character to stay on the safe side. While circumstances may contribute to making wrong decisions, they may not be used as excuses.

Spike, who grows to become Angel's foil in the long run, even more dramatically highlights Buffy's curious alliance with darkness. His role in Buffy's life emphasizes the darkness that Buffy is drawn to and drains energy from and also confirms her understanding that true romantic love lies beyond this instinctive attraction. Spike is also the one who—before his realization that he is in love—speaks from the position of the subconscious: he is the darkness who is always fought against but is never completely annihilated; he is just suppressed from time to time and when he resurfaces, he confronts Buffy and her friends with the truths that they do not want to acknowledge. Spike's realism forces Buffy and Angel to acknowledge that their idealism is incompatible with reality and that they will never have a working relationship either as lovers or as friends. As such, Spike is a real vehicle for Buffy's coming-of-age process. In *Twilight*, we have a character who is somewhat similarly positioned as Spike: a supernatural man with animalistic nature, who longs to become the protagonist's lover, but his love stays unrequited: Jacob, the Native American werewolf. Yet placing Jacob into a stereotypically presented Native American community (Burke passim) and as part of a "pack" creates shallow associations because the most defining difference between the two lovers appear to be racial and social context. Meyer's treatment of Jacob deprives the character of his individuality and accentuates the poverty that strikes Bella when she visits Jacob's home environment.[12] Jacob as a foil confirms that material wealth is a basic component in Bella's choice because of all the associations money has for her. Jacob's beauty is that of the exoticized Other (Burke 211), which is pleasing to the western eyes but would never become associated with the white power that Edward's beauty promises for Bella.

Beyond the application of foils, *Buffy* is famous for highlighting character by actions that investigate "what if" situations. This is the essential function of applying "faërian drama," a term explained by J.R.R. Tolkien and used by Janet Brennan Croft to analyze "Normal Again" (6.17). Faërian drama gives a vision for a character about a possible, alternate reality. Its "one essential goal within the experience is Recovery, the 'regaining of a clear view'"; "the participant must be in a liminal and receptive state" to have such a vision (Croft 32). "The dreamer is always an acting character in the drama," and the gained experience "cannot be dismissed as a mere dream" but should be seen as "real and 'other'" (33). As Croft points out, this technique is exploited in the Buffy series[13] and provides knowledge about various characters (or, perhaps more precisely, self-knowledge for various characters). The repeatedly used faërian drama technique ensures that the characters—including but not limited to Buffy—are confronted with certain possible consequences of the choices that they are about to make. Their experience forces them to reconsider their decisions and draw conclusions about themselves.

A similarly enlightening vision is completely missing from Bella's life experience, and she does not have anything that would come near it because the isolation that she willingly chooses prevents her from encountering such challenges in her real life. She is a teenager who does not let confronting opinions influence her; in fact, she does not ask for opinions and can dismiss her boyfriend's opinion on the basis that he is too much involved to make a clear judgment. In short, she makes a decision without actually thinking through possible consequences, insisting that there is nothing to think through because—and now we have returned to our starting point—beauty guarantees goodness. Ironically, her impenetrable mind, which Meyer later presents as her special vampire skill, an effective weapon, lends itself to being read as her ultimate weakness: her complete isolation and ignorance, as if Edward were not able to read her mind—because there is not much to read there.

Her choice should be respected, and her happiness with her fate that many find disappointing or even appalling could be accepted;

however, one must not forget that her happiness is accidental and not a logical, predictable consequence of her actions. Meyer herself must have felt the problematic nature of Bella's wish, as in her work she tries to exempt her protagonist from actually making an uninformed and rushed choice: in *Breaking Dawn*, Meyer creates circumstances that demand a quick response to save Bella from eternal death. This way the author suggests that Edward may have been right in asking Bella to give herself more time and experience to make her decision, but their love is predestined, so time would not have made a difference in the outcome (and, on the plus side, this way Bella can become as beautiful as she wanted to be). A further dilemma concerning Bella's transformation lies in the fact that only this implied predetermination guarantees that Bella will live happily ever after. Her choice to ignore the risk of her possibly turning into a beast who is controlled by her blood thirst, as most vampires are, springs from her naiveté. What turns out to be the deepest fear in *Buffy*—getting transformed into a vampire—becomes the utmost desire in *Twilight*, and these anxieties and desires address the question of what it means to be human and what gives power in the world these girls exist in.

Conclusion

The vampire lover in *Twilight* and *Buffy* embodies desires and fears that are deeply rooted not only in Bella's and Buffy's psyche but also in the nature of the worlds in which Buffy and Bella must find their places. Both protagonists are outsiders, but Buffy strives to reconnect with humanity, and beside her supernatural power, she relies on her most human nature—empathy, love and care—to accomplish her mission. She surrounds herself with people who become her friends, who help not only in the actual fights against evil, but also in tying her to a morality that always protects humanity over other values. Angel's beautiful body questions the perfection of human knowledge about good and evil, and the fact that Angel has (literally) two faces, a beautiful and a truly monstrous one, confirms the ambiguity and the instability of that knowledge. The changing, monstrous body is thus a warning about what might happen if Buffy forgets about the values that the first slayer was created to protect. It is, at the same time, also a reminder of the sacrifice Buffy has to make again and again to be an effective slayer; she is "flirting" with darkness but must never satisfy her desire for that darkness. The monstrous lover signifies the gap between duty and desire, and the power that comes from rejecting desire and choosing duty to ensure the survival of the good against the evil. As a cultural signifier, Angel's monstrosity points to an America that has faith in a clear differentiation between good and evil, a sense of morals, and the faith that good will triumph. Buffy's coming-of-age process reflects a gradual distancing from the institutionalized form of providing protection for this world (see, for instance, her refusal to co-operate with the Council when they do not give her the help she asked for), which shows a progress towards individuality, but she keeps operating as part of a team, demonstrating the need for unity and togetherness. Much of her character development is due to her trying experience of seeing Angel as Angelus, as well as understanding and accepting the necessity to kill him.

Edward Cullen's sparkling vampire body, in contrast, represents the allure of a world that does not focus on the differentiation between good and evil but directs attention to appearance that may mask goodness and badness alike. This vampire body is a cultural signifier of a contemporary America that is fundamentally shaped by its consumer culture and asks its consumers not to see behind the image because they can trust what they see. Accordingly, Bella does not want to look much behind what Edward's body may represent. She trusts the beautiful image, and the fact that she is not disappointed because the author approves of her attitude does not make her lack of consideration less problematic. The monstrous body invites everyone to appreciate beauty that is above what is attainable in a natural way for humans; it confirms that average looking people do not feel at home in the world designed to be enjoyed by the privileged. The closure of the *Twilight* series is disappointing to many not because Bella is more powerful and happy as a mother and wife but because it chooses what counts as a virtual reality to these readers; from their perspective, the vampire body signifies a dreamland as opposed to the reality which should be made better to give power for those who want to live in it.

In both works, the vampire lover embodies a choice embedded in a cultural context that significantly influences the final decisions the female protagonists make. While *Buffy* presents a superheroine in its title role, the series keeps its fans in close touch with everyday reality; through a metaphorical interpretation, the supernatural invites them to confront and discuss earthly problems; *Twilight*, on the other hand, while presenting the most average protagonist, distracts the fans' attention from actually solving problems in a way that may help them in the real world—postponing growing up for them just as Bella stops aging in the fairytale-like space to which Edward gives her access. The *Twilight* saga works more as an escapist work, a fantasy where one may stay a teenager forever; its monster embodies, among others, the alluring yet harmful ideology of a consumer society that one should question in order to arrive at realistic expectations and solutions. *Buffy*, on the other hand, is a story of perpetual growth and struggle in a consumer society, and presents vampire lovers to generate a discourse on moral values and decisions that are tied to the moral fiber of humanity, something that Bella rejects because of her infatuation with all things material.

2

Apocalyptic Monsters in Need of a Family

Daryl Gregory's Raising Stony Mayhall *and M.R. Carey's* The Girl with All the Gifts

Introduction: The Problematics of the Sentient Zombie

Vampires and zombies reside at the two extreme endpoints of the undead scale. If vampires primarily evoke associations with the aristocratic and the luxurious through their excessive consumptions of life fluid and their everlasting immortal bodies that resist change, the main agency of zombies is to warn us about our mortality, which is inherently connected to bodily corruption. The zombie is "the decomposing dead incarnate" (Abbot 161), and thus it emphasizes decay even in its uncontrollable need for consuming human flesh or brain. The aristocracy of vampires speaks about privilege; the zombie, in return, is the symbol of the disprivileged. Accordingly, the vampire is often represented as a lonely individual isolated in society, while the zombie is a monster that stands for the masses and usually appears in masses—that is, hordes. The soulless zombie of western imagination, originating from Haiti and Africa, "records a residual communal memory of slavery: of living a life without dignity and meaning, of going through the motions" (Dendle, "The Zombie as Barometer" 46). As a tool of social criticism, the zombie targets phenomena that lead to despiritualization on the metaphorical level. As "a metaphor that reflects prevailing social anxieties—such as oppression, violence, inequality, consumption, and war—that plague the contemporaneous culture that produces any given zombie narrative" (Bishop, *The Rise* 207), the zombie issues warning about "the susceptibility of the polis to outside influences, the fragility of law and order in the face of widespread chaos" (Lauro, Introduction x). It has been seen as "an objective correlative for capitalism" (Schmid 95), since its cannibalistic nature may be interpreted as "the rapacious hunger of a capitalistic and increasingly corporate society" (Lauro, Introduction x). The zombie merges existential fears that come from inside and outside. The incessant confrontation with the limits of what the human body may bear generates anxiety concerning biopolitics[1]; it addresses the threat stemming from one's physical fragility as well as the uncertainty about what may lie beyond one's material existence. This also has become a complex fear of the here and the there: the question of life after death, an ever-present angst of humanity has traditionally been linked to the idea of complete annihilation or a possible afterlife in an unknown world; but with the latest technological advancements, the idea of an afterlife links with what this world may offer to the body. The modern zombie, reinvented in the second half of the 20th century, may also embody specific anxieties of longevity generated by scientific and technological advancements, especially the fear of keeping the body artificially alive to assure existence without agency (Dendle, "The Zombie as Barometer" 52). The zombie reflects on the horrible aspects of a possible posthuman existence: it connects the exciting, promising idea of existing beyond what is human with the various fears that relate to physical decline, annihilation and/or loss of control.

The zombie, which seems to be so much limited due to its inability to take control over its own existence, demonstrates and outstanding fluidity when it comes to its interpretation. This abundance of meaning, nevertheless, is deeply rooted in the lack of agency, mostly expressed by the loss of consciousness that deprives one of taking control and thus responsibility over one's own actions—so much so that Kevin Alexander Boon in his 2007 study on the classification of zombies even argues that although zombies with consciousness appear in literature and film, they are only "labeled" as zombies, so he finds it justified to "dismiss their relevance to zombie studies" ("Ontological" 37). His definition of the zombie excludes the possibility of consciousness:

> What is absent from the zombie as reshaped during the twentieth century by western culture, is its essential self—its human soul, those qualities that make a person unique among others…. Zombies cannot retain a sense of self—a unique, human consciousness. This defining characteristic is often muddled in literature and film, but it is more central to the zombie myth than death, as you can have a zombie who is not actually dead, but you cannot have a zombie that retains its sense of identity [36].

In a similar vein, Jeffrey Jerome Cohen also claims that "zombies are never individualized" ("Undead" 403). Nevertheless, it is also Cohen who argues in his "Monster Culture" (1996) that the monster always escapes and returns, and is ready to transform (4–6), and from this it follows that even the zombie is capable of returning in different clothing.

Surprising as it may sound, the new zombie outfit of the past few years appears to be consciousness and individuality. The appearance of the conscious zombie is not a misunderstanding of the zombie concept, but a "mutation," an evolution called for by a new cultural context. The trend of creating the sympathetic version of the monster may have reached vampire literature earlier,[2] but did not leave zombies untouched, either. Zombies may walk slower, and sometimes just crawl, but they catch up with their undead relatives, and invade new, undiscovered spaces of liminality. They have bitten into the coming-of-age novel, and the conscious zombie of the maturation novel has proven that the "evolved zombie" (Bishop, *The Rise* 159) is able to serve the theme of growing up in a unique manner, thereby reforming Young Adult fiction, too. One may consider the conscious zombie as a subset of the broad category of zombie, but to leave it out of zombie studies, as Boon suggests, would be a *grave* mistake. In this chapter I will discuss two novels that utilize the zombie as a symbolic character of teenagehood, showing that having consciousness does not deprive the protagonists of the special and disturbing features that render them initially both disempowered and a curious presence that cautions about human mortality. They manifest the abilities that Wylie Lenz presents as criteria for identifying a monster as a zombie: they are indeed contagious and "disrupt a host of categories reliant on presumed binaries, destabilizing oppositions such as human/nonhuman, subject/object, and—most obviously—living/dead" (100). Yet unlike most zombie novels, in which the zombie is presented as an inseparable part of a horde and without unique features, Daryl Gregory's *Raising Stony Mayhall* (2011) and M.R. Carey's *The Girl with All the Gifts* (2014) place the individualized zombie in the center and discuss transformation in terms of the individual (as coming-of-age novels do) and society (as zombie fiction usually does), underlining the theme of taking social responsibility as a prerequisite for growing up.

Both selected works feature a zombie protagonist: in *Raising*, we follow Stony Mayhall's existence from his babyhood in 1968 to what people think to be his final death in 2010, and even beyond that, to his excavation and preparation for a burial (or a new life) in 2011; and in *The Girl*, we see a few days of the teenage Melanie's life, in which her maturation is sped up by the extraordinary situation she finds herself in. What is peculiar in the two novels is their focus on the importance of the family in the zombie protagonists' lives, even though Melanie in Carey's fiction does not have a family in the traditional sense. The protagonists' adherence to what they hold as their family is all the more intriguing because, in zombie literature and film, the family is usually used as a tool to highlight the weakness of the myth about the power of family relations, about the strength of love that allows one to reach beyond his or her own boundaries and act as a superhero to defend or save his or her beloved ones. In zombie fiction, a recurrent emotional peak comes in the form of killing a beloved one who has turned into a zombie or not protecting a beloved one in order to save one's own life. Zombies stress human failure and reflect on how late modernity brought about a crisis in the values people had once held dear. During this period, readers are well acquainted with the devaluation of various forms of connectedness (Rutherford 7), the family being probably the most important one.

As the zombie is the perfect symbol of disintegration, it can be linked to the decay of social structures; since zombies more often than not inhabit dystopian spaces, they are also indicators of the global decay that affects our planet. As Jennifer Rutherford explains, "In lieu of the modernist maxim 'make it new' zombie fictional works drive the future into a cul-de-sac of no return. They hold out no promise, no hope, only the working through of what it is that makes the present an endless prolepsis of ruin" (9). These features of zombie literature, however, contradict the general expectations of literature written for an adolescent audience. Even if we just have a look at dystopian fiction, we may note that one of the basic dissimilarities between the books written for a younger audience and for an adult audience resides in the inclusion or exclusion of hope: dystopia for young adults, as Kay Sambell highlights, successfully problematizes the moral issues by revealing their ingrained ambiguities and provides a closure that promises hope ("Presenting" 164). Thus, when zombies meet coming-of-age fiction that targets a younger audience, we may deservedly expect the subversion of the zombie symbol. But how may zombies become the carriers of hope?

Inseparable from Family: Daryl Gregory's Raising Stony Mayhall

Raising Stony Mayhall by Daryl Gregory does not fit the clear-cut category of Young Adult fiction, but the first third of the novel is almost a classic coming-of-age narrative from babyhood to the point of leaving family and starting independence. The middle part shows Stony detached from his family: he finds refuge in the society of zombies and then becomes a prisoner held in an institute run by people—a longer narrative part that allows the author to focus more on social criticism. While the interconnectedness of these narratives is evident throughout the novel, it is the closure that dramatically joins them to explore the value in human life: Stony risks his "undead life" or existence to save his niece, Ruby, and then Ruby does everything that is in her power to reconnect Stony with the family. The novel details a fantastic transformation that rejects the traditional interpretation of zombiehood: the living dead baby saved from certain annihilation grows up to become the savior of his family and mankind. As Daryl Gregory himself confirms, "the best, most efficient description of the book" that he has encountered is "zombildungsroman" (TalkTim).

Family is a key concept in understanding what makes Stony's existence as a zombie special. For the family—just as for the rest of the society—a member usually becomes an Other as soon as (s)he is turned into a zombie. The transformation immediately creates an uncanny body, a combination of the heimlich and the unheimlich, a monstrous reminder of who the person was. This process becomes reversed in the case of Stony's "life." He is an Other by birth: he is found as a baby, protected by the dead body of his human mother. Wanda, a widow and a mother of three, finds the two bodies while driving home with her children. As she is a mother herself, she cannot leave the baby's body there in the dark and cold; and then, when in the car the baby opens his eyes, she hurries home to save the boy whom she thinks is a human baby. Soon, however, she and her oldest daughter Alice realize that they took home a zombie baby. Their surprise comes not from the realization that zombies actually exist. They were already aware of this because, earlier that year, a brief zombie attack on the world's population had taken place but was successfully stopped before it could have turned the whole world into zombies. Wanda's and Alice's surprise stems from two factors: official reports claim that all zombies were destroyed (and this claim indeed is supported by the fact that people are not being attacked by zombies any more, and no new apocalyptic situation has emerged); furthermore, the baby seems not to have been bitten by a zombie but born as a zombie, while his mother died as a human. The birth of a zombie baby upsets all previous knowledge about zombies, and as zombies are known to be capable of only decay but not growth, it also seems that Stony is going to be the very first—and only—zombie who will never be capable of destroying humanity by initiating a zombie tsunami. As times goes on, Stony indeed proves to be an exceptional undead, a real wonder of his kind, although he does not stay the toothless baby that he is when the Mayhalls find him.

The incredible beginning of Stony's existence appears to doom him to stay a baby for as long as his body holds; therefore, Wanda cannot see how the baby would threaten anyone's life (except that it is illegal and punishable by law to hide a zombie, so Stony is a threat because of legal considerations). She decides to keep the baby and "raise" him in her family, though at first raising does not seem to be a good word for the care she provides, as Stony's height and weight remain constant for a long time. The change comes when Stony accidentally meets the new neighbor boy, Kwang Cho, after which he miraculously starts to grow. As Wanda recognizes the link between Kwang's physical touch and Stony's development, she asks the Korean family to allow their son to visit them regularly, assuring the parents that the strange, stone-colored baby—hence the name Stony—poses no harm to anyone.

Although it is obvious that the Cho family understands what Stony is, they become allies of the Mayhalls, and the most plausible explanation for this lies in their experience of being Others. They are new to the neighborhood, immigrants to the country, and the mother does not even speak English when they move to Easterly. In America, and especially in this very small community of Easterly, Iowa, where everyone knows every resident of the neighborhood, the Korean family is the Other. Their outsider status endows them with the necessary empathy, since they know very well that Otherness is not to be feared automatically. That they will always be outsiders in the town to a certain extent is indicated by how Kwang's name is recurrently pronounced improperly by Officer Tines even after the Chos have lived there for decades. But as Kwang develops a bond with the baby, and the Mayhalls desire his company and interpret his friendship as beneficial for their family, the Chos become embraced by at least this small part of the New World that they wish to belong to. Their status as members of the Mayhall extended family is clear: they are also invited to the "graduation" dinner that Wanda gives for Stony, and when Stony returns to Easterly with Ruby, Mrs. Cho hugs him as a mother would. The Chos offer their help and never suggest that they hold Stony responsible for the accident in which their son Kwang loses his legs.

As Kwang becomes a regular visitor in the Mayhall household, Stony grows rapidly until he reaches Kwang's size, and from then on he develops in the same tempo as his friend does, always having even the same size for clothes and shoes. This connection is never explained in the novel but noted by several of the characters as a curious phenomenon that nobody thinks is accidental, implanting the idea in the reader's head as well that there must be, after all, an explanation behind this manifestation of the special bond between the boys. His curious attachment to Kwang provides an interesting comparison between the human Kwang and the zombie Stony because the reader gets to see Kwang not only as Stony's best friend and surrogate brother but also as a very strange doppelgänger who constantly provides an example of the life that Stony will never have. For the zombie may lack an accurate yet complex definition (Dendle, *The Zombie Movie* 13) in criticism, but "zombies do all share a common characteristic: the absence of some metaphysical quality of their essential selves" (Boon, "And the Dead" 7). The undead are usually *made* from people, and are not naturally born, so the common zombie is always the uncanny form of his former self— something that Stony obviously lacks. However, when Stony begins to develop due to Kwang's "magical" touch and grows to match his neighbor in his size, it is the Korean boy who starts functioning as the human whose uncanny form is Stony. Although Wanda and her daughters love and care for Stony, the Mayhall family is made up of only females, so Kwang is the first boy who touches the zombie baby's body. It appears, then, that he is the first human who is not only young enough to become Stony's playmate but even has the right sex to become a kind of double for Stony.

For the boys, teenagehood becomes the period of experimenting with finding their boundaries. They both experience a strange combination of freedom and limitation not only due to their adolescence but also to their interconnectedness. Stony wishes to have the freedom that Kwang enjoys, allowing him to have a social life: going to school, having meals, consuming alcohol, having a sexual drive, and so on. While a human body would be a ticket for Stony to socializing in a human environment, it would confront him with various limitations unknown to his monstrous body and admired by Kwang. For Kwang, not needing food to function physically, not suffering from the effects of alcohol, not feeling pain and not getting impaired by injuries are all part of the freedom that Stony enjoys thanks to his special physicality. Correspondingly, Kwang is filled with awe by the unheard-of possibilities that his friend's zombie body displays, so he thrives to find out where its limits are just as much as Stony does.

These adolescent years give foundations for the wondrous dimension of Stony's undead existence. In fact, one may even claim that Stony becomes capable of extending his limits as far as it is shown in the novel exactly because he does have an adolescence, a phase of intense development and maturation in his zombiehood, as opposed to all the fellow zombies whom he meets later and whose living dead existence is characterized by an intense retrogression. His curiosity about his own nature is shaped by the fact that he does have a family; he is constantly in an environment that forces him to register the differences between his existence and his family members' life.

Beyond the everyday routines that they cannot share, his family members specifically make Stony more aware of how zombie existence differs from living as a human, so Stony develops a sense of self that has religious, mythological, and medical considerations. For his sister June, the zombie embodies her fear concerning salvation; she would like to save Stony's soul, as she refuses to believe that he does not have one. Although Stony thinks he actually lacks a soul, June's efforts make him contemplate his own existence in terms of religion; he researches the Bible and thinks a lot about resurrections and salvation.

While June is preoccupied by the idea of saving Stony's soul, his eldest sister Alice and Kwang focus on Stony's body. For Alice, who studies to become a doctor, the zombie body is a representation of various anxieties connected to physicality. Because no one knows what exactly turns a human into a zombie, Stony is the body of the unknowable. The fact that there is no scientific explanation for the existence of zombies (let alone the existence of a zombie who is born as a baby and is capable of growth) turns Stony's body into a warning that human knowledge has limits tightly linked to the confines of mankind's existence on the level of the individual and the global alike. Understanding zombiefication and zombiehood would give a better chance for mankind's survival in a world that has or may produce zombies any time, but due to the lack of this knowledge, Stony stands for people's fear of powerlessness and instant apocalypse. Alice's attitude, however, generates a scientific curiosity in Stony; he is eager to learn medicine in order to help research the zombie condition and he develops a scientist's mentality, which will help him later on to consciously experiment on his own body.

Kwang is also obsessed with the zombie body, but as a teenager, his reaction to what his friend may physically endure or achieve is mostly characterized by wonder rather than fear. Although Kwang never says or shows that he envies Stony, the superhero-context he places Stony in when they test zombie endurance reveals his admiration and repressed desire. Kwang is inspired by his comic book culture when he names Stony the Unstoppable. The difference in the two boys' approaches to the name is telling: Stony wants something added after the adjective unstoppable, in the manner Hulk becomes the Incredible Hulk in the Marvel universe, thriving for some kind of definition of his self, whereas Kwang insists that the Unstoppable is "like 'the Thing'" (Daryl 17). In his usage, the Unstoppable stands for the definition of Stony's identity exactly because it is as limitless as a "thing" is when it is used to define something. Not constituting an exact category, the undefined "Thing" can denote anything, so the Unstoppable emerges as the definition of the monster for Kwang, with unclear boundaries and superpower, always standing in contrast with the clearly defined—and confined—human existence. Stony wants something more concrete, as he is less comfortable with thinking of himself as a monster, but as his own existence is as much of an unexplored territory to himself as it is to Kwang, the zombie boy adapts Kwang's vision of his self when he needs to come to term with his role in the universe.

Kwang incessantly points out the positive side of his friend's Otherness, which allows Stony to create his own mythology with which he is able to identify. After he grows out of playing Unstoppable with Kwang, he discovers the zombie detective Jack Gore from the *Deadtown* novel series. From this point on he sees himself as the good and beneficial zombie, the undead hero who can make use of his special abilities to better the world. However, he must soon realize that this almost utopian vision is doomed to failure because of his monstrosity.

When Stony has to put on the old ski-mask with its mark U standing for Unstoppable, he does so for practical reasons: to rescue June from a party. His mission starts out indeed as a superhero act. Since his body is not responsive to alcohol, he is ready for action, unlike Kwang, who has drunk so much that he can hardly walk, let alone drive. But being physically able to perform an act is one thing; performing an act that needs practice beside physical ability and theory is another. Stony fails in a threefold manner because of his monstrosity: he cannot stay invisible in the company of humans because of his appearance, so the ski mask automatically marks him as Other; he is indeed unstoppable by other kids, as he is stronger than those who want to stop him, which directs attention to him; and finally, as he could not have the average life a teenager, he never gained practice in driving, which results in a severe accident. The car he drives proves to be *unstoppable* in time, and the collision with another car takes June's life and Kwang's two legs.

This event brings a complete turn in Stony's undead existence: he has to flee to save himself, and he starts thinking of himself not as a superhuman entity with the potential to become a hero but as a threat—not so much as a real threat on society, but a menace on his most beloved people, his family, who have taken great risks when they hid and raised him. He causes trouble for his sister Chrystal when he visits her later, and when the zombie apocalypse breaks out, he also thinks that the invasion is his fault, because indirectly it was made possible by his help even though he always fought against the Big Bite—the plan in which zombies launch a focused, global attack on humanity.

While it seems that this whirlpool of undesired events suck Stony in, and he finally accepts his role of being a zombie understood in the traditional sense, standing for decay on various levels, Stony's story is really about empowerment despite all odds. After he has long given

2. Apocalyptic Monsters in Need of a Family 45

up playing superhero, Stony in reality becomes the Unstoppable and the Invulnerable, a superhero who has greater power than an average human because of what his body can take. His unexplained, in fact inexplicable birth is only the sign of what he is to accomplish later; what is more, his incredible development (that he reaches well into his adulthood if we consider human lifespan, but in a strange, elongated adolescence if we consider his zombie "existence span") is made possible by all the influences that he has had as part of the Mayhall family.

His story of birth becomes a legend that justifies and foreshadows his extraordinary deeds and attracts the attention of the initiated zombies, as well as the doctor who captures him. Enjoying a privileged position in the prison due to his special background, Stony becomes a leader character, a cohesive force among the zombies who are held captive, spreading out his words secretly under the nose of the prison authorities. He continuously tries his limits, and once he has proof of Wanda's love and proof that she cared for him, his experiments, once only theoretical explorations of the possible, become practical tests about his own possibilities of obtaining freedom. When he manages to break free from Deadtown, he becomes a legendary hero, the one who escaped, the one who performed what was thought to be impossible, because he is unstoppable.

Although Gregory never makes the analogue explicit in the novel, the "messianistic overtones" (Faircloth) that are nearly completely overlooked in the book reviews associate Stony's trajectory with those of the great prophets that we know from the Scriptures. Emblematic details from Jesus's life as recorded in the Bible resurface in mutated forms in Stony's "life": he has a mysterious conception and birth; his existence is considered a threat by the authorities; he grows into a miracle-performing, prophet-like character for the zombies; he is betrayed, he dies and resurrects (several times).

Stony's first resurrection comes when he is given a chance for survival by the Mayhall family. They actually all think—rightly—that the baby is dead when they find him, and they take his unexpected opening of his eyes and movement of his limbs as the sign of his resurrection. Metaphorically speaking, they raise him from the dead when Wanda decides to raise him as her child, that is, put him under the protection of her family. But there are two more resurrections to come for Stony.

Deadtown is like the Valley of the Shadow of Death for Stony, the darkest place for zombies on Earth, which promises only one thing: the end of existence. It is an emblematic place, which fuses the real and the fictive, the imaginary for Stony because of his admired *Deadtown* novel series; and it is here where he keeps exploring how the real may be extended into the realm of the imaginary. Stretching the boundaries of his physical existence through focusing not on the body but on the power that makes his body function allows him to reach the freedom(s) he desires. He is able to leave Deadtown, which was meant to be his final grave, and he is able to find freedom beyond the limits of his disintegrating physicality.

After his legendary resurrection (surviving the shot in the head that should destroy him), Stony once again dies and rises, but as his evolution is *unstoppable*, his dying and resurrecting demonstrate Stony's transformation. In Deadtown, arranging fake death is part of his plan to escape, and thus he consciously prepares for his resurrection. Although death comes more brutally than how he calculated, he still survives thanks to his former efforts to better understand his own existence and to the practices that enable him to have control over his body even after having lost a great part of it. He even loses his brain and still stays as functional as he was before, demonstrating that the brain for him is not an organ that he needs for thinking. In Easterly, the circumstances of his death and resurrection are different. First of all, he does not *want* to die and resurrect; he wants to save people from the zombie invasion, and while doing so, he sacrifices himself, accepting the death that he always thought would come to him. He suffers death by fire—the kind of death that is known to be fatal for zombies—and he cannot expect himself to survive despite his promising experiments and practices. His resurrection is not prearranged exactly because he accepts his death, and therefore, he needs assistance to resurrect. His niece Ruby gives him the help that he used to provide for Deadtown's "sleeping" zombies who tried to put an end to their existence but were unable to.

Stony's story of deaths and resurrections is a story about seeking and granting salvation. Due to June's religiousness, Stony thinks he must be in purgatory by default, but when he indirectly causes June's death and a lot of suffering for his family, he feels that punishment is due. He risks his life because he does not care if he dies, thinking he should probably stop existing, after all. Encountering death is always a necessary step in his evolution (June's or Valerie's death is as important in this respect as his own death), each occasion allowing him to understand more about his own existence and to reach beyond the possible. His sense of guilt compels him to keep what has remained from his family safe, so his attempts at reaching absolute freedom are motivated by his sense of belonging to the people who helped to raise him. His deaths and resurrections are the means of (re-)connecting with his family. Eager for redemption, he tries to save at least Chrystal's daughter, Ruby, from death (or zombiehood), assuming that this might be the atonement that could save him and help him leave this purgatory.

Curiously, saving the people in Easterly, accepting his death, and being ready to fall into annihilation result in Stony's seemingly limitless extension of existence. By having learned how he may replace the lost parts of his body and have control over his artificial addenda, he discovers the way to connect more and more of his environment to his own self, making his surroundings the virtual extension of his body. Giving up more and more of his original body, he realizes that existence is practically independent of his own individual physicality. Therefore, the I–Suit is the only suit that ever fits him; it is the only suit that truly reveals his identity. With the I–Suit, he has no need to wish to fit in or fit a role that is expected of him. The I–Suit fits. Sarah Heaton argues that "in an amusing turn the suit designed by the leader of the zombie revolt is called an integrity suit pointing out that the integrity is the clothing itself where little else can be trusted, least of all one's flesh, whether living or dead" (153). This statement is correct as long as we speak of the general's armor, but on the final pages of the novel the connotation of the I–Suit, just as our understanding of Stony's integrity, transforms, and the suit begins to mark the extraordinary lack of physicality that does not prevent Stony from resurrecting his self. The suit signals a phenomenal integrity that transcends bodily limitations. In the end, we understand that it is not the costume that makes the superhero: after Stony has tried all sorts of costumes in search for an identity that he could accept, he arrives as a superhero who needs neither a costume nor even flesh on his black bones. The I–Suit is an emblematic embrace given by his family—Ruby. This closes the circle that begins with the fur-coat with which his mother tried to save the baby Stony. The I–Suit recalls the protection that Stony received as an infant through the fur-coat, "the image of nurturing and sacrifice which this coat, made out of skin, symbolizes" (Heaton 150). The I–Suit also recalls the suit that Stony gets from his adapted mother as a graduation present, which represents a rite of passage for Wanda Mayhall (150) and becomes also a link to Stony's natural mother, as the suit helps him visit his mother's grave. The pieces of clothes that Stony receives from his family members help him build an autonomous and firm identity, allowing him to preserve his integrity in all situations.

Stony's monstrous body is a curious signifier, as it does not have a constant shape, and the less he has of it, the more potential it indicates. The zombie body, originally a metaphor for decomposition, gradually metamorphoses into a symbol for ableness that knows no boundaries as the body thins away and the character exercises an increasing power. The body that is a continuous display of disintegration indicates the borderline not between life on earth and death, as it conventionally does, but between the expected and the imaginable. Just as Stony as a baby was expected to die but was allowed to grow with the help of his adapting family, he is also expected to die at the end of the story but is resurrected—raised again—by his family. Ruby insists on finding his bones, assembling them, and then, most importantly, she convinces Stony to acknowledge his presence to her.

Raising, referring to both education and resurrection, links family as well as death/life in Stony's experiences: he is not only brought up by his foster family, but in all the above listed cases when he is supposed to die, family—directly or indirectly—intervenes and prevents him from dying. His death and resurrection, however, give redemption not only to his family and the people in Easterly, but to humanity and the zombie world alike, as it prevents apocalypse.

Separated from Family: M.R. Carey's The Girl with All the Gifts

Similarly to Stony, Melanie becomes a savior character in M.R. Carey's *The Girl with All the Gifts*, but while her trajectory is very different from Stony's, some of the shared motifs of the two novels allow for a worthy comparison of how the monstrous is applied as the metaphor for potential and growth.

Melanie's story encompasses a brief but intense period of maturation. The reader does not get a glimpse into the protagonist's childhood; neither does (s)he see her development as an adult. The novel focuses on her coming-of-age point that is dominantly generated by two factors: the expansion of the world in a physical sense, as Melanie is finally confronted with parts of the world beyond her earlier confinements, and her growing sense of family despite the fact that she is brought up in a very hostile environment, never having a chance of living in a family.

The prison-like base is reminiscent of Deadtown in *Raising*; it functions as a research base where the captured zombies are under complete surveillance and kept "alive" for research purposes but treated as monstrous creatures that pose unimaginable threat to humanity. While Melanie does not age considerably during the accounted events, her monstrosity is the reason why we may see her as a child first and then a maturing teenager who tries to make the most responsible decision she is capable of within her limited possibilities. Due to her zombiehood that she is not even aware of, she is kept ignorant of the world that surrounds her and is able to sense only a very tiny slice of it. As a result, she lacks sufficient knowledge and displays a disturbingly limited understanding of herself and the events that she comes to take part in.

There is a considerable difference between the childhood (or adolescent) limitations that Stony and Melanie experience. Their zombiehood poses divergent levels of prohibitions on them. Stony's impediments on freedom stem from his family's love and care, while Melanie's are directly rooted in society's fear of the monstrous. Stony may have access to up-to-date, in-depth knowledge of science and other subjects despite the fact that he is not allowed to attend school. His situation may be compared to that of a child whose illness prevents him from going to school, but whose right to education and knowledge, nevertheless, is not harmed. Melanie, in contrast, participates in the institutionalized form of education whose aim is not to provide useful information for the children but to test their abilities of intellectual growth. Accordingly, Melanie learns a lot, but much of what is taught for her is irrelevant, useless or even misleading, false information. She proves to be a very curious and clever girl, always trying to make sense of all that she has learned and experienced, but due to her confinement, she shows symptoms similar to high-functioning autism, excelling at certain skills while spectacularly failing at others. She reflects on her experiences more than what she is able to communicate. Routine provides her with a sense of security, but breaking the routine causes her extreme distress. Her world (and thus her existence) revolves around the teacher Miss Helen Justineau, the only person who considers her pupils children and not monsters.

Melanie, just like Stony, is a special zombie, embodying a curiosity within the spectrum of zombiehood. Stony is one of his kind, somebody whom both humans and the other zombies consider as a unique specimen. Melanie's case is somewhat different: she belongs to a special type of zombies, a group of second generational zombies who are born as zombies (in this sense she is comparable to Stony), but she stands out even from this category because of her noticeably high intelligence. All the zombie kids in Melanie's class have consciousness and intelligence, proving that there is a subcategory within the zombies whose individuals have partial resistance to the fungus that infects humans and turns them into unconscious zombies.

But should we be happy about the existence of conscious zombies? The body of the conscious zombie is a body of controversies in both works. In *Raising*, it becomes the symbol of near-limitless possibilities but also a signifier of an equilibrium; as a messiah character, Stony brings temporary peace between zombies and humans, but warns about the fragile nature of the formed status quo. In *The Girl*, Melanie's body exposes the duality—and in fact, contradictory nature—of her role to come: her adolescent body as a conventional metaphor standing for the future generation of mankind signifies hope; her zombified body, however, warns us about the downfall of humanity.

Melanie's value system is not rooted in a direct experience of having a human family, so the zombie girl develops a special attachment to the person who has a firm role in her life and who has the least prejudice toward zombie children. Melanie has a platonic idea of a harmonious relationship between herself and Miss Justineau and works very hard not to give her teacher any reason for doubting that she is worthy of Miss Justineau's love. However, when she accidentally finds a group of children similar to her, she makes a choice and decides that the family she feels really responsible for is the group of zombie kids with intelligence and without parents, just as she is. Her zombie body becomes the borderline between human and Other, a warning that one may not belong to both groups even though the monstrous body seems to be a combination of the human and something Other. In the dystopian world that Carey created, there is no possibility for even a temporary status quo. There is something that might be interpreted as a frightening compromise: in a world of zombies, the sentient zombie (the humanized monster) may come out triumphant against the unconscious zombie hordes, but uninfected humanity is not given a chance for survival. In this space of imagination, humanizing the monster appears as an ultimate goal, the optimistic alternative in contrast to the unstoppable apocalypse of unconscious zombies.

Nevertheless, Melanie's decision is motivated by her sense of belonging, her desire to have a family, and her experience of fighting zombies to protect Miss Justineau's life. What is important for her is to keep her teacher safe, but saving humanity is never a priority to her. She protects all the human members of the team because she is intelligent enough to see that this is the practical, logical thing to do if she wants to keep Miss Justineau alive. When she encounters the zombie kids that could be like her brothers and sisters, a new sense of belonging starts motivating her actions. She still holds Miss Justineau dear to her heart. Because of what the teacher represents to her, however, she is ready to choose a path that dooms humanity. She protects the human *within* the monstrous, which she thinks is her task if she wants a "livable" future on the planet. Her vision excludes a livable future for humans—her choice is to shape a New World for zombies.

Education is a key motif in both zombie novels. In *Raising*, Stony's unorthodox education enables him to develop a scientific interest and methodology to understand his existence in relation to other zombies and the human population and then use this knowledge to stop the apocalyptic consequences of the Big Bite. Melanie's unusual education endows her with completely different skills. She knows little about science, but after she understands how the infection works, she can figure out the importance of the fungus wall that stops their fleeing and is able to use it to her purposes. The received education that determines mostly her actions is not scientific, but mythological.

Thanks to the importance of Miss Justineau's presence in her life, Melanie's understanding of the world becomes dependent on her mythology studies. Her teacher, Helen Justineau, is best perceived in the context of mythology: her first name as well as her beautiful and magnetic presence evoke Helen of Troy (R. Davis 21), implying even how Melanie will have to contest for her love with Sergeant Parks. The woman's family name, moreover, conjures up the Roman goddess Iustitia, and through her the idea of justice (21) that will drive Melanie in the end to make her decision about the future. Melanie's constant references to myths give her a framework within which to interpret her incredible experiences; as a result, the mythological context shapes the events of her life into a heroic, romantic narrative. Relying on the zombie character as agent, Carey's "semi-Dark-Age post-apocalyptic world with its own past mythology—the reader's own current, *modern* world—uses ancient Greek mythology to try and make sense of it" (Jenkinson-Brown). The body of the living dead zombie exhibits a past which is alive but monstrous, devouring, always hungry, symbolically representing the recognition of how those heroic tales seem to be incompatible with the brave, new world: the past culture cannot satisfy the needs of the culturally disintegrating future, and it may not be the cultural foundation for further development. Melanie in person becomes threatened by her educational background: "The fact that Melanie has been raised with Greek myths and romantic notions in her head seems like something that will ultimately bring about her downfall, because she clings so hard to these outdated notions of the world" (Anders). However, the plot twist at the end of the novel points out that myths still may be used as guides in one's dystopian future, but the use will be something very different from what we may expect in a "normal" world.

Heroism, courage, superpower—these features all relate to Stony as well, but as his world view, due to his upbringing, is anthropocentric, his heroism aims at saving his human family and human society he feels he belongs to despite his Otherness. The same cannot be said about Melanie, who loves a human woman because the woman's sympathy (which roots in her tragic past) makes her excel from her human environment. Melanie's superpower is not comparable to Stony's: she has special skills that humans lack, but she cannot perform as extreme, miracle-like acts as Stony is able to. Therefore, her heroism is more down-to-earth, more practical, too: she recognizes that she cannot save humanity, so she opts to save the remnants of the human that is recognizable in the sentient zombie kids. In making her decision, Melanie's education plays a major role: knowing and acknowledging the power of education, she feels that the planet might be given a chance for survival through the zombies that are capable of growth. Ironically, it is the education and care that Miss Justineau provides for her that makes Melanie care for these other children and put her trust in the possibility of educating them—whereby she dooms humanity to extinction. Generally, zombies "embody physical corruption, thus reminding us of our own mortality" (Boon, "Ontological" 34), but Carey takes this idea a step further and uses the zombie body as a reminder of cultural decline, the gradual loss of what is included in the Humanities, inseparable from the notion of being human.

Of course, one may consider the closure of Carey's novel as the possibility of a new start, annihilating inhumane humanity that is able to put aside sympathy and consider kids—infected, dangerous kids, who, nevertheless, did not choose to become Other and lethal—as beasts or objects. The lack of understanding and care for the disprivileged turns humanity monstrous, whereas Melanie grows to become a sympathetic creature who is able to care for her kind and for the planet's future. This care, however, is scary, and the monstrous body reminds us of that. Originally signaling the borderline between the human and the Other, the zombie cautions that by now the definition of the Other or the monstrous has become as decomposing and unstable as the zombie body, since the fixed point of comparison—the human—has lost its firm, unquestionable content. When the monster and the human stop functioning as each other's antithesis, always opposing each other, a partial overlapping between the monstrous and the human brings about a kind of understanding of the other, a recognition of the self in the other (and thus in the Other), and produces the sympathetic monster in literature.

Conclusion

The deconstruction of the zombie story in both *Raising* and in *The Girl* emanates from the conviction that limitation is not equal with hopelessness. This notion is fundamental in youth literature, where the teenage character confronts authority in one way or another. Hintz and Ostry, for instance, argue that dystopian narratives metaphorically reflect on the authoritative control that adolescents suffer from, as to them "authority appears oppressive, and perhaps no one feels more under surveillance than the average teenager" (Hintz and Ostry qtd. in Ames 9). This explains the popularity of dystopias where various manifestations of control, especially in the form of dictatorship are explored, and the story preferably culminates in acts of resistance, or even revolution. The zombie novel, traditionally, does not belong to this subgenre: the conventional zombie as a literary character lacks will; he is unable to control the masses, and when he is controlled, he is unable to resist. But Gregory and Carey push the zombie novel somewhat in the direction of such dystopian narratives, using as a starting point the existence of a near-totalitarian state whose formation was forced by an apocalyptic attack launched by zombies. In these narratives, therefore, the conscious zombie represents the marginalized segment of the society, defined by various limitations of his or her existence: physical limitations due to an incessant disintegration and limitations posed by society. But in both works fighting such limitations comes in forms that we rarely meet in dystopian adolescent fiction.

As Sarah Juliet Lauro argues in *The Transatlantic Zombie: Slavery, Rebellion, and the Living Dead*, "Inherently and inseparably dual, the zombie symbolizes both the disempowered slave-in-chains and the powerful slave-in-revolt" (10). However, neither of the works I examine solves the conflict with the protagonist leading a revolution, as most protagonists in Young Adult dystopias do, but opt for a different strategy. While Stony is a messiah character for the living dead and would be suitable for becoming a zombie Mockingjay (excuse me for the evoked image), he rejects to lead an apocalyptic invasion. Instead, his main ambition is to fight what makes him monstrous and is able to control: his will to bite. Even when he decides to take part in a fight, he is there not to attack but to protect both humans and zombies, always seeking alternatives to biting and turning humans in order to effect his protection. (If we stick to the *Hunger Games* analogy, he is closer to Peeta in character, rejecting aggression by all means to protect his own integrity that is inseparable from his humanness.) His resolution comes from searching alternatives beyond the usual and easily imaginable, and his belief that limitations may be challenged—his real superpower—turns him into a really incredible character. As a consequence, "in this particular incarnation [of the zombie story], zombies become a vehicle through which to contemplate the body and our relation to the physical world" (Ryle), and to ask questions concerning the power of will. As Karen Burnham argues, "a central theme of the story is the power of Will—exactly the element that the traditional zombie is thought to lack, which analysis totally turns the traditional zombie trope on its head—but Stony lacks the power to exercise much effective Will (i.e., to exercise agency) on his own behalf." Yet Stony is always ready to act on behalf of his own family, and as the story highlights, Stony's definition of his self is always modified as he gradually extends his willpower to gain control over an expanding virtual body of his own.

Extending his body and self by stretching beyond what is physical, including his prosthetic augmentations, begins with acknowledging unity with the family. This solidarity manifests in Chelsea's strategy of choosing a new name for herself (Chrystal), and then giving the name of a precious stone to her daughter (Ruby). Just as Stony's action are always driven by his attachment to his family, so does Chelsea consciously seek a way of not only helping Stony but also emblematically confirming the bond with her adapted zombie brother who gets his nickname Stony after Miss Cho's lame attempt to refer to his Otherness. While stony in Miss Cho's usage is an adjective that describes the baby boy's color and a kind of stiffness and cold that come from the lack of heartbeat (the lack of a heart, actually), his name foreshadows Stony's power that comes from his ability to unite with his natural environment. Stony cares for his stones Chrystal and Ruby, and his empowerment comes from knowing that the connection among the stones is real, so he can hide the breathing ones with his grown stony presence. As a living dead, his place should be six feet below the surface, but understanding his existence, his identity, and the possibility that disprivilege may be metamorphosed into power by accepting one's own nature allows him to perform the unimaginable.

Melanie also performs the unimaginable—not what is impossible to perform because of an assumed lack of skill or competence, but what is considered to be unimaginable because of its fatal consequences. Her character as a savior is as much debatable as that of Pandora's, whose name she craves for instead of the name Melanie, which she does not think matches her (but may in fact be read as a hint at Melanie's "dark" nature). Her mythic, imaginary name Pandora perfectly fits her, and her reflections on desiring this name at the beginning of the novel turn out to be prophetic. As the first woman created by the gods, the Greek Pandora is the representative of a new race, just as Melanie turns out to be special because she is a second-generation zombie, a "creation" of the Others, who prove to be stronger, more powerful than humans. The allusion, in this respect, is very gloomy, implying that in this dystopian world gods have been replaced by zombies and that power comes from physical force and violence. Despite these circumstances, at the end of the story Melanie seizes power exactly because her physical strength is completed with her other gifts—most importantly, her intelligence, which manifests in her ability to learn, understand, evaluate, and draw conclusions.

The title of the novel is itself a reference to Pandora and suggests Melanie's ambiguous, twofold nature. Carey himself acknowledges that he liked the title exactly because "it preserves an ambiguity: it doesn't allow you to necessarily determine whether those gifts are wonderful attributes that she has, or wonderful gifts that she's bringing to you" (Carey qtd. in Grant 17). But this ambiguity is present already in the original myth of Pandora. According to Hesiod, the gods contributed to the creation of Pandora by endowing the new creature with gifts. However, Pandora's other name is Anesidora, which translates as "she who sends up gifts," (Simon 145) describing her mythic role: she was created as a revenge on mankind, and she brought evil on people by giving people the gift of a jar (that is usually referred to as a box due to mistranslation) containing "burdensome toil and sickness that brings death to men" (Hesiod, *Works and Days* 91–2), diseases (102) and "a myriad other pains" (100). Melanie is as much a gifted girl as she is a fearsome creature whose "gift" for mankind is freeing the zombifying fungal spores by setting the fungus wall on fire (as if opening the lid of a jar and releasing the evil from it). She seals the fate of mankind because the future she envisions is that of "natural evolution, a future that will work only when the warring remnants of humanity are gone" (Bishop, "Teaching" 180). As Roger Davis puts it: "she is the hope, yet she is a monstrous hope" (32).³

Yet, if Melanie is a second-generation zombie, she is also a second-generation Pandora: she has agency, and her actions stem from empathy and pragmatism, not from a desire for revenge, so from her perspective, her actions carry hope. "Like the myth of Pandora's box, she sees not only the evils that escape from the box but also the hope that remains in the box as the yet-unopened gift, the Utopian seed in the otherwise dystopian world" (R. Davis 22). She thinks of second-generation hungries as her family and perceives them as a new race when she states that they are "the next people. The ones who make everything okay again" (Carey 456). By securing a future for the second-generation zombies, she symbolically places herself into the role of becoming mother of mankind in a new world to come after the world she knows of falls for good. This role, in fact, also links with the Pandora-myth, as it is Pandora's daughter, Pyrrha with her husband, Deucalion who are the only survivors of the deluge with which Zeus ended the Bronze Age (Ovid). They are thus the ones who repopulate the earth after the world catastrophe, and this way Pandora may be seen also as a character who made it possible for mankind to survive in a new world.

In the novel, freeing the spores from their pods will free the planet and the new race from people and their evil actions, such as launching war on the Others and dissecting them to find the cure. Melanie becomes thus a rescuer, a savior (even if an ambiguous, debatable one), showing a great deal of maturation within a very short period of time, and demonstrating her ability to fight the "stereotype threat," as Kyle William Bishop argues ("Teaching" 173–76). When we first look into her thoughts, she projects her captivity onto the space of fairy tales: she fantasizes about becoming a beautiful lady, to be rescued from her tower by a prince. From a damsel in distress she matures into a heroine who rescues others. She shuts Miss Justineau into the mobile research facility as if locking her into a tower to keep her safe from the zombie attack. She turns her rescuer into a damsel in distress this way, but only so that Miss Justineau may carry out the mission that Melanie assigned to her: to educate the new generation of zombies, who are capable of development. While Sergeant Parks appears to be the person who undertakes the task of saving the team that escapes the military base, in the end it is Melanie who saves the remains of the team (Miss Justineau) and Parks's integrity: she frees the man from his ultimate fear of becoming a zombie. From a zombie child lacking agency she transforms into a character who gradually takes the place of the adults who so far controlled her life. She becomes the driving force for education and protection, but the ambiguity of her performance is disclosed through how the human characters evaluate the outcome. Parks understands that Melanie has doomed humanity, and he does not wish to turn into a monster. Miss Justineau does not "embrace … the dawn of this new world with open arms because she views this change as a form of cleansing and consenting to the natural order of the environment," as Ruzbeh Babaee, Sue Yen Lee, and Siamak Babaee claim (53); instead, she interprets her rescue as a punishment that she deserves for her earlier sins, because "nothing is forgotten and everything is paid" (Carey 459).[4]

Melanie becomes a bridge between humanity and monstrosity, her body displaying this liminal space between the two forms of existence. The monstrous body in *The Girl*, marking the borderline between the possible and the unimaginable, provokes thoughts concerning evolution, just like Stony's body does. Both novels thus connect the knowledge earned by individual maturation—aided by the sense of belonging to a family—and apocalyptic revelations. The novels underscore the idea that "'Apocalypse' has come to mean complete catastrophe, but it has also always meant, in the biblical tradition, a revelation, an unveiling of a tremendous Final Truth" (Lukhurst 182). Through the reinterpretation of the monstrous, Gregory plays with the idea of realizing redemption by surpassing the limits of physicality; Carey, in contrast, confronts us with the idea that surpassing the limits may be seen as a gift, but redemption may in fact be a second coming that ends the world as we now know it. In both works, therefore, the zombie that is capable of growth marks the celebration of ableness that defies limitation, and allows us to read the novels that exhibit the belief that even those who appear the most powerless may become empowered by exhausting the potential in their difference. At the same time, the novels also offer a reading in which decline may be interpreted globally; however, these works go against the trend in which the zombie signals the mainstream of capitalism (McNally 2) and is often equaled with the cultural downturn manifest in "the rise of conservative meme activism, the decline of traditional literacy" (Bruin-Molé 3) as well as "the prospect of a 'post-truth' society, and 'the angry swamp monster of right-wing populism'" (Hartcher qtd. in Bruin-Molé 4). Instead, both Gregory and Carey use the sentient, evolved and continually evolving zombie to underline that the empowerment of the disprivileged becomes the only hope for giving this planet a chance for any kind of survival.

3

The Rebellious Child

Jon Skovron's Man Made Boy *and* Sarah Maria Griffin's Spare and Found Parts

Introduction: The Frankensteinian Heritage

When Brian W. Aldiss names Mary Wollstonecraft Shelley's Gothic novel *Frankenstein; or, The Modern Prometheus* (1818) as the first true science fiction story, he underlines two of its interrelated aspects that make it a seminal work: firstly, the use of scientific experiments to fulfill the protagonist's fantasy and secondly, the rejection of past authorities, whether they be religion, magic or alchemy, in order to trust science on its own (78). While Aldiss's approach may be challenged on the basis that at the time of writing this novel science as such was not a clear discipline, it is without doubt that the novel's core idea is deeply embedded in the scientific explorations and findings of Shelley's age. Frankenstein's monster owes its existence to Shelley's interest and knowledge of the technological innovations of the era it was conceived in, and the novel is "one of the first texts to examine ... the transparent technosubject" Panka (2), which directs attention to the themes of identity, technology, responsibility, as well as one's relationship to one's morality—foregrounded issues in the discussions of coming of age.[1] In our world, where scientific development shapes and in many ways improves everyday reality, yet people's inconsiderate use of technology together with their inability to trust science threaten with apocalypse, it is no wonder that *Frankenstein* has become a fundamental text that we keep returning to when we contemplate man's perplexing relationship to scientific developments that simultaneously promise the creation of utopias and the irrevocable, dystopian dangers of misuse and misconduct.

Uncontrollable Artificial Intelligence stories proliferate in the contemporary science fiction sphere, and recently the Frankensteinian theme of dangerous creation has started to invade the space of Young

Adult fiction. This, in fact, is a very natural evolution, as we live in an age where the young become more and more involved both in technological research and in creation in general; as a consequence, digital natives find Frankenstein's story as one that they can relate to. The use of computer and information technology is ubiquitous now; science and research are to a great extent defined by the technology-wise Generation Y and the older half of Generation Z kids. Post-Millennials are born into a technologically advanced, rapidly developing world, experiencing on a daily basis from their childhood on that boundaries may be pushed to venture into unforeseen territories. The widespread use of social media platforms even among the young makes it possible for children to create various "products" that spectacularly show how one's creative energy may influence his or her environment. Thanks to Internet, captured moments of creativity, as well as cuteness or stupidity alike may go viral. More and more children are now YouTubers, sharing short videos that they have created; adolescents are active on Facebook, Twitter, but most importantly on Instagram, and are keen on getting as many followers as possible. Bloggers and vloggers start their activities at a very early age now. In short, we live in an age where access to knowledge via Internet has produced a generation that excels at self-teaching, allowing children and adolescents to perform in these platforms creatively and leading numerous young adults to participate in serious research projects.

Autodidacticism plays a crucial role in the life of Generation Z, and the story of Frankenstein and his monster appeals to these self-taught teenagers. Victor Frankenstein is not satisfied with institutional education, so he seeks more on his own, whereas his creature is excluded from parental and institutional education, which leaves self-education as his only option to make sense of the world and of himself. At the core of Shelley's novel lies the thirst for forbidden, blasphemous knowledge as well as the wish to change the world by creating something that transcends past achievements. But "to boldly go where no man has gone before"[2] demands an incessant reconsideration of ethical laws. As H. Davies claims, *Frankenstein* may in fact still be read in a scientific context, informing us about medical research ethics that are still valid ("Can Mary Shelley's"). The theme of self-education and the theme of rejecting authority promise a fruitful combination for coming-of-age stories targeting today's youth especially because *Frankenstein*'s subtext addresses other important issues relevant to Young Adult fiction. The parent-child relationship with a major focus on the consequences of lacking proper parental affection, as Laura P. Claridge argues, is so intrinsic in Shelley's work that "Victor's exaggerated (and therefore unmistakable) neglect of his progeny serves merely as a bolder-than-life projection of the novel's other, more oblique family conflicts" (16). Intertwined both with this topic and the theme of dangerous knowledge is the theme of responsibility and making choices, which are pronounced subjects for youth fiction.

Yet *Frankenstein* is not only the earliest science fiction novel but also the étalon of monster literature in which equal emphasis is devoted to creator, creature, and the relationship between the two. This feature keeps Shelley's work fresh: early 21st century political-cultural discourse has been characterized by continuous attempts at renegotiating and redefining concepts of norm and the non-normative other, inclusion and exclusion, political correctness and intolerance. If anything, otherness and social tolerance at the present are hot topics; additionally, adolescents are particularly sensitive to the issue of otherness because they feel "other" by definition in their fluid state between childhood and adulthood. As social discourse nowadays largely concerns itself with the emergence of diverse social groups who finally start to claim their voice, young adults are to conform to a society in which voices of otherness become gradually audible; in consequence, the story of Frankenstein and his monster—the first literary monster with a voice of his own— may offer up-to-date, valuable lessons about difference and attitudes to otherness for those who read the novel attentively. Several critics point out that *Frankenstein* criticizes the prejudice towards disfigured people and also "questions those cultural values that circumscribe and devalue other differently enabled populations" (Marchbanks 24). In such a reading, as Anna Kérchy observes, "monstrousness does not correspond to the horrifying nature of the monster but arises from the horrendous nature of the onlookers" (33, my translation); that is, monstrosity relates to society's inhumane character that displays a shocking lack of empathy, incapability of solidarity, and practice of discrimination and marginalization. It is the shocked gaze that transforms the subject of the gaze into a monster, as it is reinforced by Jeffrey Jerome Cohen's thesis about the inseparability of the monster from its creator ("Monster" 20). The monster may be perceived as the physical projection of what Julia Kristeva defines as abjection[3]; and thus when the abjection comes to life, it is compelled to accompany the creator to the very end. This tight union is expressed by the Monster's reaction to finding Victor Frankenstein dead, as he sees no reason for his own further existence; and this inherent attraction and similarity—as well as a realization of the uncanny in the other and the foreshadowing of the collision of interests and objectives—are visualized in Kenneth Branagh's film *Marry Shelley's Frankenstein* (1994) by the scene in which creator and creature, both naked, collide in the rain soon after the monster is brought to life—a scene that captures the subtext of the Frankenstein novel, as Aldiss observes (78). The identification between child and father is finalized by a symbolic gesture: the Monster takes his creator's coat and is to roam the world in that clothing whose purpose is to mask his monstrous nature; however, in harmony with how masks functioned in classical Greek drama, this coat also reveals the true relationship between Frankenstein and his progeny.

All these marked features of the Frankenstein-myth, together with the feminist context in which it has been continuously discussed ever since Ellen Moers published her pivotal essay "Female Gothic: The Monster's Mother" in 1972, recur in the *Frankenstein*-inspired novels targeting a Young Adult readership. The two examples examined here, Jon Skovron's *Man Made Boy* and Sarah Maria Griffin's *Spare and Found Parts*, display very different takes on the theme: the former is an urban fantasy with a male protagonist, while the latter is a dystopia featuring a female protagonist. These novels, however, share three motifs that clearly serve their authors' educational and sensitizing purposes, addressing the generation of young adults: firstly, the adolescent protagonist in both novels is a monster character of some sort, who himself/herself becomes a creator; secondly, monstrosity in both novels is entwined with queerness; finally, the focus on information technology presented as a monster that is both dangerous and tamable directly links these fantastic stories to the everyday experiences of contemporary teenagers.

The Frankensteinian Heritage in Young Adult Monster Fantasy: Jon Skovron's Man Made Boy

Man Made Boy (2013) by Jon Skovron is a unique, sequence-like extension of the original Frankenstein-story set in an alternate contemporary America. The protagonist Boy is the product of Frankensteinian creation in its closest sense: he is the assembled son of Frankenstein's Monster and his wife Bride. In Skovron's fiction, Frankenstein's famous creation not only survived his creator and has stayed "alive" but also got the chance to marry Bride, who had been fully assembled and called to life by Frankenstein. Boy is seventeen, which makes him a late child in his parents' life, as the story is set in contemporary America; yet aging on the physical level is negligible in this strange family, as the monstrous bodies in question do not age and die the way human bodies do. Science-induced and magical creatures at the same time, Boy and his parents prove to be much more enduring than humans are, capable of existing for centuries, since their various worn out body parts may easily be replaced to complete the body and make it perfectly functional again. Yet just as it is with humans, consciousness is not a component that can be replaced, and a person's conscience is something that develops and evolves with age. As a result, aging plays a key role in the psychological development of some of the characters in Skovron's novel, as Boy's coming-of-age story focuses on his growth in "tak[ing] responsibility for his actions and find[ing] a courage inside himself he never knew he had" (Skovron qtd. in Kristin). For this purpose, the re-imagining of the *Frankenstein*-story in a contemporary setting proves to be a logical and effective choice.

That Skovron indeed lays emphasis on the theme of coming of age becomes evident on the very first pages of the novel. Boy believes he should change his name, since it does not fit him any more: as a magical, yet cyborg-like creature, he is seventeen now, and has said goodbye to his childlike appearance after his "mom finished upgrading all [his] kid parts to adult parts" (Skovron 5). He feels that he should complete his maturation process by a symbolic gesture, as "upgrading" has been only a mechanical procedure. Receiving a new name is a rite of passage in some cultures; for instance, as Elizabeth Pearson Waugaman points out, "in the Native American naming tradition, names should change. Children receive names that are descriptive, they may be given new names at adolescence, and again as they go through life according to what their life experiences and accomplishments are." In various mythologies, names carry a magical power, and building on this idea, contemporary writers tend to indicate a character's symbolic role through a well-chosen name. Especially in Young Adult fiction, the motif of earning one's true name, the one that reflects one's identity as an emblematic closure to one's maturation often appears, as it does, for instance, in *Coraline* and *The Graveyard Book* by Neil Gaiman, both to be discussed later. Boy in Skovron's novel longs for this symbolic change of his name, but at the outset of his adventure, he is too immature to realize that he needs to earn his name. Therefore, his expressed desire, actually, foreshadows his adventures that will bring about his real maturation.

His problems, intensified by having entered adolescence, root in his monstrous existence. The theme of monstrosity—just like the theme of taking responsibility—is presented by Skovron in a context that challenges everyday conceptions about difference. Both Shelley and Skovron gave voice to their Monsters so that they may show their perspectives and point to society's intolerance to the Other. Shelley's approach depended on the perspective of an isolated, one-of-his-kind creature confronting normative society; Boy's circumstances, on the other hand, guarantee that in Skovron's novel not only do we find a presentation of social injustice, but there is also room for subverting society's conception of what constitutes the norm and what consequences falling behind with conforming to the norm may have.

Boy lives in a monster community that disguises and utilizes its freakish features by entertaining people with theater performances. Its members fool their human audience by impressing them with various incredible stunts, which the spectators perceive as fantastic illusions, although what they actually see is a staged demonstration of the performers' monstrosity. This framework immediately invokes the tradition of freak shows once so popular in England and in the U.S. in the 19th century. The freak show, as an umbrella term, may be applied to various types of performances that grew out of "lusus naturae" exhibits of dead, anomalous specimens of species, which were completed with living humans that appeared monstrous to the audience because of the physical deviances their bodies displayed (Chemers 6).

Although "freakery" and "disability," as Helen Davies explains, are not exact synonyms, "both notions speak of the prejudice towards and marginalisation of bodies figured as 'different'" (*Neo-Victorian* 7). Yet difference in *Man Made Boy* is successfully relativized by positioning the protagonist simultaneously as an Other to the human world as well as one of the many monsters who form a community in contrast to the human world, and on top of all, as the odd one out even within the monstrous community. By such a scheme, Skovron discards the by now almost compulsory, but often very soft, politically correct criticism of a narrow-minded, conservative society that fails to embrace difference; instead, he strives to demonstrate that norm is not given but constructed and, furthermore, is dependent on a mechanism that perceives disabled people as problematic (L.J. Davis, "Constructing" 3), excluding them from culture and society,[4] and forcing them into the "deviant" zone (6).

Monstrosity in *Man Made Boy* becomes a metaphoric representation of deviance from the norm in various senses. Deviance is dependent on how society constructs normalcy. As there are two decidedly dissimilar societies presented in *Man Made Boy*, it is relatively easy to see that conceptualizing normalcy—and, consequently, Otherness—relies on the society in which one appears.

In the outside world, Boy's problems mostly manifest as those of a disabled person; due to his disfigured body, he finds it difficult to participate in the everyday life "normal people" lead. This hardship is best illustrated by his unsuccessful efforts to find a job for a long while. It is obvious that his attempts at undertaking any sort of work fail primarily not because he lacks official papers for identification but because his bizarre body induces terror or disgust. His experience greatly diverges from his girlfriend Liel's experiences. Starting her life in the city, the trowe girl is completely excluded from all social activities until she gets hold of some "glamour," a magical powder that temporarily turns her appearance not only completely human-like but also beautiful from a human perspective. She lands a job at the first place where she inquires, making Boy realize how appearances and opportunities are connected in human society. From the opposing life experiences that he and his girlfriend have, Boy learns a few things about gender-roles, beauty-cults, health-cults, and able-bodiedness.

Appearance, however, is negligible in constructing the norm in the community of monsters. In the theater troupe, normalcy is basically defined as being magically deviant from human norm, which means that all mythological creatures, let them be trolls, nymphs, fairies, ogres, fauns, werewolves, sirens, the Minotaur himself, or the Medusa, are embraced as equally important members of the community. Boy's monstrosity is what ties him to the norm in the theater company; the same monstrosity, on the other hand, links him to the deviant in the world of humans.

This dual position underscores that the norm is indeed a flexible notion through which deviance is arbitrarily constructed. Skovron highlights the irrationality of such a construction by demonstrating that seemingly homogenous communities may not have a commonly agreed upon norm. While Boy and his family play essential roles in running the theater company smoothly as indispensable members of the technical crew, Boy recurrently experiences some of the monsters' prejudice towards him. Shaun and his friends regularly bully Boy because of his Otherness, but the faun's attitude does not come from his enmity about physical deviance; rather, he is a "racist" in a way Voldemort and his followers in the Harry Potter series are: just as Voldemort looks down on Mudbloods, Shaun also thinks that Boy and his parents are not pure magical monsters, as their existence is dependent not exclusively on magic but also on science and technology.

The manifestation of difference, in Skovron's work, is shown in the most diverse manners so as to encourage readers to reconsider the everyday practice of marginalization. Boy and Liel both reflect on difficulties that may be met by anyone whose body is deemed deviant by society, but Skovron directly links the discourse of being ugly in a beauty-promoting society to living with serious physical impairments when Boy's body becomes truncated after his stitches burn and cannot hold firm any more. His temporary dysfunction suggests the correspondence between looks and able-bodiedness, allowing readers to understand his ugliness as a marker that isolates him from the able-bodied part of the society.

While in *Man Made Boy* most of the discourse on difference concerns deviance detectable on the outside, this novel is actually a prime example of embracing Otherness. Relativizing is one of the most successful strategies that Skovron applies to underline the injustice of disprivileging the non-normative. Not only Boy's ugliness but also the other end of the spectrum, beauty, emerges as a notion that lacks unanimous definition. Boy considers Liel in her trowe form beautiful and finds her strange as an attractive woman who can fit into human society with the help of glamour. Yet he himself is taken aback by Adam Iron, the clockwork man, calling Bride "such a beauty" (Skovron 191). Monstrosity is revealed as a contested concept when monsters are presented as the default state in a monstrous community and as an Other in a strictly human environment. Finally, disability also proves to be a relative idea when, for instance, Boy and his father are able to take advantage of their Otherness to serve the needs of their troupe and save others from harm. Boy's dependence on technology, that is, his feature that ostracizes him in the monstrous environment, allows him to switch to a low-functional mode. Disconnected from the part of his brain that is responsible for his emotions, he comes to lack the ability to perform in all areas in which he is otherwise competent. But this temporal disability is, at the same time, Boy's superpower that turns him into a hero when he uses both his skill and then his knowledge about the backlash of this superhero skill to save his community and to stop his creature who calls itself VI, an abbreviation for Viral Intelligence (Skovron 142). Highlighting how much these concepts lack stability, Skovron confirms that no homogenous normalcy exists, thereby questioning the legitimization of marginalization that operates through othering and monsterization.

Another effective strategy that aims to deconstruct Otherness is not acknowledging difference at all. Queerness, for instance, is an attribute that is never brought openly into the discussion of difference yet develops into a recurring motif. Skovron chooses not to give any specific reaction to certain characters' gayness, informing the reader only casually of the characters' sexual orientation. If the narration happens to include any response to the text where gayness is suggested at all, it is not judgmental in the least, which makes the point that sexual orientation in itself is insignificant.

Nevertheless, queerness, as Robert McRuer points out, is a social construct produced by the same mechanisms as disability is. McRuer contends "that the system of compulsory able-bodiedness that produces disability is thoroughly interwoven with the system of compulsory heterosexuality that produces queerness, that—in fact—compulsory heterosexuality is contingent on compulsory able-bodiedness and vice versa" (301–2). In *Man Made Boy*, monstrosity and queerness sometimes overlap. For instance, the elf Leurellen and the mechanically constructed Adam Iron are revealed as gay characters, but queerness is not what constitutes their monstrosity; on the contrary, queerness embraced by a monster character appears to be an important link to humanity. Leurellen can enjoy his Otherness in a gay club once a week, and as he uses lots of glamour to make his Monday nights very special, he is perceived in the gay club as one of the many gay men as well as a very special gay person. He performs queerness to the extent that it would be best defined as fabulous, which Tony Kushner explains as "one of those words that provide a measure of the degree to which a person or event manifests a particular, usually oppressed, subculture's most distinctive, invigorating features" (vii). Leurellen thus somewhat "overperforms" his queerness, which in return disguises his monstrosity (elvish nature) and allows him to pass as an extraordinary person with homosexual orientation.

Less open is the discussion of Adam Iron's gayness. The text emphasizes his emotional attachment to his friend Allen, who cared for him for so long, and who died months before the narrated events take place. Adam's confession that "Allen was … [his] everything" (Skovron 191) and Mozart's confirmation that it is Adam who misses the late Allen most of all (191) are subtle hints to the special bonding of the two characters, which becomes more specific when Adam tells about the peculiar way he was moved into the house they were to share: unable to walk on stairs, he had to be put into a box and rescued from the place where he had been staying before. Adam reminiscences about that event with an obvious reference to the post-wedding ritual of the groom carrying the bride over the threshold of their new home.[5] Adam's arrival in a box, furthermore, may be read as a subtle hint that Allen is "unboxing" Adam, that is, helping him to come out of his closet or, in this case, his box. As Adam was for a long time hid in the basement of an old house and was only accidentally discovered, his moving into the house with Allen is symbolic because he surfaces from where he was hidden. A crane is used to haul him up from bellow, freeing what so far was repressed, his monstrous and queer self that someone has unconditionally embraced, and this allows him to become "the sweetest old gay uncle" Sophie claims to have (Skovron 201).

In both above-mentioned cases queerness is presented as a natural part of one's integrity and in an environment where queerness does not mark the character. This is contrasted with the overall presentation of monstrousness, always a showcase of confrontation in which Otherness is a painful and disprivileging experience. The underlying argument of this strategy seems at first glance ambiguous because it differentiates between *otherness visible* and *otherness invisible*. It shows that while the two types of deviance are similar in nature inasmuch as both derive from a condition that one does not choose to have, they are differently received: the more visible one's otherness is, the more disappointing and hurtful experience (s)he may have. However, this simplistic conclusion is successfully subverted by providing differences in the actual circumstances as well as by some related scenes that point to the complexity of the issue.

In the novel, queerness is shown to be a non-issue for queer people, queer monsters and non-queer monsters, and the reaction coming from those who constitute the norm in human society is excluded. What is emphasized here is what McRuer claims about the role of the "severely disabled," represented by monsters in the novel:

> "Severely disabled" ... would reverse the able-bodied understanding of severely disabled bodies as the most marginalized, the most excluded from a privileged and always elusive normalcy, and would instead suggest that it is precisely those bodies that are best positioned to refuse "mere toleration" and to call out the inadequacies of compulsory able-bodiedness [306].

In short, monsters teach tolerance in Skovron's work, and I venture to propose that what they perform is something we may term as "enabling tolerance," standing in opposition to what McRuer considers "mere tolerance." Monsters have no judgment about either queerness or monstrosity (even if they may be afraid of some manifestations of the monstrous). What is more, monsters prove creative in transforming their otherness into productive efforts and *enable* themselves or other monsters to use their potential in a fruitful way. But while this is so, the novel also points out the disadvantageous position of those who are forced to do that "under cover." The theater and film business provides safety for the various monsters, but they cannot be themselves in the eye of the human community, and they need to pretend that they perform a role of assumed identity when in fact they perform their own true selves. This keeps them safe, whereas suppressing one's own true identity, as Liel's case demonstrates, may lead to disastrous consequences: she can pass as a human woman only with continuously consuming glamour that attacks the sanity of anyone who is not supposed to live with this magical "drug."

With their amazing diversity, monsters in *Man Made Boy* raise awareness about the intricate complexity of what one may call otherness or deviance as well as the need for inclusion as opposed to discrimination. Some of the monsters that get a major role in the plot warn about specific borders that they emblematically embody. Claire and Sophie, sharing one physical body and having two personalities (according to which even their bodies transform) as an attribute inherited from the Jekyll and Hyde experiment and the family traumas that it created, are presented as the fantastic translation of a person suffering from dissociative identity disorder. The multiple personality monster, understood as the metaphor for a person with mental disorder, a serious disease of the psyche, extends the scope of difference that is addressed in the novel, stressing that all forms of deviance, let it be disfigurement, mental disorder, or sexual preference, are treated unjustly in society on the basis of an assumed norm that should be challenged to create an inclusive, and thus less traumatic world.

From a certain perspective, Claire and Sophie also connect to the theme of queerness, as Boy falls in love with both personalities (with distinct physical manifestations) of the monster girl, ending up in a humorously presented polyamorous relationship with the girls. But since Claire and Sophie inhabit one monstrous body, it is not Boy's sexual orientation that becomes the focus in this non-exclusive love relationship, but his process of maturation in which he learns to accept difference that is strange even from his own, monstrous perspective. In addition, Claire and Sophie also provide a case of science going wrong, an analogy of the Frankensteinian overreaching, thus recreating in modern version part of the Victorian literary scene, where important monster narratives fictionalize the dangers inherent in the misuse of science generated by human hubris—and this time one may be confronted with the realization that disastrous consequences are still detectable generations later.

Indeed, the key to understanding the novel as Boy's coming-of-age narrative lies in the recreation of the conflicts that are explored in both Shelley's *Frankenstein* and in Robert Louis Stevenson's *Strange Case of Dr. Jekyll and Mr. Hyde* (1886). Like the earlier texts, *Man Made Boy* reflects on the issue of collective responsibility, which should also evolve in time, producing a kind of coming-of-age narrative for humankind.

The recreation, in this particular case, is based on expanding the Frankenstein universe in time (allowing for the Monster to survive and start a family of his own), using as premise the notion that Victorian literary monsters were real and their descendants are now to be found in real life. Besides monstrous creatures of Victorian fiction, Iron Adam, an actual Victorian automaton, makes his appearance in a re-imagined

3. *The Rebellious Child* 69

form: as a combination of man and machine, who needs to be wound up in order to function. He is much more than an additional creature in Skovron's monstrous world, as Adam Iron was, already in his age, a direct reflection on the *Frankenstein* theme. In the 1880s a certain Mr. Hornburg of Sidney built two steam-powered automatons christened as "Graaf von Frankenstein" and "Parnell," respectively, to which he added a third one, a clockwork man that he named "Adam Iron" (Hoggett). The name of the very first Hornburg steam man speaks for itself: Graaf von Frankenstein references the monster in Shelley's novel, although, as also Reuben Hoggett notes, the name reveals the usual mistake of referring to the monster with its creator's name. In the novel Adam Iron is the clockwork man, but he has a history of having been first a steam-powered automaton, an implication that he is in fact a transformation of the original Gaaf von Frankenstein automaton.

This matters because creature Boy himself becomes a creator when he writes and unintentionally releases a supervirus for computers, which makes the relationship between creator and creature a main theme in Skovron's fiction. Boy draws the conclusions from the consequences of his bold acts, but only when he has enough experience to understand the responsibility of a creator. The various creator characters that he either meets or hears about, all acting as foils to him, clarify where he has made mistakes and make him understand that mistakes are to be acknowledged because, while deeds may not be undone, wrong decisions may be corrected if one takes responsibility for one's actions. Absent creators, among these Hornburg, who built Adam Iron, are bad parenting examples in this novel, and their most important crime is the lack of responsibility they display. Hornburg is revealed to be "pretty erratic," not caring about winding Adam up on a daily basis, which ultimately results in a long "sleep" that easily could have brought about Adam's final destruction had Allen and Mozart not found him accidentally. Hornburg, additionally, is also accused of being too practical, not providing his creature tear ducts (Skovron 192). While this appears as a marginal comment from Adam, his complaint actually suggests that responsibility should be rooted in emotions. Hornburg lacks the awareness that would lead him to acknowledge that Adam belongs to not only the machine world but also humanity. Not recognizing his creature's needs to show his emotions the way humans do indicates, in fact, the rejection of parental responsibilities. Adam may have been his "thing of darkness," but Hornburg never said "I acknowledge mine" (Shakespeare, *The Tempest* 5.1.275–6).

This rejection is at the root of all the other creator-creature conflicts that Boy learns about in all sorts of variations. Of course, he is familiar with his own family past, knowing the tragic story of his father, who was abandoned by his creator. The moment his Monster comes to life for real, Frankenstein understands that his desire to create life just as God did is doomed to failure because it represents his utter hubris. He is a man, not a god, so he cannot create human life from scratch; his attempt to do so represents a transgression, which is why the result of his scientific experiment is the monster. Yet, the monster is not diabolic, as Boy's experience suggests. His father is a kind, responsible parent, caring about his own creation, and this contradiction is the one Boy needs to understand during his adventure in the human world, bringing about an intense maturation for him.

What Boy learns from the various encounters with creators or their stories is that monsters who appear evil in the eye of human community are created by trauma. Boy's father is traumatized by Frankenstein's rejection and abandonment that stem from the creator's recognition that he could give life only to something that he identifies as Other. This recognition induces horror; Frankenstein's creature turns to violence to force acknowledgment of the monster's right to suffer from the human condition. He wants bonding, but he is not loved by his creator. He wants what his creator cannot give him, a partner in life. Yet Boy may also conclude from his father's example that trauma may be processed, and a traumatized creation may find a way to cope with his own monstrosity. Ontological monstrosity is a permanent condition; moral monstrosity, in contrast, is temporary. Being evil is not part of ontological monstrosity but an association that comes from society's prejudice towards difference. As one matures into an adult, one should ideally develop the ability to differentiate between these kinds of monstrousness—and this is what happens to Boy.

Boy's coming of age is a process of making sense of his own existence, which is to understand his identity in a creator-creation relation. The adventure he has is triggered by his changed position: from his status of being a creation he raises to the status of being both a creator and a creation, driving him to ponder his experience in a more complex form. His maturation route has several important stations in which new creature-creator stories shape his own ideas about crime and punishment—but most importantly, about responsibility. He hears about negative examples of parenting but also talks to nice creations, such as Claire and Sophie, who were quickly deemed as "bad creations" (Skovron 220). Furthermore, he learns important lessons from positive examples of creators, his parents and Kemp, the Invisible Man, who deeply care for their creations. These junctures in Boy's road trip continuously shape his opinion about his place in the world and enable him to come to terms with his own role so that he can right the wrong that he produced as the creator of an artificial intelligence.

Skovron makes a crystal clear claim about the inseparability of the monster and its creator when he makes Boy's creature, VI, solve certain problems for Boy in its first phase of existence without its creator's consent or even knowledge. VI in this context performs the subconscious wishes that Boy has in his dire situations: sending a message to Liel to make her look for him, getting rid of his flatmate who would be an inconvenience now that he has Liel, and stealing enough money for the both of them to live on. The monster works as the resident of the subconscious, and the act of creating it is a wish-fulfillment that is an abomination at the same time. Boy's monster performs all the acts that its creator himself feels would be wrong to do. By creating an entity that is separate from him yet performs his dark desires, his monster becomes a technosubject evoking Mr. Hyde's character. Accordingly, VI soon runs havoc and becomes uncontrollable.

That Boy's monster is a computer virus turns the *Frankenstein* topos into a modern example that is easily accessible to today's teenagers. While many contemporary paraphrases present the monster as a robot or an android, Skovron's choice directly links the theme of responsibility to widely known social media, such as Facebook or Twitter, where things may quickly "go viral." Boy's extraordinary feat of creating a super intelligence, in this way, does not appear as an extrapolation of a scientific dilemma but as a parable of what dangers our everyday reality holds for us right now and why responsible use is inevitable if we want to keep our technologically-advanced world safe. VI's behavior warns us that one's acts have greater effects than what one assumes. This lesson is deducible already from Shelley's novel, but in *Man Made Boy* "greater" stands for immediate *and* global, unlike in *Frankenstein*, where the direct consequences are local and personal (because they target Frankenstein's close environment), and the global effects emerge only as a vision of breeding monsters, which makes Frankenstein abruptly abort his forced project of creating a female monster.

Taming the beast, as a result, will also have global consequences in *Man Made Boy*: VI is recreated in an updated form to assist in protecting the monstrous world in hiding. It joins the show as part of the technical crew, but the effects of this act have a greater impact. Helping The Show keep a low profile and appear as an entertainment company minimizes the possibility of shocking interactions between humans and monsters, and thus protects the whole of humanity. Resurrecting VI gives a second chance for creature and creator alike, and giving it a function to co-ordinate between two worlds recognizes and endorses otherness as an important constituent of the world one lives in.

The Frankensteinian Heritage in Young Adult Dystopia: Sarah Maria Griffin's Spare and Found Parts

In *Spare and Found Parts* (2016), Sarah Maria Griffin also utilizes the Frankensteinian heritage to present a complex discourse on coming of age. Just like in Skovron's *Man Made Boy*, the young protagonist must cope with family issues and the responsibility attached to the act of creation, both being a part of her greatest problem—her difficulty in fitting into a community where she feels deviant and even monstrous.

One of the very first narrative devices that contextualize her isolation comes from the multiple binarism of space. Griffin's story is set on an island that is spatially divided into two parts, dividing the citizens into two as well. In this text, the rule is that "the sick in the Pale, the healed in the Pasture" (Griffin 5), which emphasizes the fundamental idea that the population is differentiated on the principle of health (or rather, as it turns out, completeness versus incompleteness). Griffin sets the whole island against the rest of the world: the borderline between the community that we are introduced to and the world beyond the sea that surrounds the island is sharp, yet the difference between the two spaces are, naturally, not much detailed, as no one knows what the outside world is like. The island, "disconnected from the rest of the world" (Griffin 41), is thus bordered by something that is known to be there but is mostly defined by its lack of accessibility: one may not go there, see it, get into contact with it, learn about it. A firm ground within a world of uncertainty, the island is a place within a space that the islanders mostly register as emptiness, since it is practically nonexistent for them.

The spatial binarism rests on a temporal division. The Turn, signaling a vaguely referenced catastrophe that was brought about by computers and then resulted in a devastating epidemic, changed the course of history due to the island's choice to rebuild society without computer technology; therefore, before the Turn and after the Turn are phrases that point to two different worlds. The Turn signals a decision whereby the island's community detached itself from what is defined as the Old World, which is old in the sense of the temporal, rejecting the idea that what was destroyed may be rebuilt with the use of technology that shaped the world in the past; however, old is also used in the sense of the spatial, rejecting the rest of the world, which seems to have dismissed

3. *The Rebellious Child* 73

the idea that civilization needs such a radical re-structuring. From the protagonist Nell's perspective thus her home is a catastrophe-defined reality, with limited possibilities for advancement, whereas what lies beyond the sea is the land of possibilities—the Old World (which, of course, successfully subverts our conventional associations between the Land of Opportunities and the concept of the New World).

The symbolic binarism of the here and there as well as the real and the possible that relate to the island's history is strongly tied with Nell's personal history, which is also shaped by absence, isolation, and the seemingly unreachable possibilities that she craves for. Nell's life is anchored to the absence of her mother—and what connects her to her mother on the symbolic level is itself lack: the lack of a biological heart. For a long while Nell thinks that her heart condition—and its consequence, that is, an artificial heart ticking in her chest—results from her mother's lethal illness, some kind of "bolt-from-the-blue toxic aftershock of the epidemic" (Griffin 385) that earlier afflicted all the islanders, causing various forms of disabilities that resurface in the coming generations as well. However, at one point she realizes that her deformity is the direct result of her mother's aspirations to reach posthuman existence. The absence of the heart, furthermore, turns out to have been a shared condition, since Cora intentionally aimed at replacing her biological heart with a machine as one of the steps that would have turned her into a cyborg. The emptiness filled with a machine in Nell's chest is, therefore, a symbol of the most complex kind: it evokes the absent mother and the monstrous mother; it signifies monstrosity as Frankensteinian fantasy, which prefers knowledge (matters of the brain) to sentiments (matters of the heart, metaphorically speaking) and directs attention to the themes of construction, creation, assemblage, replacement, hubris and responsibility; it indicates Nell's empty emotional life that the girl attempts to fill with a robot; it continuously reminds us of Nell's hybridity, which makes her both similar to and very different from the rest of the islanders (similar because others also have bodily defects but different because their disabilities are visible and may be turned into pride by spectacular artificial replacements that lend superhuman power to their owners); and with its ticking, it is a (monstrous) warning about what the above listed, complicated set of issues may do to the character, who functions as a ticking bomb about to explode—promising injury to herself and to her environment alike.

In a world where "contribution" to the society is the prerequisite for coming of age, and in a family where contribution has been defined as technological invention, Nell feels pressed to prove worthy of her family history and her over-occupied father's love. She wants to step out of "the shadow of what her parents had made" (Griffin 18) so she wants to create something that is not even imaginable for others. Once she finds a hand—part of a mannequin that the sea brought on shore—she focuses on her secret contribution project, thinking she has begun to walk on a path that has never been stepped unto. She does not know that her secret contribution project very much echoes the efforts that her mother made years ago and her father is making now, simultaneously with his daughter's experiments. Ignorantly, and due to different reasons, she repeats her parents' acts of hubris when she decides to construct a robot and thinks "he" will provide her the company that she lacks and desires.

Nell's process of maturation is a struggle for independence in various ways. She wants to be appreciated in her own right and not because of her family's prestige. Winning independence from family influence means that she can choose her own vocation and make her own decision about her romantic life. These desires appear as the conventional components of teenage life; the latter, however, is a more complicated problem for Nell than for most young adults, as she is not attracted to either sex. In fact, she is not attracted to people in general, and that is why she thinks that a machine may fill the emotional vacuum that people around her seem to embody.

Building the robot, therefore, would have a twofold function: it would serve as an extraordinary contribution presented for the Youth Council as well as a companion for Nell. The girl's aspirations reveal her inability to conform to the norm set by the island's leaders. The island is distinguished from the rest of the world by its renouncing the use of computers; therefore, Nell's aspirations count as rebellion. What is at stake here is not simply breaking the law of the island but also bringing about the threat of breaking nature's law, reminiscent of Nell's mother's scientific experiments on herself.

Cora's research on her body and mind aimed to transform her into a hybrid being—a monster as defined by Cohen ("Monster" 6). Not only does she desire to get connected to a computer so that she can have access to unimaginable, seemingly limitless information but she also wants this experiment to modify her human body, part by part, to produce a more durable one, which would allow her to exist in a masterly enhanced, posthuman manner that would ensure longevity. She is guilty of the same hubris that Frankenstein is and her failed attempt at transforming her own existence into a Frankensteinian creature will inform her daughter about the importance of embracing life as opposed to an aspiration for immortality.

Looking at Cora's actions from a Freudian, psychoanalytical

perspective, we may observe that her body modifications aim at creating a new ego and superego. She desires a different form of existence, so her operations are testimonies to her non-normative, already posthuman attitude that react to the abject differently than humans usually do. The abject, argues Kristeva, "is radically excluded and draws me toward the place where meaning collapses" (2). Corpses, for instance, are powerful manifestations of the abject, as they "*show me* what I permanently thrust aside in order to live" (3; emphasis in the original). Cora Crane, however, wants to stretch the boundaries of life itself. From her perspective, her human body is what should radically be excluded from her existence. The human body—including its organs and not just what they excrete—qualifies as abject to her. She considers her living body what the corpse is to other humans: "the most sickening of wastes, [which] is a border that has encroached upon everything" (Kristeva 3). She thinks of her living body already as an uncanny one, familiar and unfamiliar at the same time: not as a whole that provides "home" for her human existence, but as a set of parts that together remind her of a living person but, actually, is unhomely (unheimlich) to her self, an uncomfortable case that hinders her evolution. Aspiring for a posthuman existence, she privileges information over embodiment, which from a posthuman perspective is just "the supplement to be purged, an accident of evolution" (Hayles 12).

Her research diary is a testimony of how she tries to get rid of various parts of her body to compete with the machine, or, as Nell puts it, "an electric god" (Griffin 384). Her consecutive operations are like repetitive actions that recall Kristeva's explanation of how vomiting is an act of rejecting the abject:

> since the food is not an "other" for "me," who am only in their desire, I expel myself, I spit myself out, I abject myself within the same motion through which "I" claim to establish myself. ... "I" am in the process of becoming an other at the expense of my own death.... During that course in which "I" become, I give birth to myself amid the violence of sobs, of vomit [3].

For Cora, birth—her entering the world as posthuman—comes at the expense of her own life, and the long process of discharging her body parts so that those be replaced by metal is like excreting waste from her being.

The mother's rejection of her own body of organic matter and desire to unite her personality with a computer lies at the root of Nell's problems. While Nell believes her difficulties with fitting in the community stem from the special type of defect she has, the revealed past suggests that even that defect is the signifier of the psychological dimension of the problem. In the usual course of a child's psychological development, the mother "becomes an abject at that moment when the child rejects her for the father who represents the symbolic order" (Creed, "Horror" 68); Nell, however, does not have this chance of "normal" separation from the mother; instead, it is Cora who rejects her early, already in her womb, when she keeps preferring metal to organic matter and finds the electric voice of the computers more alluring than her human life. Nell's vague memory of her mother, as the Prologue shows, is about the lack of warmth that her mother provides for her as a child: "You put your ear to her chest, looking for warmth, listening for a heartbeat. There is none" (Griffin 3). Cora envisions her daughter not as someone in whom her human life continues, but as a scientist-to-be, in whom her own scientific curiosity lives on, that is, someone who will be able to push further the experiments that she already started. This is the emotional vacuum that determines Nell's personality even if she does not remember precisely. Her memory, however, is just as much of an assembled entity as her mother and the robot that she comes to build to ease that emptiness she suffers from. The opening sentences, therefore, foreshadow the Frankensteinian theme by referring to the mother and the idea of assemblage as the origin for Nell's life: "When you grow up, you'll never be sure if this happened or not. Never sure if it was just something your grief stitched together from the parts of her you remember and the questions still in your throat" (Griffin 1).

Nell's highlighted moments of growing up come when she learns the truth about her mother and she is able to readjust her relation to these stitched together memories. This gradual realization has two remarkable scenes: the first one is the discovery of her mother's body that she thought to have been cremated and buried but is kept for a last but failing experiment, that of resurrecting the body; the second is finding and reading Cora's diary, which makes Nell understand—and reject—her parents' real characters.

The first scene is about confronting the abject, her mother's corpse. The mother's body must be pushed aside because it is an abject both as a corpse and as the mother who has already been transformed into memory in order to allow the character to live. The body, therefore, is pushed into the lake so that Nell be able to go on living with the knowledge that her mother is gone. Putting her own mother into the lake is a symbolic gesture that allows Nell finally to see her mother as an abject and separate from her. The rejection of the mother, however, is not generated by the relationship Nell feels for her father, who should stand for the symbolic order (Creed, "Horror" 68). It is indeed the father who turns the mother into an abject, but he is the disturber of natural order, one who seeks the resurrection of his wife's corpse. By discovering and sinking the body, Nell rejects her mother as corpse and her father as a liar and a (failed) Frankensteinian overreacher. The girl is thus left on her own—except for the robot that she built.

The second emphatic scene, in which Nell discovers and reads her mother's diary, gives depth to the previously discussed one and pushes Nell to finalize her separation from her parents. She realizes the tragedy behind her mother's death: the fact that the real genius and overreacher was her mother and not her father. She also realizes that her father is a much more serious liar than she thought him to be. Julian Crane claimed that he was the genius who designed and built his prosthetic left arm that garnered fame and respect for him, whereas it is Cora who should be credited with the achievement that brought a flourishing business for Julian.

When Julian claims his wife's intellectual properties as his own, he recreates the patriarchal mindset that Mary Shelley faced as a female author in her time. Because her name was not written on the first cover of the first edition of *Frankenstein*, her creation, readers could assume that the author was a man.[6] The issue of authorship in Griffin's novel brings to mind the publication history of Mary Shelley's *Frankenstein* and connects the theme of coming of age to a number of other topics, such as gender-biased power relations, one's creation proving the creator as valuable and respectable, and plagiarism, which attacks the self because it claims a part of one's integrity. Protecting the self from various attacks is to secure one's integrity needed for an independent, mature existence. Nell's defensive mechanism is the act of pushing aside the father who has turned into an abject: as Kristeva points out, the liar and the impostor are abjects, just as their crimes are, because they expose how feeble the law is (4).

For Nell, her desire for independence manifests in building a company—on her own. This is a deed that exposes her maturation process, characterized by a longing for breaking away from parental influence and having a life in which she is both in a relationship and has her integrity. As Oliver Kelly keeps approaching her with his marriage (and business) proposal, and she feels the weight of his persistence less and less bearable, she finds comfort in the idea of creating a computer-driven machine as a friend and a contribution project that would demonstrate her ability to be a useful member of her community.

The hand Nell's friend Ruby thinks useless is a real treasure for Nell and comes to represent a rich symbolic content, just like Nell's machine-filled chest cavity. Nell is inspired by her find, and immediately feels the connection that the strange object offers. "Ready to be held" (Griffin 9) and "posed as though it were holding something invisible" (14), the hand implies the possibility of a connection that is to be explored. The promised bond is twofold at least. Ruby sees the hand as "masculine" (15), while Nell thinks of it as the hand of a boy. When Ruby jokingly suggests that Nell keep it as a kind of solution to the problem Oliver poses, the idea of actually creating a boy for the hand begins to form. The hand presents the unfulfilled desire to have someone who would understand her, which explains why Nell expresses her fascination with the object by "locking her fingers with it" (14). The hand calls for assemblage: to be connected to a body and then to be connected—as part of a whole—to someone who would appreciate the body completed by the hand. Yet this "strange piece of the old world" (43) signifies connection to another body that is invisible to Nell: the world beyond the sea, mysterious but imagined as something like the hand itself wrapped by plastic: protected from the changes of time that transformed the island's society after the Turn.

The hand to be part of the completed robotic body is the signifier of the absolute taboo on the island, as computers are completely banned. Constructing an AI with a strange body is breaking the law, but this is not the most important transgression Nell performs: when she kisses her own creature, she violates the rule of separation between the human and the computerized-mechanical. Although she does not aspire to posthumanism the way her mother did, her symbolic gesture expresses her momentary desire for a self-defining union between the human and the robotic, the living and the inanimate, the limitation with the potential, virtually repeating the sin of her parents. It is a brief union with the abject, for it is the mechanical that Nell would like to purge from her body were it possible for her to exist without it. The robot, furthermore, is the replacement of the abject body of the mother's corpse attached to a machine. However, what differentiates Nell from her parents is her recognition that this kind of violation is unnatural and thus wrong—the same realization that drove her to sink her mother's body and to disown her family legacy, which culminates in the symbolic act of expelling the father from the house. The sudden realization of wrongness brings the collapse of meaning to Nell and results in her desperate attempt at pushing aside the abject. She runs away and nearly dies of her efforts. When brought back to life with a new, advanced artificial heart in her chest, she is symbolically reborn and has a chance to reconsider her mistake as well as the possible uses Io (the robot) could be put to.

The mannequin hand is a substitute for a prosthetic arm that would be the natural choice for building a robot (if building a robot were a natural act at all especially on the island). Prosthetic body parts have become commonplace objects on the island, and two biorobotic hands would make the robot more capable, but Nell insists on building the whole robotic body around the found object for the symbolism it holds for her. Beyond the already discussed symbolism of bonding, in the subconscious realm of her psyche, the hand must represent a direct connection to her father's skills, as the very first smart kinetic limb in the community was his. This limb, moreover, is thought to have been designed and built by him. The father is identified by and with the arm, whereas Nell wants to be identified as someone who is able to build a complete body around a hand. As Nell thinks of her contribution as a male body, Io competes both with the father's contribution and the father himself. As Julian is more occupied with working behind closed doors, trying to resurrect his wife's corpse, than being there for his daughter as a supportive father (although he is supportive as a scientist-mentor), Nell becomes more attached to her creation than her "creator," the father who replaced her heart with a machine.

The hand evokes association with the mother, who is a builder of a new body (and the creator of the new building project, which is also about constructing a new, huge body—of a statue). The hands perform directly the actual work that is needed to build new bodies, so using her mother's gloves for the work Nell does carries emblematic significance. The gloves and the dresses that Nell inherits from her mother keep her attached to her mother emotionally, so abandoning them in the end signals a new phase in Nell's life. In Nell's memory fragment, Cora says to her that "you're cut out of my cloth" (Griffin 2), but Nell discovers that this truth does not have to predestine her to follow her mother's steps. She can use her heritage—her scientific talent and curiosity—and still take a different path, based on the lessons she could learn from her parents' various failures. Her robot will be a means to bridge isolation, reconnect with the old world, and better people's lives in a responsible manner.

Conclusion

Among the many *Frankenstein*-inspired works that appear on the Young Adult book market,[7] *Man Made Boy* and *Spare and Found Parts* are intriguing examples because one of the central themes that connect the two works is the ambiguous nature of computer technology, featuring as a threat that may lead to catastrophe and as a means to provide connection and even safety if used correctly. This theme, therefore, marks computer technology as the most threatening science of our contemporary world, a menace that may bring about the disintegration of the world. While the authors set their stories in radically different environments, both Skovron's urban fantasy and Griffin's post-apocalyptic dystopia use the *Frankenstein* theme to warn against the fragility of the world that has become dependent on computer technology and argue, at the same time, that refraining from the use of science is not a solution any more. In such a context the role of individual responsibility becomes necessarily highlighted as an attitude that may either keep the world intact or help an already disintegrated world heal and unite.

Disintegration and integrity are, therefore, accentuated themes in the examined novels. The image of a collapsing world appears in *Man Made Boy* when VI, the super virus, is able to infect and reprogram computer-driven technology via the Internet to attack humanity. In *Spare and Found Parts*, computers played a role in the apocalypse that resulted in the infection rendering the community of the island disabled and in the decision to cut the island off from the rest of the world and start living without computers. The act of assembling, as a consequence, stands for the individual's act of aspiring to create integrity, which can be a successful attempt only if the individual has matured enough to claim his or her own integrity. For Nell, the process of building the robot mirrors her own character development, step by step, allowing her, finally, to stand up for herself. Boy's falling apart in the fire and then his complete reassembly signals a metaphorical rebirth, after which not only his stitches hold more but his character becomes firmer and more responsible, too. This new beginning allows him to come to the conclusion that VI needs a second chance, too, so he annihilates the supervirus completely, reconstructs it, and makes it his ally to keep the world safe.

In both works, claiming one's integrity links with a better, more complex understanding of the world and one's place in the world. In this spirit, the *Frankenstein* theme is used to teach about attitudes to otherness as well as responsibility as core factors that shape one's process of coming of age and transform the world into a better place by questioning otherizing and normalizing practices. Adaptations that rewrite the *Frankenstein* story for a younger audience tend to present redemption in the place of the despair and isolation that the original *Frankenstein* novel ends with (Coats and Norris Sand 245), and these novels are not exceptions. The fundamentally optimistic closure, however, underlines the necessity of learning from earlier mistakes. This recognition acknowledges the practice of making fatal errors and warns that seemingly smaller issues may have world-wide consequences in our contemporary world, where all things are connected via advanced computer science.

4

Oppressed Daughters and Oppressing Fathers

Theodora Goss's The Extraordinary Adventures of the Athena Club *Series*

Introduction

Theodora Goss's *Athena Club* series (2017–2019), a fresh take on the Frankensteinian theme, discusses aspects of coming of age with a historical dimension within the space of the fantastic. Just like Jon Skovron in his *Man Made Boy* and Sarah Maria Griffin's *Spare and Found Parts*, Goss employs the motif of the monster to examine the consequences of one's act of creation and to emphasize the importance of taking responsibility for one's deeds. She also endeavors to present her theme with a special focus on diversity, combining various examples derived from Victorian monster novels, just as Skovron does, to make her point about those who transgress various borderlines (either because they create recklessly or because they are created and thus embody transgression). Goss's primary interest, however, lies in the investigation of what makes certain types of transgressions possible; therefore, her main theme is the female condition as monstrous otherness in a patriarchal society. Such a focus aligns Goss with Griffin through gendering the Frankensteinian theme especially since both authors endow the missing mother character(s) with a symbolic content that indicates the power relation between women and men in the given society. In *Spare and Found Parts*, female characters claim power through acts of transgressive creation: both the mother and the daughter character turn out to be overreachers and are contrasted with the husband/father character, who originally seems to be the only one capable of powerful creation. Subverting the classical trope that power is attached to the creator whereas the "product" of creation is disempowered and disprivileged (especially in comparison to the creators), Goss strives to empower the creations that occupy a liminal position as a result of the scientific experiments that turned them into monsters. Accordingly, her trilogy's monstrous daughter characters roam the space of feminism in an utterly patriarchal world and offer new ways to think about power relations and social issues that do not exclusively concern the Victorian era.

The various monster characters that inhabit the alternative 19th century London in the *Athena Club* series were shaped by scientific experiments that were carried out in the hope of improving humanity by transmutation, that is, hybridization. In focus are the female monsters, whose liminal positions are accentuated by the contrast they provide to various groups of characters: as women, they are considered to be inferior to men in Victorian society, which results in a number of confinements in their everyday lives; as daughters, they are subjected to the ambitions and desires of their scientist fathers and/or creators, respectively; as monsters, they suffer from their disprivileged position due to their deviance from what is accepted as the norm in human society; and finally, as monstresses, they provide even contrast with the similarly transmuted, male creatures. The first novel of the series, *The Strange Case of the Alchemist's Daughter*, disguises itself as mystery fiction, but there is much more at stake in the presented investigation than finding a serial killer who takes various body parts of street women. What is a criminal case to be solved by Sherlock Holmes and his associate Dr. Watson (for how can we have a really curious Victorian detective story without them?) is, for the female protagonists, a complex and dangerous search for their own pasts and an opportunity to face and heal from their traumas. Storytelling is instrumental in this process of maturation for the central characters: by telling their own stories, they are to take control over their own narratives and thus their lives, claiming power that they were deprived of because of their gender and monstrosity. This psychological benefit of storytelling is accompanied by a very practical use of turning experience into story: it becomes a source of income, thus a means of gaining independence not only in a psychological but also in an economical sense. For this purpose, Theodora Goss introduces a writer character among the monstrous gentlewomen, thereby creating a fictional alter ego for herself, through whom she may directly reflect on the importance of storytelling and may highlight its function to give space for female bonding via acknowledging a common experience, a *herstory* throughout the course of history—but at least from Victorian times until our present days.

The series expands the Frankenstein universe by giving voice to (either familiar or previously unmentioned, that is, newly invented)

4. Oppressed Daughters and Oppressing Fathers   83

daughter characters of the most famous 19th century literary ("mad") scientist characters. Thus the first part of the trilogy, which provides the core material for the present discussion, features Mary, the daughter of the scientist Dr. Jekyll, and Mary's sister Diana, who is fathered by the transformed scientist, that is, Mr. Hyde (from Robert Louis Stevenson's novella *Strange Case of Dr. Jekyll and Mr. Hyde* from 1886); Beatrice Rappaccini, the Poisonous Woman (from Hawthorne's short story "Rappaccini's Daughter" from 1844); Justine, Frankenstein's monstress, who was to become the bride for Frankenstein's creature and was completed by Frankenstein (unlike in Mary Shelley's *Frankenstein; or, The Modern Prometheus*, in which she is destroyed before completion); and Catherine Moreau, the Puma Woman (who is not half-finished, as in H.G. Well's *The Island of Doctor Moreau*, but fully transformed). In the third part, two other characters join the Athena Club: Lydia Raymond and Lucinda Van Helsing. Lucinda is the fictional daughter of Abraham Van Helsing from Bram Stoker's *Dracula* (1897). Her father's scientific experiments turn her and her mother into vampires with extraordinary strength and senses and the curse of being able to feed only on blood. Lydia Raymond is the fictional daughter of Helen Vaughan from Arthur Machen's 1890 novella *The Great God Pan*. Lydia is the third woman in her family to possess mesmerizing abilities. She inherited her special mental skills from her grandmother, who was transformed into a mesmerist by an experimental operation,[1] carried out by the grandmother's own husband, Dr. Raymond.

All of these above listed women characters of the Athena Club go through a transformational phase in their lives, so while technically all have come of age except for the fourteen-year-old Diana, the novel presents their coming-of-age narrative(s). On the one hand, the criminal cases to be solved force them to confront their own pasts and relationships to their creators/fathers; on the other hand, the investigation compels them to transgress their own limitations and become integrated into society by challenging the concept of monstrosity, deviance—challenging, at the same time, the normative and redefining traditional concepts of (wo)manhood and family.

These ladies form an untraditional family based on sisterhood created by their common experience: monstrosity. They all have fathers or father substitutes (scientific creators) who, as the daughters feel, betrayed them, since these overreachers cared more for science or themselves than for their own daughters or creatures. Mary, the focal character, was left without a father when she was only seven. Her father was believed to have died, but Mary learns that she was abandoned by her father Jekyll when Hyde took full control over him. Her father's hubris thus is the direct cause of her troubled childhood as well as her dire situation that she finds herself in at the beginning of the narrative: her mother succumbed to insanity because of her husband's terrible secret, died early, and left Mary with no income or property in money, as Jekyll transferred all their money previously to an account that only his transformed self, Hyde, could have access to. Mary would have been left completely on her own if the housekeeper had not refused to abandon her despite Mary's inability to pay her. This gesture foreshadows the numberless examples of female solidarity that characters witness during the adventures and paves the way to aligning not only the female monster characters but women characters in general, which strengthens Goss's underlining argument that the female condition and the "monstress condition" are naturally connected.

The strange family unit begins to form when Mary learns that she has a sister living in a Church-financed home for fallen women. On the surface, the family reunion is natural: Mary feels responsibility for her younger, ill-fated half-sister, so she cannot leave her in the home even though she does not feel much drawn to her newly found relative. However, this union is far from being natural, as it is that of two monstresses, even though they are not aware of this then. Both Mary and Diana are results of Jekyll and Hyde's scientific experiments. Mary has a very logical, rational character because her father had already started experimenting with separating his two selves when he fathered his first daughter. As a result, Mary's father is "purely" Dr. Jekyll—without his most beastly inner self, the later released and strengthened Mr. Hyde part. In contrast, Diana's monkey-like features, such as her climbing skills or complete ignorance of etiquette, may be explained by how she was conceived. Her father is Mr. Hyde without Dr. Jekyll's self. As a letter suggests, Hyde wanted to have a second offspring only to continue his transgressive research, and he considered his future child—preferably a daughter—a subject of scientific experiment. In the end, he abandoned Diana just as he abandoned Mary, but as Diana was born into much poorer circumstances, this meant that the younger daughter lived in poverty for most of her life.

All the five protagonists of the first volume thus fall into the category of the monster as defined by Cohen.[2] Mary and Diana are special cases because it becomes apparent only after some research that their fathers' attitude to science and his transformation into a monstrous character altered the girls' identities, as Sigmund Freud speculates in *European Travel*. Yet even though the girls appear perfectly human, their fathers were unnatural creations themselves and thus the daughters count as hybrid, liminal characters. It is easier to see how the other

4. Oppressed Daughters and Oppressing Fathers

female characters who gradually join them also classify as monsters. Justine's hybridity is that of the classical Frankensteinian monster; her body combines the living and the dead, not respecting nature's law of death that separates those who live and those who do not. Catherine, the Puma Woman embodies the transgression of the borderline between the human and the animal, while Beatrice became a Plant Woman as a result of her father's experiments, so her body functions as an incessant reminder of the transgression that does not respect the borderline between the human and the vegetal.

These characters' gender and their monstrosity, both forcing them into a liminal position, are curiously intertwined: their otherness is the result of gender-biased science, as girls were experimented on and considered better subjects of gene manipulation than male patients. The limitations imposed by their femaleness are often paralleled with constraints resulting from their monstrosity. To survive in a patriarchal, Victorian society, they need to prove much more active agents than what society would expect of them (or would generally allow them); their coming-of-age stories, therefore, reveal extraordinary power—and outstanding cunning. These ladies partially may have inherited/received their rational, logical thinking or their instinctive inventiveness from their biological or symbolic fathers (whether they like this idea or not), but it is strongly suggested that their various skills have also developed due to their extreme situations that demanded exceptional solutions. In fact, the stories these ladies tell and also the method of storytelling imply that, while the male scientists aimed at forcing a directed evolution to accelerate the bettering of mankind, the natural course of evolution that took place enabled the women to empower themselves in their own way.

Coming of Age: A Struggle for Independence

As noted before, in Goss's work being a woman and being a monster are intertwined, thus behaving monstrously often appears as the equivalent of behaving in an unladylike manner. To put it in other words, not displaying proper manners expected by social conventions is, in effect, demonstrating savageness; therefore, transgressing social norms aligns the characters. Rebelliousness and monstrosity share the same formerly uncharted space in this story; accordingly, monstrosity becomes a metaphor for one's rebellious nature.

The backstories of the monstrous ladies reveal individual coming-of-age stories whose leitmotif is rebellion against the father creator, symbolically reiterating the Monster's defiance against his creator in Shelley's *Frankenstein*. Rewriting and thereby creating more complex backstories for the Bride, the Puma Woman and Beatrice Rappaccini function not merely as a tool for the author to write a fun monster mashup. Revising their stories actually keeps these monstresses alive: it erases their deaths that were recounted in their original hosting fiction and thus frees the ladies from the fate that would have befallen on them because of reckless men. Instead of presenting them as ultimate victims of a patriarchal society, Goss turns them into active agents. Beatrice consciously "seduces," that is, slowly poisons Giovanni so that they may be together. Later she does not automatically agree to drinking the potion that would normalize her—a decision that saves her life, as it turns out. Her real defiance, however, comes when she turns against her father, leaves him, and starts co-operating with his enemy, Baglioni, who promises a cure for her. Her absence from the poisonous, corrupted Eden eventually kills her father, who cannot cope with the garden without her. In a similar manner, Catherine turns against her creator and kills him out of revenge, while Justine beats Adam, Frankenstein's Monster, to unconsciousness so that she may flee from him. While Adam is not literally her creator, he may count as a perpetrator in the act of creation, as it was he who ordered Frankenstein to assemble and animate Justine for him. Ironically, in all these cases, the creators suffer death or defeat in a symbolic manner: Rappaccini dies of the poison that he used to turn his daughter into a poisonous creature; Catherine strangles Moreau with the very chain that he put on her; Justine is able to fight Adam with the use of her skillet—an emblematic object signaling her oppressed status as Adam's woman and mocking the love-relationship that Adam said he would want to share with her. We may add that Frankenstein also dies as a consequence of creating Justine: it is Adam who kills him because he is outraged that Frankenstein gave Justine the education that he never received from his creator. The irony is strong here: Adam in theory would like to have a partner not to be alone, yet in practice he is mad that his woman has a sharp intellect (and thus would be able to engage with him in meaningful conversation, for instance). And while he is actually upset because he feels even more abandoned by his creator than before, it is indeed Justine's intellect that hinders their happy union. Justine loathes him because she perceives Adam's immorality. Additionally, both Catherine and Justine enjoy extraordinary strength as a result of how they were created, and they both use their physical power to battle their oppressors.

The manner of defiance listed above indicates how the manner of oppression itself offers a tool for empowerment—a point made several

4. Oppressed Daughters and Oppressing Fathers 87

times in the novel beyond the above instances, as well. The experience of the monstrous and the feminine become allied, which turns marginalization into power. Just as the means of oppression are used by the monstresses to gain freedom, we see a much broader circle of characters taking advantage of their own marginalization. During the investigation presented in the novel, women characters recurrently exploit men's general understanding about women being inferior and negligible. While Holmes talks to Dr. Seward, Mary can easily observe the room and copy an important letter without being noticed because Seward would not assume that Mary could be a partner in the detective work Holmes conducts. She easily passes as a secretary who simply takes notes of the conversation because a man like Seward would never conceive that a woman could have a more intellectual job. The same mindset leads the male doctor to accept Mrs. Poole's confusing, non-informative reply to his inquiry about what institution they represent. As he is convinced that one should not expect much of an intellectual performance—let alone cunningness—from a woman, it never occurs to him that the simple-looking Mrs. Poole deliberately distracts his attention.[3]

Goss's trilogy is set in the Victorian world and Victorian society, so the feminist ideas usually appear in form of conflicts or contrasts between men and women. In spite of the 19th century setting, the spirit in which Goss writes is recognizably that of a 21st century, intersectional feminism, rooted in Kimberlé Crenshaw's theory of intersectionality. By criticizing "how dominant conceptions of discrimination condition us to think about subordination as disadvantage occurring along a single categorical axis," Crenshaw emphasizes that various forms of discrimination relate to one another, so it is impossible to look at them independently of one another. Prominent examples of how the Athena Club members represent intersectional monstrosity are provided by Megen de Bruin-Molé, who observes the "different systems of oppression that impact women of differing social classes" (83). De Bruin-Molé also highlights Catherine's role as a "'brown' colonial subject" (84) in authentically voicing the link between the discrimination against women and the discrimination against people of color.

Intersectionality thus recognizes diversity within oppression; such a take was heralded by Chandra Talpade Mohanty in 1988 (that is, one year before Crenshaw coined the term of intersectionality in 1989), when she argued at length about how one should not consider "the 'Third World Woman' as a monolithic subject" (61). A similar approach is palpable in Goss's feminist fantasy as "crucially, none of the women in the *Athena Club* series stands in for all women" (de Bruin-Molé 83). Yet Goss presents diversity not only through including variations of monster characters and female characters but also of men who think outside the box in their time. Holmes's character is indispensable in creating a more complex representation of society as well as making clear the criticism concerning the depicted patriarchal environment. As Holmes is of an outstanding intellect, someone who has garnered fame by his skill of deduction, his appreciation of the female characters provides a reassuring contrast between him and the average Victorian male, repeatedly confirming that highly intelligent men consider women as equal partners with important skills and equal rights. Nevertheless, Holmes's character is also useful to underline that even the most intelligent people may fall into the sin of being inconsiderate due to the prescribed social roles that are assigned according to gender. Dr. Watson's character equally emphasizes that progressive and tolerant as he seems in many respects, the subtext of his words and deeds often reveal that he has an inherent prejudice against women; for instance, he gives out dubious compliments about Mary's remarkable intellect (which render other women in general as a category with inferior intellect) (Goss, *The Strange* 76), but he does not acknowledge Mary's importance in his account of the detective work that they did together (Goss, *European* 16).

By telling their stories as a conjoined series of adventures that unites them, the diegetic narrators and the non-diegetic narrator allow us to read monstrosity and feminism as associated concepts, both rooted in the patriarchal practices of society oppressing women. Yet Goss not only highlights the roots of feminism in England but she also writes a very postmodern novel by which she creates an opportunity for herself to reflect on the situation of women today and present a historical link among women that is not only established through their liminality but also through their solidarity. The feminist issues that she keeps returning to include the unequal financial opportunities for women; society's beauty and fashion expectations that turn women into spectacles; the normalizing attempt of society that should be replaced by an inclusive approach that accepts diversity (still in the focus, in an extended form, of third wave feminism); and most importantly, women's and other marginalized people's liminal state that allows violence directed towards women by men—or, on a more general level, violence directed towards disempowered people by those in hegemonic position—and also ensures the silencing of the suppressed (let us think of the metoo movement revealing several thousands of silenced stories).

One of the first components through which Goss's monstresses invite an association with women of the 21st century is their financial situation that is both a result of and a contributing factor to their

4. Oppressed Daughters and Oppressing Fathers 89

marginalization. The comment thread on the novel's epigraph immediately focuses on the characters' financial situation, revealing that the novel is being written because the ladies "need money ... as usual." This observation may appear as a funny comment to start an adventure book with, yet it is a fundamental statement because what Goss actually investigates in her book is not a series of mysteries but the methods of marginalization and the possibilities to fight one's liminality. And while *The Strange Case* is a monster fantasy and thus one is tempted to consider monstrosity as the reason for the characters' liminal position, Goss argues that the characters' monstrosity, just like many other problems that they have to cope with, is the unfortunate consequence of their gender. Mary's financial situation, as clarified early in the novel, is not a question of having been born into poverty or wealth, but a consequence of women's legal position in Victorian England. Mary, daughter of the once well-to-do Jekyll, is left with a big, unsellable house to maintain and no money to live on after her mother dies and she can no longer rely on her mother's life-income. Male heirs in England, as Beatrice is quick to point out, did not find themselves in such a situation (Goss, *The Strange* 7). Just as Mary is in a single state, which most women in 19th century England considered as "a fate to be avoided like the plague" (Perkin 3), so are the other monstresses, and this state defines their lives as much as their monstrosity.

English Common Law, which restricts Mary legally and thus economically, may be considered as the long-established legal framework that justified the male scientists' experiments on their daughters in the *Athena Club* series. "The law undoubtedly regarded almost every woman as under tutelage to some man, usually father or husband. Being physically and economically the weaker sex their dependence, the theory went, was for their own good" (Perkin 1). This male privilege being taken for granted is detectible in the originally London-based Moreau's hypothesis "that the female brain would be more malleable and responsive" to the transmuting experiments (Goss, *The Strange* 87)—a conjecture that affected all the other members of Goss's fictional Société des Alchimistes and motivated even the Italian Rappaccini as well to experiment on his daughter. The legal doctrine of coverture deprived married women of agency: as Joan Perkin puts it, "In Orwellian language, [a feme covert] became an 'unperson'" (2). But before marriage, it was the father who exercised control over his daughters who had not reached adulthood, so from these male scientists' points of view, the experiments performed on a daughter did not greatly differ from those that others performed on animals or dead bodies.

It does not take much power of conception to relate the above discussed legal and economic discrimination to 21st century practices of discriminating against women. Even in western countries, where legal equality is taken for granted, gender pay gap is a hot issue: "On average, full-time male employees across the EU and 35 other countries were paid 13.8% more per hour in 2014, according to figures from the Organisation for Economic Co-operation and Development" (Rubery); and as of today,[4] only Iceland has passed a law that makes it compulsory for companies to provide equally pay for men and women (Rubery). Sadly, some men who enjoy the privilege of gender-biased higher pay justify their good luck by claiming that women earn less money than they do because their pay is commensurate with their intellect. Let us just remember Polish MEP Janusz Korwin-Mikke's contribution to the gender pay gap debate in the European Parliament in 2017, during which he actually claimed that "women must earn less than men, because they are weaker, they are smaller, they are less intelligent" (Vonberg).

The motif of the spectacle, associating monstrosity with the female condition and allowing the reader to see Victorian women related to present day women, further supports the notion that women have often been expected to function as decorative components of a patriarchal society. Their assumed role is to please the male gazer; accordingly, implied in this idea is the inferior intellectual capacity of women compared to the omnipresent, giant male intellects. In the novels, female characters keep complaining about their clothing (to various extents). Their desire to wear nonconformist clothing comes primarily from the experience that their dresses are not practical and they impose an actual limitation on their personal freedom, which is immediately contrasted with how men may enjoy rational clothing and how, on top of it all, wearing men's clothes in itself guarantees greater liberty simply because clothes indicate the gender and its privileges. Strangely enough, this debate is still an ongoing one concerning women's fashion—and for instance, the lack of pockets, something that Goss's Victorian women characters complain about, is a phenomenon that women try to fight even today (Lower); in fact, not until 2018 has data been collected to prove that the pockets on women's clothes are either too small to be practical or they are simply decorative, non-existent (Diehm and Thomas). While the great cultural quest for pockets on female clothing was undertaken already by the Rational Dress Society that Beatrice advocates in the novels (Goss, *The Alchemist's* 192), Jan Diehm and Amber Thomas still conclude from their 2018 survey that "men's pants pockets are basically the pockets of our [i.e., women's] dreams." And while pockets seem to be a minor issue in our world when we contemplate gender bias, the mentality that robs women of pockets—the mentality that considers women objects of beauty rather than subjects of intelligence—is behind the unequal opportunities for education, which is still not a negligible concern. It is not by chance that the lack of education for women (that especially Mary suffers from) is repeatedly underlined in the novels—together with highlighting Beatrice's and Justine's exceptional educations due to their exceptional pasts as contrasts.

The fact that society's beauty and fashion expectations deprive women of agency appears on the metaphorical level through the presentation of actual spectacles. Beatrice, Catherine, and Justine are all characters who, for a period of time, sustain themselves by becoming spectacles to please and/or terrify an audience hungry for curiosities. Posing as objects of the gaze, they let others define them as freaks and monsters, in accordance with Slavoj Zizek's assertion that "the gaze denotes at the same time power (it enables us to exert control over the situation, to occupy the position of the master) and impotence (as bearers of a gaze, we are reduced to the role of passive witness)" (2).

Appearing in the right clothing in order to further support expectations and maximize the eerie or horrific effect is also part of the job these women do and supports the notion that appearance serves as the basis for judgment in society. Beatrice's beautiful, elegant appearance that turns her into a perfect femme fatal is as much part of the show as Catherine's fake cat tail and hood with ears. The constraining, yet decorative appearance in the social space is metaphorized via the image of the spectacle: the ladies' stage performance is a reminder of how men oppress women by controlling their appearance—whether it be through science or societal norms, such as fashion, defined by patriarchy.

Closely related to the image of the spectacle is the theme of beauty linked to the body image accepted as norm—although what is communicated as norm matches rather our concept of the ideal, as Lennard J. Davis (*Enforcing* 24) warns. Falling short of society's beauty expectations, then, is easy, to say the least, and the consequences may be devastating. Recent works, such as Deborah L. Rhodes's *The Beauty Bias* or various chapters in the essay anthology *Beauty and the Norm* (Liebelt, Böllinger and Vierke), explain in detail the way society punishes those who are not found attractive. But the *Athena Club* trilogy, just as Jon Skovron's *Man Made Boy* or the various other Frankenfictions de Bruin-Molé discusses, problematize the normalizing practices of a society when presenting a micro-community made of monsters, which renders normal what originally may be considered as deviance from the norm. Goss's monstresses specifically question society's norms concerning beauty and body image and society's assumptions concerning them. For this reason, Beatrice and Justine remind us of how inscribed—and wrong—our notions concerning the meaning of beauty are. Beatrice's beauty disguises her poisonous body, but it also doubles the danger she poses because people may not assume that such a beautiful, young woman may be lethal to her environment. Her extraordinary beauty suggests norm[5]—and thus a pleasant feminine appearance and safety. In contrast, Justine obviously does not meet the normative expectations concerning a lady's beauty and body. She is taller and stronger than most people are, and as a consequence of these masculine traits, people expect her to behave in a stereotypically masculine manner. However, she is the gentlest monstress of the Athena Club, and despite her strength, she has the tendency to faint due to emotional stress. She is very pious and looks indeed lady-like in her dresses; so besides her biologically determined bodily features, where she clearly transgresses the gender boundaries of the age is her education.

These female monsters resist conforming to the beauty standards of Victorian society, systematically question the societal assumptions linked to them, and also fight the notion that youth is a determining factor in a lady's attractiveness. Age, to start with, is a relative concept in their case. As monsters, both Catherine and Justine are created as adult women endowed also with a matching, fully developed intellect, but considering their monsterhood—the time they spent as monsters— Catherine would count as a child, whereas Justine would be a very old woman. It becomes difficult or almost not possible to speak about their ages because, considering how they were created, their life expectancies do not conform to "normal" human or even monstrous expectations. As Justine is stitched together from dead body parts, her body is not subject to change in the same way that the bodies of her fellow monstresses may change, so she could live a much longer time than an average human or an average monster. (She does not seem to have aged at all for the past one hundred years.) Catherine, in contrast, may die much earlier if she is to have a puma's average life expectancy especially because she was transformed into a woman from a fully developed animal (Goss, *The Strange* 378–79). These anomalies of the characters also question fixed categories (such as childhood versus adulthood, coming-of-age, youth, maidenhood versus spinsterhood) created by a normalizing society, in which especially women were judged based upon their status that was linked to their age.

The *Athena Club* novels point to various areas where discrimination against women has changed somewhat and yet we still can see the long-lasting after-effects of these imprinted discriminating practices. They draw attention to the subtle mechanisms that result in the marginalization of the Other (such as women, people of color, the poor), but also underline the not so subtle method of physical violence, which forms the basis of the series' concept. On the whole, these monstresses' origin stories are painfully meaningful to today's society because they also address the issue of physical violence against women, highlighting that a great percentage of such aggression belongs to the category of domestic violence. The paternal transgression has transformed all of the daughter characters into Others. Mostly, the fact that they are monstresses is not something that may easily be deduced from their appearance—not even from Justine's— suggesting that such trauma is usually invisible on the outside but life-determining in nature.

The absent mother characters, therefore, signal the lack of female power in a patriarchal society on two levels: on the level of family unit, this vacuum stands for the much needed, powered presence that may have given protection for daughters; on the societal level, the lack of mothers suggesting that the female voice may be erased in a society defined by men. There are two notable exceptions when we meet the mother characters and are actually allowed to see them as protective shields that save their daughters from their fate. In *European Travel*, Mrs. Van Helsing dies in the fight while protecting her daughter, and in *The Sinister Mystery*, Mrs. Raymond sacrifices herself in order to save her daughter from the sure death that would befall her. In both cases, protection results in the immediate death of the mothers, reinforcing the notion that the protection coming from the mother may not hold for long in such a world. In an environment full of men who experiment with creation, the lack of a strong and enduring motherly presence stands for the moral transgression that defines this world and considers women as tools for glorifying humanity defined as *man*kind. The *Athena Club*, however, gives space for the rise of formerly oppressed women and becomes a story of gaining voice through the process of coming of age that is inherently linked to the act of storytelling.

The Empowering Effect of Storytelling

The book that we may read as *The Strange Case of the Alchemist's Daughter* is the novel being written by Catherine, one of the monstresses. She starts writing the novel because it offers a way out of their dire financial situation. Storytelling, in this context, is a life-creating activity: it provides a means for the Athena Club members to survive. Yet beyond its very practical function of earning money to live on, storytelling—through its method—signals a metaphorical relation to life. Catherine comes up with "a new way of writing," the outcome of which

Justine identifies as monstrous because it is "as though it's been stitched together of various parts" (Goss, *The Alchemist's* 206). She considers the novel a Frankensteinian creation, which Catherine actually finds an apt idea. "Well, we're different. I have to tell the story in a way that fits who we are," she explains (206). Her words primarily justify the narrative technique she chose: her novel is indeed assembled from various parts, symbolically repeating Frankenstein's (or, for that matter, any of the other transgressing scientist's) act of creating monsters; moreover, the embedded narratives are first written by the characters whose stories need to be inserted in the main narrative, thereby supporting the idea of producing a chimera-text. The novel, eventually, is a monster-narrative on multiple levels: it is a mystery story about finding overreachers who created monsters; it is a narrative that includes the origin stories of various monstresses as its integral part; and finally, due to the previously mentioned writing technique, it displays monstrous features in its structure, doubled by a twist in the narrative strategy, as Catherine/Goss even includes the various characters' commentaries on what Catherine is actually writing. By doing so, Goss not only returns to Mary Shelly's heritage of giving voice to the monster but also makes the point that a produced text reflects identity. Storytelling, furthermore, shapes identity and is, therefore, as much life-creating as the experiments of the alchemists featured in the book.

Although the female protagonists come from various backgrounds and have had greatly differing experiences, this disenfranchised state bonds them instantly. Mary is not only a very intelligent, rational character but also a highly sensitive (though not very emotional) one, and these personal traits practically attract the other, similarly disempowered characters to her life. She needs the other young women in order to solve her family mystery (and, perhaps, her financial situation connected to it), so it is a rational decision to find them and talk to them; her sense of responsibility and her realization that they are natural allies, furthermore, keep the new acquaintances together and allow them to form a family of sisters in the end. Their lives have been shaped by the irresponsibilities of scientists with a god complex, and this is a connection that Mary understands. She sympathizes with the other ladies, and more importantly, she starts making up for all the carelessness that the male scientists displayed: she rescues those who need help and offers a home not only for her half-sister but all the other monstresses, too. Caring for those who were similarly abandoned by a father character, Mary makes these women understand that they belong to the same house—and so she treats her new friends as family. Lucinda knows that becoming a member of the Athena Club "meant becoming part of a new family

4. Oppressed Daughters and Oppressing Fathers 95

in which she would always be welcome" (Goss, *The Sinister* 416), and Mary makes sure that Alice/Lydia considers the Jekyll residence not a place of work but a home where she belongs (429).

The "monstrous" narrative that Catherine assembles accommodates the characters' life-stories and provides shelter for them, just like the house itself does. The epigraph *"Here be monsters"* seems to simply establish a thematic connections to monsters who will later make their appearance in the novel, but it is a more complex, multilevel reference, which also suggests the novelty that comes from the recounted adventures and Catherine's new method of writing. The phrase itself is a modification of "hic sunt dracones" (here be dragons), generally believed to be a warning about uncharted and thus dangerous territories on maps.[6] Accordingly, it is a suitable motto to give warning (as monsters should)[7] not simply about the monsters to be encountered on the pages but also on the characters' endeavors to venture into uncharted territories. At first sight one may think the epigraph points to the Société de Alchemistes, since they are the ones who transgress nature's laws, discovering unknown territories—those of science. However, the main narrative in these texts belongs to the female characters whose life experiences compel them to transgress not the laws of science but those of society.

The origin and coming-of-age stories that the monstresses recount are as much transgressing in their nature as their very monstrous existence is. Since they find themselves in extraordinary situations, which society is not prepared to have laws or etiquette for, their actions often do not fit society's expectations of what a lady should do. Hence they define themselves as monsters and not ladies—not simply accepting monster as a technical term that refers to their origin but also as a common term for the immoral. Catherine, Beatrice, and Justine share the fate of murdering someone during the course of gaining independence, but telling their own stories has a liberating effect. Firstly, allowing the (diagetic and non-diegetic) readers to have a glimpse into the protagonists' own perspectives ensures that society's judgment does not define the story. This provides the story with an authentic voice. Secondly, by distancing the story this way from society's prejudices, telling the story becomes therapeutic because it is finally told; in fact, the story is shared almost in a group therapy situation, where similar traumas are revealed and discussed. As a consequence, the story is met with understanding and support, which in itself subverts social conventions. This is the point where liminality becomes questioned and turned into agency; storytelling highlights how marginalization is not the shame and fault of the disempowered and indicates that the act of telling one's own true story may question and resist the dominant discourse as well as legitimize transgressions of norms that stem from and inscribe inequality. Understanding the legitimate nature of their transgressions that come from unfair, unequal power relations empowers the characters with the agency that they have sought in the less extraordinary part of their lives.

The inserted narratives that provide the background stories for the protagonists work as confessions in Susan David Bernstein's understanding. Bernstein's feminist criticism of Freud's and Foucault's (*The History of Sexuality*, 60–61) theories of confession argues that, depending on one's gender, the confessional subject has a differing experience in the same confessing situation. As Bernstein points out, "the male standards that implicitly define sexuality and power for both Foucault and Freud" question these theorists' conclusions concerning the possible empowerment stemming from the act of confessing, as testimonies given by female subjects seem to inevitably confirm and reinscribe dominant ideology (27). However, Bernstein maintains "that narratives of transgression present descriptions of domination that might be starting points for questioning the rhetoric and structure of power" (32). Relying on Judith Butler's theory on gender identity, which explains that agency "is to be located within the possibility of a variation on the repetition" (Butler, *Gender* 145), Bernstein proposes that the discourse of testimony instead of the discourse of confession may offer a useful variation "on the redundancy of power relations that mark women as confessional subjects" (Bernstein 33) because it is testimony that is able to give someone voice. "Confession is mute, silent, secret; testimony breaks the 'bondage' of this silence and liberates the unspeakable" (Bernstein 34).

In *The Strange Case*, the above noted duality of women's confessions is tangible: we may hear the monstresses' own, often self-accusatory voice; however, as the confessors do not belong to the dominant, patriarchal hegemony, instead of confirming the interpretation that comes from the inscribed dominant ideology of patriarchy, we meet a confirmation of the transgression as justified.

Storytelling is the tool for the characters to come to terms with their own identities through understanding their own traumas and perceiving a larger pattern into which their life stories fit. Such a recognition is empowering too: it allows them to see their own narratives as stories reflecting social issues on a larger scale and suggests that revolting against socially imprinted marginalization may not only be part of one's individual coming of age but may also promote social transformation, pushing society closer to a symbolic coming-of-age phase, too.

Conclusion

Wherever men have considered women's possible claim for power as unnatural and frightening, women who rejected patriarchal oppression and demonstrated deviance from the social norms prescribed by a male society have been associated with a perceived monstrosity in a normalizing society whose default status has always been designed by and for men. *The Strange Case* highlights many of the conflicts that contemporary feminists still fight for, but even more importantly, it also suggests that inscribed conventions are invisible and thus suitable to normalizing problematic phenomena, such as the inferior status of women. As Caroline Criado Perez has recently demonstrated in her eye-opening monograph entitled *Invisible Women: Data Bias in a World Designed for Men*, these conventions have so much permeated our world that it takes a very systematic research to demonstrate that even phenomena that we would cherish as clear examples of equality discriminate against women.

Storytelling can empower the liminal, and this is shown by one of the most insightful comment threads that the novel provides at the end, in which Mary Shelley's heritage is specifically evoked and discussed within the fictive space of Catherine's novel. By reinterpreting Shelley's *Frankenstein* novel as *partially* true and explaining the divergencies from the truth as female solidarity towards Justine so that she may be free to live—allowing her, this way, to tell her own story later—Catherine underlines that writing, that is, storytelling, has the function of providing protection and support for those who share experience of liminality as well as the role of shaping one's own story. Also, it may be a source of wisdom and encouragement for those who are determined not to stay silent and thus voice their own experience in real or in fictive spaces. As Catherine explains in the first novel's concluding paragraph, she feels Mary Shelley's presence and encouragement as an author: "Whenever I'm not sure what to say, when the words don't come and I sit there staring at my notebook, she says something encouraging, one author to another. I swear, sometimes I can see the shadow she casts. ... And then I nod at the chair, as though she were really present, and get back to writing" (Goss, *The Alchemist's* 400). Goss uses her alter ego Catherine, who writes the adventures of these women for the diegetic audience of Victorian women fond of mysteries, to create through an evocation of Mary Shelley a monster-narrative history from Shelley to Goss, who uses ellipsis to suggest silently her place in this group of writers and make the point that the writer can state a lot even by omission (similarly to what Shelley is suggested to have done to Justine's story).

When Catherine ponders the difficulties of writing, she thinks about the practical methods used by writers, such as the use of typewriter versus a pen. She compares Shelley's tools to hers, "marveling at the typewriter and how much faster is that than a quill pen" (Goss, *The Alchemist's* 399). As the reader is looking at the actual book, (s)he is aware of Goss's 21st century method of using a computer and creating a digital file for the publisher; the reader has no problem with filling in the virtual gap in the suggested evolution of writing methods and considering Goss as an author who, through writing the stories of various liminal characters, also shaped her own identity as a female author of monster narratives.

Storytelling, emphasizing the connections between various manifestations of marginalization during the course of history, does not only assist individual empowerment but encourages maturation in a social and historical context. Coming of age in the *Athena Club* series, therefore, is a process that empowers the *his*torically disprivileged and gives power to women through the gift of creating *her*story, even as that story includes accounts of oppression stemming from sexism, adding up to a continuous narrative voicing what was silenced for so long. In the end, with a symbolic gesture, it loudens Mary Shelly's voice, too. It does not only boost a new interest in her novel but also reminds the reader of *her* story: on the first published edition of *Frankenstein*, the author's name did not appear (Gordon vii). Later, when the author was publicly identified, Mary Shelley had to suffer gender-biased criticism that tried to deprive her of the voice she had as an author of a popular and well written work. As Ellen Moers observes, "Her extreme youth, as well as her sex, have contributed to the generally held opinion that she was not so much an author in her own right as a transparent medium through which passed the ideas of those around her" (94). But now her name is inseparably tied to Frankenstein's, and her voice now, in the age when monster literature flourishes, is louder than ever.

Part II
The Monstrous Wilderness of the Teenage Mind

5

Dangerous and Safe Spaces
Neil Gaiman's The Graveyard Book *and* Coraline

Introduction

Coming of age is a complex and difficult process that brings about a change of perspective. When you have grown up (or at least stepped out of the shell of childhood), you interpret the very same phenomena differently than before. Growing up, thus, is inherently connected to gaining experience and knowledge that helps adolescents understand their own existence, allowing them to view the space they leave (childhood) and the space they enter (young adulthood) from a new perspective. In the two best-known coming-of-age stories written by Neil Gaiman, *The Graveyard Book* (2008) and *Coraline* (2002), the protagonists learn to reevaluate their relationships to the world. Monsters are active agents in this process, even though the specifics of their role greatly differ, as they are determined by the space they belong to. In both works, the interpretation of the monsters and the worlds they inhabit provides the key to understanding what the transition from one space to another means.

The Allure of Monstrous Safety:
The Graveyard Book

We are used to reading about monsters whose fate (or function in the text) is to become slain. We almost take it for granted that in fairy tales, as well as the classical forms of fantasy, the hero will prove his aptness and worthiness by passing the test of battling and overcoming at least one monster. Less conventional is Gaiman's approach to the monstrous in his *The Graveyard Book*, where monsters are the ones who protect the sacredness of childhood and teach the rules of the world to the protagonist Bod. This subversion of the literary convention is not unprecedented[1] and fits well with Jeffrey Jerome Cohen's theory about the various functions that monsters may fulfill, as we will see. However, Gaiman's attempts at subverting the strategies of coming-of-age literature extend to his use of narrative methods. In *The Graveyard Book*, the spaces standing for the real and the fantastic realm are clearly distinguishable, and the transition between them may be decoded as the metaphorical representation of the protagonist's maturation. This solution seems to correspond with a classical method of fiction writing, in which the specifics of the portal fantasy serve the purpose of providing space for coming of age.[2] As this process is about transition, portal fantasy appears to be a very convenient and logical choice for writing about growing up: portals allow passing from one space to another, and the newly discovered world offers ample and diverse space for education and moral growth. Gaiman writes portal fantasy, making his protagonist Bod cross the borders between the two contesting worlds a number of times, eventually making him leave his home and set on a new adventure in what is an otherworld to the teenage boy. However, Gaiman subverts the rules of writing portal fantasy: he reverses the expected direction of Bod's adventures,[3] as the starting point resides in the world of the fantastic, and the destination point in the mundane world; in addition, he does not employ only the rhetorics of portal-quest fantasy, but instead, he occasionally combines it with the language characteristic of liminal fantasy.[4] The difference between the two rhetorical strategies are compelling: in portal fantasies the fantastic is elaborately described, and its wondrous nature is continuously contrasted with mundane reality (Mendelsohn xix), whereas in liminal fantasy, the fantastic is taken naturally, thus the language of the narration suggests that the boundaries between the two realms are fluid and insignificant (179). These subversions have an effect on how we see and interpret the monstrous in *The Graveyard Book*, and they also reinforce the idea that the change of perspective is a central factor in growing up.

Gaiman makes sure that already at the beginning of his story we readers discard our conventional assumptions concerning monstrosity and humanity: we are quickly confronted with an act of human ruthlessness in the mundane world, followed by an act of kindness performed by monsters in the realm that appears fantastic to us. As a coldhearted murderer intrudes the peacefulness of everyday reality and stabs the family members of the then toddler protagonist to death, the child needs a safe space in order to grow up. Life has become too perilous, so the space of death provides the necessary safety for the escaped boy. This becomes possible by an unexpected turn: the dead mother's ghost makes a last request of those who may still see her: the inhabitants of the graveyard into which her son fled. Her request is heard, discussed, and finally the Lady of the Grey (a kind of Angel of Death character) declares that "the dead should have charity" (Gaiman, *The Graveyard* 15), and thus convinces the cemetery ghosts to accept the child into their community. The Owens couple adopt the little boy, who has no one to take care for him among the living, and name him Nobody Owens (Bod for short). Their helper becomes the neither living nor dead Silas, a vampire who, unlike the ghosts, is able to leave the graveyard, so he undertakes the task of providing necessary items for the child from the world of the living.

The charity of the dead (and the neither living nor dead) turn the graveyard into normalcy and the safest place possible for Bod, and this is where a doubled perspective arises from the narration. What functions as a natural playground with a cozy home for the child Bod is a disturbing reminder of human mortality to the readers. The anxiety that we now relate to burial places is a cultural product. Before the atheisticization of western culture, the cemetery used to be an integral and sacred place of the cities, as Foucault explains, but that has changed with time. As death came to be seen as an illness that actually brings decay to those who are in proximity, the graveyard lost its original function and place: it was pushed to the outskirts of the cities, or even beyond the city borders; as a consequence, it grew into "'the other city,' where each family possesses its dark resting place" ("Of Other" 25). To the living, the "grave's fine and private place"[5] is a Gothic counterpart of the city inhabited by people, a kind of dark double where residents are deprived of the possibilities that regular city dwellers may enjoy. In this story, the reader must continuously negotiate between the two possible functions of the cemetery, especially when, during the coming-of-age process, even Bod's interpretation becomes unstable.

In Bod's early childhood, interpretation—just as the space he inhabits—is limited, and thus practically unchallenged. The cemetery is safe, the monsters are protectors, educators, friends and family; going outside the graveyard is dangerous and prohibited, but the cemetery gives a special freedom, the Freedom of the Graveyard, which only those who are members of the graveyard community may enjoy, so, in effect, it constitutes limitation (Rusvai 101). With knowledge and experience, however, comes reinterpretation. As Bod is maturing, he starts to feel ambiguously about the graveyard: instead of enjoying the Freedom of the Graveyard, he experiences restriction and longs to go outside, gradually understanding that beyond the graveyard wall a different kind of freedom awaits him. But while in his learning phase, he must face again and again the fact that although going outside is exciting and adventurous because of this new kind of freedom, it is still the graveyard that offers kindness and protection against the corrupted nature of the city characterized by murderers (the Jacks of All Trades), kidnapping (the pawnshop episode), and bullying (the school episode).

In order to mature into accepting the world of the living as his own space, where he truly belongs, Bod needs to learn how to differentiate between the two spaces between which he must choose. The monsters—the ghost teachers, as well as the vampire Silas and his substitute werewolf Miss Lupescu—educate the child not only by giving formal lessons, but also by their sheer existence. Looking at Jeffrey Jerome Cohen's theoretical basis for interpreting monsters,[6] we may notice that (at least) three of his theses concern the relation between monsters and borders. Thesis III, stating that "the monster is the harbinger of category crisis" (6), emphasizes the monster's hybridity, which denies clear borderlines, and "breaks apart bifurcating, 'either/or' syllogistic logic with a kind of reasoning closer to 'and/or'" (Cohen "Monster" 7). The hybrid nature of monsters, accordingly, informs us of how humans and monsters fundamentally differ in their relation to respecting certain borders. This is the idea that Cohen further elaborates in his Thesis IV, which claims that the monstrous body reveals the kind of difference that the monster as a metaphor signals (7). Thesis V, moreover, assigns the monster the role of policing "the borders of the possible," the transgression of which threatens the offender with becoming a monstrous entity (12).

In harmony with the above observations on what a monster is, the undead Silas conforms to his expected role of teaching Bod to perceive being dead and alive as separate, opposing categories. He explains his hybridity as a limitation when he unveils to Bod why he does not take part in the danse macabre: "You must be alive or you must be dead to dance it—and I am neither," he says (Gaiman, *The Graveyard* 67). He also stresses his difference from humans, who live and die as opposed to him, whose undead existence denies him these experiences. Silas tells him, "You know you're different. That you are alive" (79). He starts his discussion on the subject with Bod, which he later completes, with a reflection on his own self: "I am, as you say, not alive. But if I am ended, I shall simply cease to be. My kind *are,* or we are *not*" (80). His vampire body demonstrates what border he guards: the one between the living and the dead.[7] His body is deceptive, as it seems to be a normal human body (he can order pizza without problems in a restaurant), but it lacks most life functions.

The danse macabre is central to Bod's maturation—and thus, symbolically, is placed in the center of the book (Becher 102). During his dance with Death, Bod learns that leaving the graveyard does not mean departing from the dead for ever; in fact, leaving the cemetery is the way to live and then reunite with the dead. This "comfort in the certainty of a sublime and beautiful death" (103) to come when it is time crowns Bod's efforts to understand life and death in their relation. The revelation leads to Bod's coming of age, and thus the borderline between the dead and the living, marked not only by the cemetery wall but also by Silas's body, is also the boundary between childhood and young adulthood. Silas, who in his role of the guardian watches over Bod's life, as the member of the Honor Guard "protect[s] the borders of things" (Gaiman, *The Graveyard* 132), and as the monster of the cemetery guards the graveyard wall and gate, is a constant warning about the necessity of guarding. Growing up, after all, is a transition of this role: he who needs to be guarded must learn to guard himself.

Equally important, the werewolf Miss Lupescu and the vampire Silas are examples for combining nonhuman and human(e) nature, which is evident in their bodies, too, especially since both are in a way shapeshifters: Silas may actually become bodiless, a ghostly presence,[8] an absence of what a human is at first glance, while Miss Lupescu may turn into a hound, demonstrating her beastly self. Both of these hybrid entities actively help Bod become able to discern humans and monsters, or, more precisely, what everyday language terms as monster (with the connotation of evil) and the word that "simply" aims at identifying his monster friends' special form of existence. (In effect, he studies Cohen's monster theory at a graduate level, doing mostly field work, taking no proper lecture course, but consulting a professor when he is at a total loss.)

The complex knowledge that the monster-shaped instructors provide to Bod, then, is not only about mortality but also about morality. Monsters, furthermore, teach about perspective, as the boy's task is to become aware of the distinction between seeming and reality. Not all those who look like monsters are "monstrous," that is, evil, in their nature. And the tough lesson: monsters are created, constructed; consequently, you may also be or become a monster to someone else (which happens to Bod when he saves Scarlet by tricking the Sleer into taking Jack the murderer).

The ability to differentiate and to see things as they are tightly links with the ability to become and stay visible. It is not by chance, then, that the motifs of seeing, as well as being visible and invisible recur in the novel and clarify what coming of age means for Bod. The boy's safe existence in the graveyard is completely connected to his invisibility—as visitors to the graveyard are unable to note his existence; he thus becomes a "half-ghost entity" (Becher 102). A special vision comes with the package, so he can see in the dark much better than ordinary humans can. His acquired ghostly abilities include Fading, allowing him to turn invisible even outside the graveyard—but only if no attention is paid to him.

Bod's various adventures conclude with seeing things in a new light. Nowhere is this gain better presented than after his escape from the world of the ghouls. When Miss Lupescu and he reach the boundary between the lands of the ghouls and their space of familiarity, Bod wonders at the beauty of the starred sky. "Now he could see the Milky Way, see it as he had never seen it before, a glimmering shroud across the arch of the sky. The sky was filled with stars" (Gaiman, *The Graveyard* 67, 44). The new perspective brings changes in his attitude to Miss Lupescu and studying: he becomes enthusiastic about gaining knowledge, proudly enumerating to Silas what he knows about stars and constellations, and he cherishes the idea of Miss Lupescu's visiting him again to give further lessons, whereas before the adventure he considers his teacher a burdensome presence who came not to substitute Silas, but to make him suffer.

As Bod needs to learn how to see constellations that are always in the sky yet stay invisible to you if you do not know how to spot their presence, Bod also needs to become visible so that the world may welcome his existence. The boy's process of coming of age is connected to the realization that although invisibility seems to be convenient, safe and fun in childhood, it becomes an obstacle to someone who is growing up; thus, he begins to feel the need for agency. Bod loses his invisibility in school when he decides to act against bullying, so the lesson to learn is very direct: if you act, the world will take notice of you; consequently, you lose your invisibility. Such a change in one's attitude to one's environment may be dangerous but is necessary in order to become an active participant in life. Visibility, therefore, equals agency, and agency means that one may fulfill one's potential in life.

As in most of Gaiman's texts, names are of special significance, marking and revealing important qualities about characters, and *The Graveyard Book* is no exception.[9] Bod's names relate to the above explained two important aspects of coming of age: the issue of visibility versus invisibility, as well as the change of perspective that is inherent in the process of growing up. While the toddler receives the name Nobody Owens from his ghost foster parents because, as Mrs. Owens insists, "he looks like nobody but himself" (Gaiman, *The Graveyard* 13), Silas points to one of the functions of his name when he notes that this name "will help to keep him safe" (13), assuring the boy some sort of visibility. At this point the name, in fact, denotes this childhood safety I discussed before, stating that the child has no body that could be seen or that could act as "somebody" in the real world. The lack of such a body denies existence in the usual way, and thus reflects the ghostly presence Bod has, which comes with invisibility and hiding. The short version of his name makes us even more conscious of this meaning: we know that the full name should contain the word body, but the child has only a partial body, as the name "Bod" indicates. (Thus Bod, as a word, in effect "embodies" the lack of a complete body.) While in many works a new name signals a new phase of life for a character, often as a result of coming of age, in *The Graveyard Book* seemingly no such change marks the new level of maturation that Bod reaches. Using the more formal Nobody in the end instead of the informal Bod does not fall into this category of indicating transformation, especially since the name Nobody has also been in use during the course of the events that the novel relates. Yet the meaning of the name Nobody shifts as the story unfolds, as we—together with Bod—come to understand that Nobody in the first official document that the boy possesses does indeed mark the end of childhood. The name is there to prove identity, existence—belonging to the world of people holding such documents. The passport is a new means to *pass ports*, that is, borders, of unexplored kinds. It grants for the boy the ability to cross borders within the realm of the living: it is the Freedom of the World, the token of a yet unfamiliar, but earned freedom, which will be lost only when the Freedom of the Graveyard is regained—after death. But until that it is the space of human potential.

The new name signals this potential from another angle, too: the name Nobody itself reveals that the person attached to it has no fixed boundaries yet. Nobody is a person who is just at the outset of a journey that will shape him into somebody, having the potential to become *anybody* that he chooses to become.

As identity formation is closely attached to one's relation to one's family, the name in the passport, Nobody Owens, is also an indication of Bod's renegotiated connection to his families. After destroying the members of the Jacks of All Trades, including the Jack who murdered his family, he becomes reconnected with his own roots. He learns the truth about his own past, and he also understands that knowing what happened to him does not change his identity, only his knowledge about himself and the world. He is what he has learned to become in the graveyard: a child who was raised by ghosts and monsters because they had charity when the child needed it. It is not birth that defines one's identity, but the experience that one has, the novel suggests. However, the first experience that Bod has in the cemetery is an act of kindness that he owes to his birth mother, who loved him so much that she tried to assure her child's safety even after her own death. Bod needs to destroy the Jack not only because he is a threat on his life but also because this is how he may pay his tribute to the family he also belongs to.

After his triumph over the Jacks, Bod begins to lose his ghostliness, and instead of his hybrid existence he is able to develop a complex, firm identity that acknowledges both families that he belongs to, and links him to the world of the living. Yet, his new identity is characterized by independence, a partial departure from his families. Symbolically, the gestures of departure are twofold: Bod is able to get rid of a haunted family past by destroying the Jack; then he needs to leave his home, the graveyard. Leaving is immediately connected to seeing differently: the boy cannot see clearly in the dark any more, and Silas's reaction, asking, "Already?" (Gaiman, *The Graveyard* 131), suggests that this change is the expected result of the coming-of-age process that concludes with Bod's arrival in his new world, which comes with completely losing his special, yet ghostly abilities.

As Sandor Klapcsik observes, Gaiman takes it literally that we forget our dead (N 9, 207), our past, and consciously builds on the premise that this past does not only exist but is a space that may—and should— actively shape our character, our identity. Coming of age, in this reversed portal fantasy, deals with the very central topic of understanding death as a preparation for understanding and embracing life. As death and life are interconnected, the process Gaiman presents in his Young Adult novel is actually very much about understanding death in terms of what it means to the living, but first one needs to understand what living is. From a child's perspective, death is incomprehensible, and therefore does not pose a real threat. From an adult's perspective, death is understood as the closure of life, and it may be feared or desired, but Gaiman makes sure that he presents it as something that should not be either feared or too soon desired. Through Bod's story he subtly criticizes today's taboo on the issue of death noted by Foucault and helps to reestablish a connection to death as a natural part of one's life circle—building "a healthy relationship with death" (Becher 103).

When as a child Bod claims that death is no big deal, he points out that all his friends are dead. As his claim is based on the notion that his friends are not part of the living world, from the readers' perspective this may be translated as a statement that defines Bod's environment as other than the real world we know. The graveyard, consequently, is a metaphorical wilderness, an uncanny jungle, but this wilderness is of the mind, of imagination. Childhood is where monsters, the products of imagination, provide protection against reality, and what seems as real as the world one lives in. Childhood imagination is the space you need in order to grow up and become a healthy adult. Monsters are there to help because they prepare you for the journey that you will need to undertake. But growing up means that the world of imagination and reality becomes clearly separated for the human mind. Crossing the borders of the graveyard and leaving the space of the fantastic behind indicate Bod's mental growth, as a result of which he is able to make a clear distinction between what is imagined and what is real.

In the end, Bod is able to cross the once prohibited borderline without the need to return quickly, and without punishments. What used to be the site of danger has become the space for deserved adventure. This experience seems to be the gift of the monsters in the novel—but this gift, in effect, is extended for the readers. Bod seems to benefit from gradually forgetting his early life in the graveyard, which allows him to fully appreciate life; in a parallel manner, the readers benefit from a gradual realization of what Bod's mental growth implies. For Bod grows up to become a young adult, whose manner of looking at the world recognizably resembles ours, allowing the readers to conclude that all that they read in the book is a realistic representation of coming of age. We are all Bods, after all—grown-ups who have become unable to remember our childhood, where monsters kept us company and protected us from the discomforts of life. An echo of our lost memories surfaces when we withdrew from annoying reality and explore realms of the fantastic with the help of books and films. And when we read *The Graveyard Book*, we believe that before this life we live, we lived in a space which was as kindly monstrous as Bod's graveyard.

In *The Graveyard Book*, the representation of monsters relate both to the process of coming of age and the sense of forgetting. Gaiman uses a very special space, that of the cemetery, to communicate about transformation that concerns individual and community alike. How Bod is shown to forget his space of carefree childhood corresponds to how western society has grown into forgetting about the cemetery as a safe space that established and embodied an eternal connection among members of communities, the living and the dead. The idea of the extended family in the novel thus invites cultural interpretation. The graveyard functions as a connection to the dead, to the past, which is not to be forgotten on the communal level; instead, the knowledge that we may get from our ancestors and history in general is to be appreciated. The graveyard may be a disturbing place, but it is also a place for memory, just as monsters are part of our collective memory, too. This is the space we are born into: something that Jung calls collective unconscious, which is real but manifests on the level of the fantastic, in unreal images and dream moments, and communicates some hidden, yet eternal truth. It is humankind's psychic landscape whose monsters we recognize.

The Dangers of Staying a Child: Coraline

Coraline's adventures in the mirror image of their house appear almost claustrophobic compared to Bod's in *The Graveyard Book*, and they are much more limited in time, too. However, the two juvenile works have numerous points in common, and may be considered as each other's variation. If *The Graveyard Book* is a text that exhibits the collective unconscious in the form of fantasy to tell a story of coming of age, *Coraline* is a variant that closely relates to the personal unconscious—although these two concepts are difficult to clearly separate, especially since the personal unconscious is rooted very much in the collective unconscious.

In both novels the process of maturation links to an uncanny space. Gaiman's use of the graveyard as a home with invisible ghosts and monsters makes us see the cemetery as familiar and unfamiliar at the same time, and insisting that the difference is not perceivable by human sight lends credibility to the presentation and suggests that it is part of the collective experience of humankind that we all grow up to forget to see the hidden dimension of a graveyard.

In *Coraline*, Gaiman applies a different approach to the uncanny. Instead of an important communal space, the heterotopic graveyard, he focuses on the presentation of the most private space of all: the human brain. Much in the same manner as Emily Dickinson wrote of the human mind when she drew a parallel between a haunted house and the human brain that contains more to fear than what the outside world holds for someone ("One need not be a Chamber..."), Gaiman presents trips into an unheimlich house to show the mostly suppressed anxieties and horrors of the adolescent mind. Although the story reveals the girl's real life situation, and thus we may see her fantastic adventure as a metaphorical representation of her mental growth, the use of archetypes, especially that of the monstrous mother, assures that we may read this text too as a fantasy that reflects on the general process of growing up.[10] Again the transformation links with the exploration of a monstrous space, the notion that the key to coming of age is the change of perspective, and the necessity to experience a renegotiation of family bounding, as well as to understand the importance of life through perceiving the significance of death, too.

The novel's structure highlights the theme of transition: we meet

Coraline after her family has moved to a new house, so she is to explore a new environment, and soon we see that the transition from one concrete place to another leads to the transition from a concrete house to its uncanny equivalent with unstable boundaries. The unexplored space will be that of imagination—or, more precisely, a trip to Coraline's unconscious[11]—which we may witness as a story of dark portal fantasy. Accordingly, the space of the fantastic is inhabited by monsters who are to represent borders between childhood and young adulthood and take an active part in shaping Coraline's identity.

Coraline makes two trips into the house she discovers, and what may strike the reader is that while the portal is the same and the house she enters in both cases appears to be an altered version of the house where she departs from, the two trips lead to spaces that have distinct dissimilarities. One may say that Coraline's first adventure takes place in the uncanny version of their new house, and when she reenters, she finds the uncanny variant of this earlier explored Other House. This is important to note because the differences between these mental projections are dependent on Coraline's perspective, that is, the phase in her process of growing up. Just as Bod sees the graveyard differently as a child and as an adolescent boy who is more drawn to the outside world, Coraline has a different evaluation of what this uncanny space means to her.

When she first steps into this Other House, her mental landscape proves to be that of childish desire: it exhibits itself in the form of wish fulfillment (Gooding 396). She is promised the kind of freedom that she does not have, since she is not a small child anymore, so only in her fantasy could she have everything according to her desire, including her clothes, her room, and her parents' attitude to her. Yet this freedom, similar to the Freedom of the Graveyard for Bod, masks the real limitations that the girl would have by accepting the utopian aspects of this brave, new world. Coraline would need to agree to have buttons sewn in the place of her eyes as a price for the luxurious life that the Other Mother lures her with.

Obviously, this bargain is about perspective. The offer that demands "an eye for an I"[12] is based on the premise that one's identity depends on forming one's own perspectives, thus, giving up the right to see things as they are is to give up one's identity. The monster who makes the offer signals the very boundary between having a fix identity and having no identity, as well as the anxiety that connects to the loss of eyesight or, on a more abstract level, perspective. Agreeing to the button eyes would make Coraline similar to the Other Mother, who is blind to see one's true self (Kotanko 177).[13] Gaiman cunningly draws attention to this relationship by visualizing the importance of the "I" standing against the mist that will appear as a threat to the whole otherworld.[14] When it is suggested that Coraline draw something, she prefers writing a word, but makes, in a way, a picture of it:

M ST
I

The mist, which threatens with the loss of perspective, hiding details, and gradually devouring the otherworld, surrounds the I, ready to devour it, too.[15] When Coraline makes her second trip, what was an unconscious play with letters proves to be a foreshadowing that warns against the attack on the psyche of the protagonist. The fog itself acts like a monster: it has no graspable body, but is able to act as an animate entity; it does not only obscure but eats away the clear boundaries of the Other House, threatening with a claustrophobic sensation of the world as a result of the child's perspective, which is so much more limited than the adult perspective. Yet, the mist is only one of the many signifiers that communicate about the dangers of staying a child.

The uncanniness of the Other Mother (alternately called as the Beldam) in itself indicates the identity crisis that Coraline experiences, since the button eyed, scary variant of the girl's mother denotes Coraline's transformation. The Other Mother is a reminder that Coraline has started to see her family—and thus her place in her family—differently. This change of perspective comes primarily from the girl's maturation, and as her relationship to the world is not that of a child to a completely safe playground, the guards of her once reliable safety are now perceived hostilely. The monster characters embody the fear that comes with the loss of careless childhood. But as the process of coming of age is about transformation, the monsters relate to the hybridity coming from experiencing the amorphous phase between childhood and young adulthood. As a result, both the angst connected to childhood and the distress linked with adulthood are embodied by the monsters. Just as Coraline fears losing her childhood safety, she also worries about the possible consequences of not stepping over the boundaries of childhood. Staying a child for ever is possible, and in a way desirable in the alternate world that Coraline enters, but it threatens with an abominable dependence on the Other Parents. The button eyes would also turn Coraline into an uncanny "bad copy" (143), something that is only reminiscent of the person she is—evoking the image of stuffed toys, inanimate objects—with no agency of her own. In effect, the Other Mother is as much devouring as the mist that threatens the "I" of Coraline. This notion is supported by the Other Mother's vampire-like peculiarities, such as her pale skin, long fingers and nails, her craving for the life—that is, souls—of humans, and her lack of reflection in the mirror, traditionally associated with the soulless vampire since Dracula's appearance on the literary scene. The mother as a vampiric character is the representation of the monstrous female's imaginary *vagina dentata*, which Barbara Creed links with the female vampire (*The Monstrous-Feminine*, Ch. 8). The Beldam is the archaic mother, ready to devour her offspring to maintain her power.

The Gothic elements of the novel "operate rather obviously as metaphors for unconscious depths," as Karen Coats notes ("Between" 77). Gaiman, as both David Rudd and Richard Gooding examine in their studies, makes complex use of the uncanny, specifically building on the anxieties that Freud lists in his study "Das Unheimliche" (1919), and are connected to "the immediate granting of wishes" (Gooding 392), doubling, "involuntary repetition," "breaching the divide between animate and inanimate," castration (including losing eyesight) (Rudd 161–62), dismemberment (connected to castration), the dead (Gooding 392), and being buried alive in "the prospect of being sutured to the mother forever" (Rudd 163), to mention only the most important ones. Coraline must overcome these anxieties by seeing and understanding her own identity—especially in the context of the new place she is about to claim in her microcosm, her family. As a result, the monstrosity of the other world is primarily concerned with seeing and metaphorical blinding—that is, seeming.

Again, due to the novel's mirroring structure,[16] Coraline's real world experience anticipates the events that will unfold in her other world. We see how she assumes the role of the explorer in her new environment, and then we see how she is forced to explore the various fears that her unconscious holds. We are also shown how some of the events forewarn what will happen in her next trip, and in the end we are also allowed to observe how that affects Coraline's reality. The mirroring effect is amazingly complex, and accordingly, the function of the theater scene goes well beyond demonstrating what Gooding notes, namely, that this first encountered other world is a wish fulfillment not only for Coraline, but for others, as well, including Miss Spink, Miss Forcible and even their dogs (396). In fact, the brief theatrical moments that Coraline has a glimpse into clarify the foci of the novel, directing attention to its three essential, interrelated issues: acting, distracting, and identity formation.

The performances that Coraline witnesses combine well-known utterances from Shakespearean plays. The line from *Romeo and Juliet*, hinting at the relationship between name and character ("What's in a name?"; Shakespeare, *Romeo* II.ii.47) relates to Coraline's identity crisis that manifests also in how the people around her mistake her name for its less unique variant Caroline; this is similar to how people in *The Graveyard Book* automatically take Nobody Owen's short name, Bod, as Bud, derived from Buddy.

The other Shakespearean quote gives a more subtle hint at the nature of the game that Coraline has entered to play. In the source play, Macbeth's question—"Is this a dagger that I see before me?" (Shakespeare, *Macbeth* 2.1.41)—presents a manifold dilemma. The hallucinated dagger is the product of Macbeth's unconscious, an object of fear and desire, revealing both aspiration and guilt, corresponding to Coraline's unconscious wish to grow up and have the power to act, together with a sense of guilt that she does not want to stay a child forever. Like the components of the other world to Coraline, the dagger is real and unreal, which Macbeth connects to the ability of seeing when he states: "I have thee not, and yet I see thee still" (2.1.43). Therefore, "the dagger of the mind, a false creation proceeding but from the heat-oppressed brain" (2.1.46–7) touches upon the idea of illusion as a possible catalyst for action—an idea that *Coraline* utilizes several times.

Creating a convincing illusion in order to generate the needed response is a recurring motif in the novel; not only does it constitute the central action in Coraline's adventure but the girl's trip to the Other House is framed by the highlighted instances of camouflage. At the beginning of the novel, Coraline learns from a television program what protective coloration—the art of distraction in nature—is; then in her psychic journeys, she experiences how it works and makes use of it; finally, when she returns to her reality, she rehearses her unconsciously mastered skill to defeat the Other Mother. In all cases, the ability to mislead someone by providing an illusion is presented as a skill that concerns questions of life and death—a game of survival, that is.

In the otherworld it is the Other Mother who provides the very first such illusion simply by luring Coraline into her fantasy of wish fulfillment, trying to direct the girl's attention away from the significance of her real parents. She enchants Coraline by providing her with the illusion in which she presents a familiar looking, yet in many aspects more attractive family to her. Then, by keeping Coraline in her Other House, the Beldam kidnaps and magically incarcerates the girl's real parents. Coraline needs to deceive the Other Mother twice after this: first to reclaim her parents and leave the shrinking world of her childhood; then to get rid of the Beldam, whose hand crosses the border of the real and the imagined, thereby turning the portal fantasy into intrusion fantasy.

But the significance of illusion and the idea that seeing through deceptive tricks is crucial for survival (in this case, for surviving the terrifying end of childhood) return in other forms, as well. The game that Coraline needs to play in order to save herself—that is, to surpass the confinements of childhood and mature into the next phase of identity formation—is about seeing and finding. She must see through the Other Mother's trap in order to see the snow globe which holds her parents and which was exhibited on the mantelpiece all along. But even before this, she needs to find the souls of the ghost children to set them free from their mirror-bound existence. To do this, she uses the stone with the hole in it to see through it—in effect seeing through the camouflaged reality with which the Other Mother tries to blind her vision, as if the gift that came from the real world provided an opening in the texture of the imagined world.

Macbeth's famous monologue part associates *Coraline* with the Shakespearean play through its themes of seeing and seeming, reality and fantasy. It also evokes the importance of prophecy, especially since Miss Spinks and Miss Forcible read Coraline's future from the tea leaves as if they were two of the weird sisters from Shakespeare's imagination. (In fact, Mr. Bobo appears to take the role of the third weird sister: his otherness with his mice circus that he keeps speaking about is emphatic; in addition, he also warns Coraline not to go through the door—a message from his speaking mice, as he claims.) The dagger speech indicates that Macbeth's mind has begun to disintegrate, which, at the same time, is an obvious sign that the protagonist's downfall is soon to come. Consequently, the Macbethian line uttered on stage by the Other Miss Forcible is a complex warning of what awaits Coraline if she fails to overcome the obstacles of the otherworld.[17]

Among all of Coraline's anxieties, the fear of disintegration—the process opposite to forming a unified, harmonious identity—is especially underlined. The monsters of her second trip, including her two old ladies and even her father, have amorphous bodies, as if the clear boundaries of the bodies have already been dissolved. In fact, "the body," the component of the otherworld has been partially devoured by the mist, and decomposition affects the Other Mother too when the otherworld collapses, as she transforms into a threatening hand—a monster of fragmentation.

The song that Coraline hears in her dream before setting on her journey foreshadows that she "will have to contend with forces of fragmentation and disintegration" (Gooding 394). The song promises the

5. *Dangerous and Safe Spaces* 115

fall of the girl ("we will be here when you fall") (Gaiman, *Coraline* 12), and since her adventure will bring about the destruction of the otherworld, that is, the fall of the House (of Others), Poe's famous short story "The Fall of the House of Usher" is evoked in the verse sung. Such an association stresses the common themes of doubles, family, the house as the metaphor for the anxiety-ridden mind, and the process of all-encompassing disintegration. The dream song, in its capacity for predicting the adventure to come, hints at the dream-like nature of Coraline's exploration of the otherworld. While dreaming, the girl's unconscious turns the mice that allegedly live with Mr. Bobo and have given warning to Coraline into "black shapes with little red eyes and sharp yellow teeth" (12), that is, rats—the uncanny variants of mice from the otherworld.

The cautionary message about Coraline's fall is thus connected to the rats, who are under the Other Mr. Bobo's command. In the space of Coraline's unconscious, the strange neighbor transforms into a Pied Piper character, whom we may best know as a character in a Brothers Grimm tale, published originally as "Die Kinder zu Hameln" (George 69). The Pied Piper comes to the town of Hamelin and helps the town get rid of its rats by playing music and leading the rats into the river to drown there. However, the town does not honor his services; thus, he returns to play his music again, but this time it is the children who follow him (73–4). The variants of the tale propose diverse endings, but the town loses its children independently of what exactly happens to the Piper's captives.[18] The Piper's character is a peculiar form of threat to children, a musician, associated with rats and death, and thus relatable to the pipe-playing devil of the *danse macabre* (77). In *Coraline*, the Other Mr. Bobo exhibits all these characteristics.[19] He is not simply a commander of rats, but a monster, who at one point transforms into a nest of rats, displaying how his monstrous body is a reminder of disintegration. His existence defies boundaries and clear categories, shifting between a human form and a mound of rats, and giving a warning about how human life is subjected to the threat of death. The song his rats perform links him with music, and although this music seems to be far from luring, the warnings that come from mice and rats equally encourage Coraline—not by enchantment, but by marking borders that invite transgression, offering space for the rebellions against the adult world's order, which are inherent in the process of coming of age.

The rats' dream-song, an uncanny equivalent of the mice's circus performance that Mr. Bobo speaks of, does not only suggest the threat of disintegration but also confirms the significance of performance in

Coraline's experience, which the theater scene puts in the foreground. Acting, as Shakespeare's Hamlet explains, is to hold "the mirror up to nature" (Shakespeare, *Hamlet* 3.2.22), and Gaiman takes this literally, since the lines from the staged performance, as we have seen, point to the main aspects of Coraline's adventure. The theater performance or the show works to demonstrate correspondence between art and reality, as much as between the imagined and the real. The whole of Coraline's trip to the otherworld is a show, then, in which the repressed is staged, and as a result, Coraline may rehearse the role that she will have to assume in the real world. Gaiman's version of the idea that "all the world's a stage" underlines performance as a key component in forming one's coherent identity.

Coraline learns that one's performance determines how her environment sees and interprets her. Accordingly, she acts like an adult when she realizes that, in the absence of her mother and father, she needs to undertake adult tasks if she wants to save her parents. She garners her courage and thinks of her brave father to remind herself how to act valiantly. But when the hand of the Other Mother intrudes into her real world, Coraline realizes that she needs to give a performance of her childlessness to make the uncanny monster believe that she is an easy prey, and thus poses no threat to it.

Performing is surviving, a lesson very much reminiscent of the one Bod learns in his coming-of-age process, and just like in *The Graveyard Book*, this knowledge is associated with ghosts. In *Coraline*, the ghost children embody the meaning of the danger that the Other Mother threatens Coraline with. Unlike Bod, Coraline is not a half-ghost entity, but she is presented with a vision of what that would actually mean: no agency and no capacity for change, that is, development. The captured children are stuck in-between two worlds: as ghosts they belong neither to the living nor the dead. They are kept behind the mirror, and thus occupy an imaginary space even within this uncanny otherworld, as opposed to the ghosts of *The Graveyard Book*, who consider the cemetery as their natural home.

The ghost children, accordingly, emphasize the importance of being in the right place. This is a theme that Rudd identifies in terms of emotions,[20] but Gaiman presents as a literal search. As the purpose of Coraline's adventure is to make her see where she belongs, where her new place is in the world, her tasks demand that she see things in a misty world, find the sought items (the encased souls of the ghost children, and her parents in the snow globe) in the place that they do not belong to, and relocate them to their new, fitting place. While in *The Graveyard Book* Gaiman utilizes the idea of the heterotopic cemetery as a metaphorical place to show where Bod belongs, in Coraline it is the semi-heterotopic mirror that fulfills this function. The mirror is a multi-purpose signifier of what the Other House in its complexity is, for it is a mirror (as the theater is), in which Coraline may observe her own character, and the very absence from where she is observing. As Foucault explains in detail, the mirror is halfway between utopistic and heterotopic places:

> The mirror is, after all, a utopia, since it is a placeless place. In the mirror, I see myself there where I am not, in an unreal, virtual space that opens up behind the surface; I am over there, there where I am not, a sort of shadow that gives my own visibility to myself, that enables me to see myself there where I am absent: such is the utopia of the mirror. But it is also a heterotopia in so far as the mirror does exist in reality, where it exerts a sort of counteraction on the position that I occupy. From the standpoint of the mirror I discover my absence from the place where I am since I see myself over there. Starting from this gaze that is, as it were, directed toward me, from the ground of this virtual space that is on the other side of the glass, I come back toward myself; I begin again to direct my eyes toward myself and to reconstitute myself there where I am. The mirror functions as a heterotopia in this respect: it makes this place that I occupy at the moment when I look at myself in the glass at once absolutely real, connected with all the space that surrounds it, and absolutely unreal, since in order to be perceived it has to pass through this virtual point which is over there ["Of Other" 24].

Looking into the mirror and seeing the ghost children allows Coraline to reconstitute herself as a character who is on her way to becoming such a ghost child if she allows the Other Mother to triumph over her. By freeing the ghost children's souls from the magical neverwhere, this timeless and placeless mirror-space, Coraline reclaims time and place, and allows the ghost children to fully experience death. As time, finally, may have its full effect on the ghost children, they can leave this place of the living. They make their last uncanny appearance in Coraline's dream, where they can assure her that leaving this place is necessary for them to find the place they belong to. Understanding the significance of death is an essential step that helps Coraline reconnect with the (more mature) life that she will lead as a young lady, so by saving the ghost children's souls, she directly saves her own soul.

The situation of the kidnapped parents whom Coraline sees shut behind mirrors when she returns from her first trip, and whom she later finds shut in a snow globe, mirrors that of the ghost children. The parents are forced behind the glass, so they have no agency, and they are only reminiscent of their real selves, since they appear as miniature figures in a decorative object. They are clearly not in their right function and place; furthermore, they also signify the reversed relationship between child and parent that Coraline unconsciously fears. In this uncanny world, Coraline is the one who needs to take care of her parents and saving them from dangers. Accepting this task contributes to Coraline's maturation and marks a new phase in her family relations: the child's dependence on the parents is transformed into a growing independence, and the relationship between child and parents is characterized by reciprocity.

Coraline's adventure turns the girl's "fear that that the increasing independence her real parents demand of her amounts to rejection and abandonment" (Gooding 397) into a realization that her real parents act out of love and care, and that the real parents are "real," and therefore imperfect. As the parents have no memories of their captivity, their attitude to their child does not change but Coraline's perspective transforms. She learns to make fair judgment of her parents, doing justice to them (Saravia Vargas and Saravia Vargas 89). Now appreciating the safety provided by her home, she may safely perform her deceptive role of a child in order to trick and defeat the Other Mother's intrusive presence.

While the appearance of the hand in the real world reveals that Coraline still has a lot to be afraid of, her confident management of the problem proves her maturity. The novel does not promise a conflict-free (or, for that matter, nightmare-free) life for her; she may need to put back the hand into the well again and again, just as the Other Mother had to put her own (other) mother into the grave repeatedly, but now she has the strength to cope with the repressed anxieties that may surface at any time.

Coraline's growth is recognized and rewarded by her environment: the people who always mistook her name for Caroline now use her name correctly, as if from one moment to another they all could recognize her true self. With maturation Coraline earned her name, a constant signifier of who she is—and a symbolic stage in her process of coming of age. It indicates her identity (the girl who is not to be mistaken for anybody else) and since it is the name her parents gave her, it points to her renegotiated relationship with her parents. With this turn, finally she stops being an uncanny presence in the real world, where her identity is signaled with a name that is both familiar and unfamiliar. She is her true, familiar self in a familiar world.

Conclusion

Both *The Graveyard Book* and *Coraline* show childhood and the problematic, alarming process of coming of age in mental landscapes shaped by the archetypal images of the unconscious. The monsters of the fantastic world are active agents in the protagonists' maturation process, as their presence reveals the borders that the maturing child needs to learn about and cope with. Independence versus lack of agency, freedom versus limitations constitute the basic conflicts for the characters who are on the threshold of leaving childhood and entering young adulthood. These notions are connected to the parent characters, and the resolution of the conflicts is complex: the young characters need to destroy the monster(s) who threaten their sense of safety in the world they belong to; and as a result, the characters gain a new perspective of who they are and what their relation to the world is.

The use of monsters is somewhat different in the two examined works, although their primary function, broadly speaking, is to aid the children's coming of age. For Coraline, the monsters are the reflections of her unconscious fears, thus they may be considered as part of her coping mechanism: once the monster is given a concrete body, it can be destroyed (even though Coraline's experience underlines that destruction is never complete). For Bod, the Jack and the Jack's society embody the monsters he really fears and needs to destroy so that he may return to the world of the living. His existential fear is similar to what Coraline feels: he is scared of the otherwise desired independence and agency, and thus he connects his childhood in the world of the living to trauma and victimhood (just as Coraline imagines herself as a victim, who is left on her own because her loving parents have been kidnapped by evil forces). The children defeat their monstrous enemies in the space of imagination, which signifies a symbolic triumph over forces that attack integrity, but as Coraline's mental landscape is indeed her personal unconscious, her monster is indestructible, and from time to time she will need to overcome its effect and repress it. One may argue that the monstrous home that gave Bod safety against the cruelty of the real world becomes similarly repressed once Bod reaches maturation and the graveyard is unable to provide him the Freedom that ensured the carefreeness of his childhood. In *The Graveyard Book*, the sympathetic monster in a space that appears uncanny to the adult spectator—that is, the world of the marvelous graveyard—signals a coping mechanism that differs from Coraline's: for Bod, the mental landscape is a real refuge, which serves to postpone facing the real and its perils as long as possible.[21]

Gaiman's coming-of-age novels, however fantastic the world they are set in, feature a psychological realism that does not deny the fairytale-like closure that children need, while the triumph over evil is presented with a fair forewarning about adulthood's difficulties that will not disappear magically from one's life just because one successfully passed the phase of childhood. Gaiman's monsters—whether scary or caring—tell you the truth: the Other Mother's hand never waves you a real goodbye; and in your unconscious, you will always know that you will join the *danse macabre* to remember it as only the dead do. But monsters help you understand that all this is natural, and growing up gives you a perspective that allows you to see it so.

6

Destructive and Healing Psychic Landscape

Siobhan Dowd and Patrick Ness's A Monster Calls

Introduction: Trauma as Out of the Ordinary

After Siobhan Dowd's painfully premature death by cancer, Patrick Ness was approached by his publisher to inquire if he could possibly write the monster novel that Dowd hoped to but had no time to write (WHSmith). It appeared that a monster called and it demanded Ness to tell his story—which is, at the same time, Dowd's story for all of us about coping with trauma, and the struggle to accept loss, all cloaked in dark fantasy. Dowd's legacy combined with Ness's imagination and mastery of his profession engendered a compelling story in which coming of age relies on an intense, demanding initiation into the complexity of life troubled with unexplainable adversities, incomprehensible situations. The monster, in this work, is an unstable signifier that constantly seeks definition; as a consequence, clarifying the monster's function and intention promises the kind of revelation that may be needed for the protagonist to cope with his trauma.

The alarming situation in which the thirteen-year-old protagonist Conor O'Malley finds himself in *A Monster Calls* (2011) is generated by his mother's terminal illness, which leads to a number of other conflicts in the boy's life. As the basic unit of the family so far consisted of Conor and his mother, who divorced Conor's father, the looming death of the mother threatens Conor with the loss of all stability that he has had in life. Conor feels that no one provides him proper support in this time of anxieties: his father refuses to take responsibility for his son, and instead it is the grandmother who comes to take charge, although she is more like a stranger—and even an enemy—in Conor's eyes. His school environment, additionally, gives a double torment to the boy: his schoolmates bully him, while the teachers overlook his misbehavior, understanding how difficult his situation is now; their sympathy and good intention, however, destroy for Conor even the illusion that there is normalcy in the world. He tries to cling to his mother, while subconsciously he is aware of the truth that his mother's death is unavoidable and very near. And if that were not enough, a strange tree monster starts visiting him, disturbing him with stories that hurt him and threatening him with its demand that the fourth story be told by Conor himself.

Understanding the significance and signification of death may be considered as an integral element of coming of age. Bod in Neil Gaiman's *The Graveyard Book* can leave the safe space of childhood when he is ready to join the living, that is, after he has come to a full understanding of the difference between life and death. In a similar manner, the protagonist in *Coraline* by the same author also matures by helping the ghost children find their places and thereby understanding that the dead belong *elsewhere*, not sharing the space with those who are alive. Conor's experience, however, is very different from Bod's or Coraline's. It is not death as other than living which he must perceive on an abstract level, but it is the dying and the death of his mother that he needs to suffer through and make sense of. He is so much in pain exactly because he already understands the significance and the finality that death promises. This experience is not part of the "ordinary" process of coming of age; it is unnatural and violent, breaching the unwritten rules of the "normal" process of maturation. In accordance, Ness chose to apply the rhetoric that best suits capturing the nature of this unnatural and destructive attack on the everyday reality of maturation, the rhetoric of intrusion fantasy, to accentuate that the monstrous experience is tightly aligned with the protagonist's trauma.

The Vegetal Monster

When the monster appears in Conor's life, it is narrated as a real intrusion into Conor's reality: its presence disrupts consensus reality as it commands the boy out of his room, and while the monster does not enter the house, parts of it (yew tree berries) still penetrate Conor's space of familiarity "through a closed and locked window" (Ness, *A Monster* 54). But even more important is how the rhetoric fits the theme of the novel. As Farah Mendelsohn argues, "The trajectory of the intrusion fantasy is from denial to acceptance.... For all that the intrusion fantasy appears—usually—to be a 'this world' fantasy, the narrative leads always toward the acceptance of the fantastic, by the reader if not the protagonist." Acceptance is a key theme in *A Monster Calls*; yet curiously, in this novel it is not accepting the fantastic which is at stake, but rather accepting reality which the fantastic communicates and brings to the surface from the depth of Conor's unconscious. Fantasy and reality are inextricably bound: in a similar fashion that Coraline's adventure in the Other House functions, the monster's emergence in Ness's novel may also be seen as the representation of Conor's coping mechanism. For Coraline, there is an otherworld which as a magical theater gives a show of what is repressed, but for Conor, there is no portal, no sharp borderline between the real and the fantastic. The monster may appear in various places for Conor, and unlike in *Coraline*, it is always part of the protagonist's familiar reality (even though it also creates a context of the imaginary for itself via its stories). Conor's monster is as real—and credible—as any other elements of the boy's reality, as he "experiences feelings of dissociation—that he is not doing things himself" (Ghoshal and Wilkinson 1). Of course, Conor does wonder after the monster's repeated visits if the encounters were real or only part of his dream, as the rhetorical rules of intrusion fantasy dictate. Nevertheless, the focal issue from Conor's perspective is not how real the monster is; his anxiety concerning the monster is that independently of how real his visions of the monstrous encounters are, he recognizes the truth that the monster represents to him—but he is not ready to acknowledge the truth of the monster.

Yet, if the monster were easy to interpret, if its image could be seen as a one-to-one correspondence between signifier and signified, the lesson would appear as a simplified lie about the boy's life situation. Then the tree could be a monster for small children, perhaps. But this monster links with Conor's very complex coming of age, teaching much more than what Conor already knows albeit resists to acknowledge. What the monster represents and conveys through its stories is "complexity itself" (Cavanagh 9), taking the form of paradoxes (Carlin 770). Relying on the use of dream interpretation, Nathan Carlin's psychoanalytical approach demonstrates how the repeated ambivalence in the resolutions of the stories that torments Conor corresponds to the boy's paradoxical feelings concerning his mother's struggles against her illness: his wish to have his mother and his wish not to see her suffer any more—that is, his wish for his mother's death.

The monster's body itself reveals what kind of knowledge it possesses and tries to teach to Conor. As a "humanoid-tree monster" (Cavanagh 2), he is a manifestation of the Green Man, an ancient representation of life and death—a paradox that has filled mankind with awe and fear since antiquity. Carlin sees in the monster a connection to the tree of life and death from Genesis, but there is a closer and more convoluted link to the Green Man whose images combine vegetation and a human face.

The monster identifies himself by various names, all suggesting that whatever name it takes, it is *"this wild earth"*[1] (Ness, *A Monster* 50). The specific mythological names he mentions highlight the eternal aspect of its existence that keeps renewing and manifesting in altered forms. *"I have had as many names as there are years to time itself!* roared the monster. *I am Herne the Hunter! I am Cernunnos! I am the eternal Green Man!"* (50). The mythological equivalence between these named characters point to complexity and continuity, while the associations concerning them underscore the paradox nature of the intricacy relating to human existence that they stand for. Herne has been suggested to be a variant of the Celtic Cernunnos god (Thompson; Monaghan 245). Being a horned deity, "his semi-human, semi-zoomorphic form" (Green 88) denotes Cernunnos' ability to willingly change his form (86). A similar hybridity and transmogrification (form-changing ability) are evoked by Ness's tree monster, who reveals clearly anthropomorphic features when he needs to act. His functions as a god are manifold: he is "lord of the beast" (94), a god of crop-growth (95), prosperity, fertility, regeneration (92), and healing (94), whose chthonic aspect at times is suggested by his subtle underworld imagery (92). He is also identified with the Dagda, "father of all the gods," whose magic club emphasizes the dual character of the god: "With one end of the club he can slay his enemies and with the other he can heal them" (Berresford Ellis 77), exhibiting the seeming contradiction that the same representation may denote life and death. This feature of Herne/Cernunnos links with the Green Man motif, which has evolved from the foliate head of Roman art as early as the second half of the first century AD and has become the best known representation for the co-existence of human life and nature because "though pagan in origin, the motif evolved within the Church and, during the early Middle Ages, became part of its symbolic language" (Basford 19). Associations of the Green Man with the Roman Sylvanus, the god of the oak or the woodland god (Varner 153–4), highlight the regenerative power of nature people bestowed upon the leaf mask representations. However, writing about the Green Man images in churches, Kathleen Basford points out that "while it is possible that some of these leafy faces might allude to the May King or to the idea of the revival of nature in springtime, the Green Man more often evokes the horrors of the *silva daemonium*" (19). The leaves are often in a parasitic relationship with the human face, as especially the "blood-suckers" images, foliated heads from whose eyes and mouth leaf stalks suck out life, indicate (19).

Green Man representations on Christian tombs and memorials remained popular long after the motif was disposed of as a favored form of decorative motif in churches, but this use had its ambiguous content, too: it may allude to the idea of resurrection as "a life out of death symbol," or could stand as a suggestion for "man's fallen and concupiscent nature, or to his brief life on earth" (Basford 20).

Yet, Herne the Hunter, Cernunnos, and the Green Man are not only variants of the archetypal character denoting the same complexity of human existence, but they are all linked to the Celtic heritage of England; moreover, the Green Man who appears in the monster's first story is emphatically associated with the area where Conor lives. For Conor the monster is not only the reminder of the impending death of the mother, but also a warning of his multiple isolation. Conor's cultural heritage, expressed by the monster's body, becomes accentuated because the boy's father belongs now to another world: America. In Conor's experience, the separation within the family has led to a separation of worlds, indeed. The father seems to have been shaped by the culture he chose when he started a new family in the New World. The misunderstanding between father and son repeatedly manifests in the cultural content of details: Conor thinks his father speaks funnily because of his American accent and vocabulary—whereas the awkwardness of his father's words originates, in fact, from the father's estrangement from his first family. When he explains why he cannot spend more time with him, he blames American culture for it, saying that "Americans don't get much holiday" (Ness, *A Monster* 118). He cares about Conor in his limited way but does not think his responsibilities reach beyond spending some time together in the holidays now that he has another family and belongs to another woman and another child.

In effect, then, the vegetal monster signals the destructive and healing power of nature as well as points to Conor's first trauma, the separation of his family. The loss of his father as an active parent deepens the trauma he is facing right now, threatening Conor with losing all anchors to what he knows as a normal, workable family.

The Story-Telling Monster

The marked transformation of Conor's family life begins when his grandmother comes to take care of the boy while the mother is hospitalized. The appearance of the grandmother indicates what will happen to Conor when his mother dies, and Conor must realize that his father would not reclaim his role as an active parent in his life. Although his father invites Conor over for holiday, the boy perfectly knows that this is an empty gesture. His father's house has no room for Conor, and the boy easily grasps the meaning of this symbolic lack, comprehending that his father has no real space for him in his new life. For the father, divorce meant separation from his son, too, which is underlined by the huge distance between the two continents. Conor, however, has no other father figure in his life, no alternative family to find refuge in. As a result, the boy naturally considers his grandmother as a weak substitute for the father, who could have been a weak substitute for the mother, anyway. Conor's fear of losing his mother is intertwined with his anxiety springing from the recognition that he has lost his father for the second time, too. This is the situation that provokes the first encounter with the monster.

The night after Conor's first conflict with his grandmother the monster makes its visit to tell the first story that it had promised. As the monster previously revealed that it comes because Conor summoned him, the boy secretly hopes that it came to aid him in his fight against his "enemy," but the monster's story turns out to be one that connects in a metaphorical manner to many more of Conor's issues than this single fight between the boy and his grandmother. In what follows, I will rely on Freud's method of dream-interpretation[2] that also Carlin applies to disclose the various meanings of the story, completing Carlin's suggestions. Details in Freud's theory, of course, may be questioned, but the phenomena Freud bases his theory about the function of dreams on is a familiar experience to all of us who dream. Ness's authorial intent is clear: he refrains from putting overtly didactic tales into the monster's mouth and instead makes these scenes psychologically realistic by granting the monster's stories dream-like characteristics, which allows Conor and the reader to relate to their meanings. As Ursula K. Le Guin observes, "The great fantasies, myths and tales are indeed like dreams: they speak *from* the unconscious *to* the unconscious, in the *language* of the unconscious—symbol and archetype" (57; italics in the original). They are especially suitable for suggesting truths concerning reality because fantasy as an art form is "not anti-rational, but para-rational; not realistic but surrealistic, superrealistic, a heightening of reality. In Freud's terminology, it employs primary, not secondary process thinking" (79). The same relationship between myths and fantasy is also noted by Brian Attebery, who writes that "fantasy spins stories about the stories" (Attebery 3). This observation is a key to understanding *A Monster Calls*. Story-telling is so central in Ness's fantasy that it features a

6. Destructive and Healing Psychic Landscape 127

monster who tells old stories for a boy who somehow needs to make use of these tales: he must re-contextualize them and recognize the connection between the stories and his own life.

The Freudian approach highlights four important dream processes: condensation, displacement, symbolization, and secondary revision. Due to condensation, dream elements may generate numerous associations, so they do not have a clear meaning and may refer to a number of ideas, revealing a network of desires and anxieties. Displacement relocates a wish or an anxiety into a different context. Symbolization turns logical connection into visual images, while secondary revision attaches some meaning to the content of the dream. All these processes may create seemingly mutually exclusive readings, but in dream interpretation "contradiction is the rule, not the exception" (Carlin 770).

The beginning of the first tale makes a metaphorical statement about Conor's life situation, foreshadowing what is going to happen to him. The monster speaks about a king who had to secure the borders of his kingdom by terrible battles. His attempts turn out to be successful, but he also has to face the fact that guaranteeing peace for his land had a high price, as he lost his four strong sons, who all suffered a violent death, which left the king with only one heir: his infant grandson.

At this point Conor interrupts and comments on the fairy tale-like quality of the story. His note is an intrusion that helps us see the significance of the hidden content: for the structure of the story does in fact echo that of the fairy tales; however, in fairy tales it is the number three that dominates, so the number four stands out from the monster's story, especially that he promised four stories to be told, implying also that the stories may be of help. As we will learn later, the stories indeed play a defining role in helping Conor face the tragedy that awaits him, leave his stage of denial in his anticipatory grieving and go on to experience further stages of his grief: anger, bargaining, depression, and then, finally, acceptance.[3] This part of the story implies that the violent deaths of four sons of the king may be viewed as the price for peace. The kingdom is the symbolic equivalent of Conor's personal kingdom, his life, whose borders that were secure so far are now aggressively attacked. The four sons signifying the four stories do not promise comfort but struggle and painful payment for regaining integrity. Additionally, the result of the successful battle brings about a loss of power: the heir of the kingdom is an infant, which points to the fall of Conor's position as well as the ambiguity in his situation. He is in charge of the land, but once powerful, now he is wasted away by sorrow, so the new ruler of the land, in theory, becomes an absolutely powerless person, symbolically expressed by the image of an infant. In fact, the paradox duality of Conor's traumatic adolescence is captured by this double equivalence: he should be the king (and have power over death), but feels like an infant, as he believes has no real power in his hands until he actually grows up.

The next part of the story focuses on family relationships. The king remarries after his wife dies, and when the king dies, the new queen takes over the ruling of the kingdom until the prince comes of age. She is rumored to be a witch, though, and people suspect that the king died because she poisoned him to obtain power. When the prince is just a year away from coming of age, and he falls in love with a farmer's daughter, the regent queen feels threatened, and she makes plan of having a marriage between herself and the young prince to secure her position as a ruler. The prince and his bride, however, choose to flee rather than make the queen's wish come true.

The situation that the prince finds himself in mirrors Conor's position, who suffers from the loss of the two parents. While technically his father is alive and healthy, Conor feels that he has lost him when the father does not offer taking him and making him part of his new family. He also knows that he practically has lost his mother due to her illness. The new queen, then, as Carlin observes, may be interpreted as Conor's grandmother, whose plan to make Conor move in with her seems as unnatural and hideous to Conor as the new queen's desire to marry her stepgrandson prince (Carlin 770). (Note that Conor finds his grandmother strange: she is not a stereotypical old woman, looks young and energetic, which corresponds to the assumed old age of a witch hag, which the new queen allegedly disguises with the illusion of youth and beauty.)

The rest of the story centers around the themes of death, sin, punishment, and justice—the issues that mostly torment Conor because he has developed a very strong sense of guilt due to his hidden wish for his mother's death. The story reflects on this secret wish that manifests as murder. After the prince and his love flee and spend the night together under the yew tree (which is the shape the monster took then, as well), in the morning the prince finds his bride murdered. He tells the people that it was the queen, having acted out of revenge. The people capture the queen that they think to be a witch anyway, and prepare to burn her alive, but the monster intervenes and saves her because he knows that it was actually the prince who murdered her bride, claiming that he acted for the benefit of the country.

The queen, thanks to the dream process of condensation, may stand for either Conor's father or his grandmother (Carlin 770), as the boy considers these people as his antagonists in his life. Furthermore, "according to the dynamics of the dream-work, the murderous desire of the son in this story is *displaced*; the prince kills his bride, not the father (who is already dead) or his (step)mother" (770). As Carlin suggests, "Conor's Oedipal wish to have his mother sexually" is presented in the scene where the prince and his bride sleep together, while Conor's complementary wish to have the mother for himself is actually a wish to murder his father, just as the prince wishes to put the queen to death. The prince's act of murdering his bride suggests the boy's wish to kill his mother (770) for the good of the country—that is, his own integrity.

But the most important part of the story for Conor is the resolution that he finds illogical and unjust. The queen is saved, because even though she is an evil witch, as people believed, she is innocent of the actual crime she is accused of; whereas the prince, who murdered his own bride to blame it on the queen receives no punishment and will become a good and loved king of his country. Strangely enough, injustice carries the seed of hope for Conor, promising that he could be saved, just like the evil queen was (Carlin 770) or just as the prince could avoid his punishment.

The monster's unexpected move of saving the queen from the punishment that Conor thinks she deserves until the moment the monster reveals the identity of the real murderer foreshadows the repeated contradictions between what is expected to happen and what actually happens both in the stories and in Conor's life. Conor has a number of false assumptions concerning what the monster represents and what his purpose and mission are, and when he starts trusting the monster's ability to save people from troubles, he first believes that the monster came to save him from the grandmother's control, then when his belief grows, he hopes that the monster actually came to save his mother from dying. Just as this first story concludes with an unexpected turn concerning who is to be saved, Conor will be very surprised to find that the monster came to help him (who is innocent in the sin for which he blames himself).

The story initiates Conor into the illogical and unpredictable nature of life, as also Ness confirms in an interview: "Conor is caught between childhood and adulthood.... His realization that he can think two contradictory things at the same time—to me, that's a step into adulthood" (WHSmith). This is an important stage in the boy's maturation also because he understands that the laws and rules he learned as a child are not always applicable in practice, and when such a breach of law takes place, it may not even disturb the universe; life goes on. It is a monstrous knowledge, something that destroys the safety of childhood order and binds Conor to the world of adults, from which childhood's easy binarism of good and evil has vanished.

The tree, that is, the monster as a tree, brings this bitter knowledge again and again in his stories, giving it new shapes, but focusing on the same idea. We may also notice that the components of the stories that emerge as the result of symbolization gradually take shapes that become easier to see as relevant signifiers of Conor's problems, because they more directly address the boy's problems. The first story is, on the surface, about intricate court conspiracies to obtain power by all means, and Conor's wishes are displaced so effectively that one needs to work hard for recognizing the matching components. The second story addresses more directly the main issue in Conor's life: illness, death, the question of possible cure, and in relation to these: faith, or rather the consequences of lacking faith.

The circumstances of telling the story are peculiar: Conor now is in his grandmother house, where he breaks her clock because he cannot bear listening to its ticking sound. While his fit of anger takes place at nine in the evening, due to his destruction, when the clock stops running, the hands show the feared "12:07." Although Conor does not now the real significance of this time, it is still the time of horror, as the monster chooses to make his visits at this time of the night. Breaking the mechanism of the clock is symbolic of Conor's attempt at stopping time, stealing some time for his mother and himself. He is devastated by the loud bongs that would announce the passing of another hour from the little time there is left for them; he is overwhelmed by the warning that does not allow him to escape the recognition that time is up. So, when the monster visits again, it tells a story which needs less time for Conor to interpret as a story that speaks about his own life conflict. Also, while the first story is mostly just narrated by the monster, who shows only in the end the parts that were omitted from the narration previously, this time the whole story is both narrated and presented as a miraculous theater show for Conor, bringing the story-experience closer.

The case of the greedy Apothecary and the faith-lacking parson starts with a conflict because of the yew tree growing in the parson's garden. The Apothecary would like to cut the tree so that he may process its parts and turn them into expensive, yet very effective medicine; the parson, however, in the name of enlightenment that trusts science as opposed to old ways of healing, denies the medicine man's request and leaves the yew tree intact so that it may provide protection for the church in foul weather. The parson's two daughters, however, fall so ill that no modern treatment may help them, and the parson, in his ultimate despair, turns to the Apothecary for help. The parson promises that he would stop preaching against the medicine man and would give up his belief if the Apothecary cures his daughters, but this offer appalls the Apothecary. He rejects the request, and this results in the death of the parson's two daughters.

The story directly explains why the monster comes in the shape of a yew tree: it is revealed that the yew tree is the basis of strong medicine. Since the monster who appears as a tree is in a synecdochic relationship with the whole of nature, one may assume that the yew tree is to represent the healing power of nature, but in fact the yew tree represents the natural world's healing and destructive power alike. A few chapters later we learn from Conor's mother that the active substance processed from yew is used for a type of medicine for her illness[4]; however, knowing the mechanism of chemotherapy, it is evident that the healing potency of the medicine comes from its poisonous effect: the poison needs to attack the ill cells—but we also know that it cannot intelligently attack only the malignant cells, so the medicine does in fact poison the patient's whole body. In the monster's story, the yew tree potentially is the source of healing power, but the same yew tree—indirectly—becomes a cause of deaths, as the conflict over him "poisons" the relationship of the two people and leads to the Apothecary's denial of help.

As Carlin points out, both of the main characters in the monster's story may stand for Conor (772). The parson manifests the lack of faith that Conor has in his mother's recovery, which he thinks deserves punishment. This wish is expressed in this dream-like story. Carlin also identifies the Apothecary with Conor through the medicine man's use of magic, and argues that this identification reflects on how Conor experiences the process of growing up:

> The Apothecary also can be seen as Conor, though at a younger age of development, in that the Apothecary practices the old ways of medicine, of "magic," we might say, just like Conor once believed in magic and monsters as a boy. But as a teenager, Conor has given up—or is trying to give up or is being forced to give up—the ways of boyhood on his way to becoming an adult [772].

My reading on the link between the Apothecary and Conor is somewhat different, although it stems from the same observation concerning the discrepancies between the two approaches to healing presented in the story. The emphasis on the Apothecary's traditional, from the parson's perspective nearly witchy practice of healing, which stands in contrast with the spirituality and the science the parson represents, creates indeed a connection with Conor, who instinctively starts his own healing process in the most traditional manner, as it is his psyche that responds to his conflict. *How* it responds seems fantastic to Conor's environment (and the readers), since his imagination creates a monster "as a dissociative coping mechanism and as an outlet to deal with his feelings of grief and anger" (Ghoshal and Wilkinson 1). While Nishan

Ghoshal and Paul O. Wilkinson see Conor's strategy to fight his condition as an example of "maladaptive coping mechanism" (2), it still turns out to be a successful attempt to manage the boy's emotional response and reach the stage of acceptance in the end.

Before the monster would start relating its second story, Conor suspects that this one will be again a "cheating story" (Ness, *A Monster* 123), with an unexpected, even unfair turn in the end. The monster assures him that this story will be different, and reveals that "it is about a man who thought only of himself.... And he gets punished very, very badly indeed" (124). This clue leads Conor to think that the monster will punish the Apothecary in the end. He considers the medicine man to be the villain of the story, because he thought only of himself when he did not help the parson and allowed the death of the innocent girls. The monster, however, explains that the parson is also guilty of selfishness—so much so that he would abandon his faith that made him the leader of his congregation. He would not care about the people trusted to him if this were the price of his egocentric wish. Implied in the monster's explanation is that the Apothecary may even be seen as a less despicable person: he would not give up his profession, he would go on serving—and charging—those who need his help, but denies cure "only" from the person who prevented him from making the most effective medicine he could have produced.

At the end of the story, what was formulated as a suspicion before turns into scolding: Conor challenges the monster who promised a story without tricks, but the monster repeats his former claim: "*I said this was the story of a man punished for his selfishness. And so it is*" (Ness, *A Monster* 135). The repeated statement calls special attention to the themes of selfishness and punishment, underlining the tragic consequences of self-centeredness. Curiously, the fact that there are actually two opposing characters guilty of egocentrism may indicate that Conor has two wishes, both selfish—and on top of all, these two wishes are mutually exclusive. Conor's wish for not letting his mother go places his own needs above his mother's wish, ignoring his mother's suffering. His wish for his mother's death also reveals his selfishness: when he is forced to tell the truth about what happens in his recurring nightmare, his explanation concentrates on his own feelings: "I can't stand it any more!" he cried out as the fire raged around him. "I can't stand knowing that she'll go!" (220). In Freudian terms, what Conor actually experiences is "the conflict between the id and the superego" (Carlin 773). His wish to get punished (for selfishness, for wanting to be free from suffering) derives from his superego, but his desire to escape his situation comes from his id.

6. Destructive and Healing Psychic Landscape

The idea of selfishness, however, is tightly connected to the notion of sacrifice, which also forms part of the monster's story. It appears that the tale focuses exclusively on the parson and the Apothecary, but there is a third protagonist: the monster itself. The monster as a yew tree seems to be the most passive character in the story: he is argued over, but he has no say in the conflict. When he comes to act, however, he appears to be the most active, most potent agent, an irresistible power of destruction. But what really strikes Conor is the monster's disclosure of what could have been the right course of events.

> *I expected him to give the Apothecary the yew tree when the Apothecary first asked.*
> This stopped Conor. There were further crashes from the parsonage as another wall fell.
> "You'd have let yourself be killed?"
> *I am far more than just one tree,* the monster said, *but yes, I would have let the yew tree be chopped down. It would have saved the parson's daughters. And many, many others besides* [Ness, *A Monster* 134].

Beyond Conor's latent wish to be punished for selfishness the suggestion that sacrifice may be a viable and beneficial solution to problems appears. But even more important could be the monster's teaching about what sacrifice means: it means death, but the monster also emphasizes that it is not complete death but giving up a part that represents what or who one is. While it appears that sacrifice demands the whole of one's existence (because one's existence depends on making the choice of giving up his or her own wish and well-being), he should know that this is only how it *feels*. In Conor's situation, giving up his mother would mean giving up a very important component of what defines his existence—but the sacrifice is survivable.

In this second story the paradox becomes resolved in destruction. In Conor's experience, the destruction of the parson's house in the monster's narration merges with the real destruction that he does not even recognize he is performing until he has finished it. The border between fantasy and reality becomes fluid, indicating the unity of the monster and the one who summoned it, which will result in an even more intense experience when the monster tells its third tale.

The monster's first four visits take place near midnight and hence appear to grow out of a dream-like experience. The first three encounters are interpreted by Conor as very vivid dreams, in which the boy is only a passive listener and spectator. The next visit, when the second story is told, starts similarly, but its closure suggests more clearly that it was heard and acted upon already in an altered state of consciousness, generated by a violent dream that Conor actively joined, while the third occasion when the monster tells a story is presented as an interactive experience, which Carlin identifies as a narration of an altered state of consciousness (774). Instead of 12:07 in the morning, the monstrous intrusion begins in the middle of the day, at seven past noon—a symbolic shift displaying how the repressed, traditionally presented in the Gothic as actions of the night, come to invade the diurnal social self. How the repressed emerges manifests in the gradual change of Conor's participation in the storytelling. The monster's stories and their real-world effects question the borderline between reality and imagination, and the third story confirms the overlapping between the two. This phenomenon is in line with how the stories become more and more transparent in mirroring Conor's situation.

The third story is a direct reflection on Conor's circumstances; in fact, it is an immediate response to what happens to him, so the monster intervenes when Conor feels that the situation has turned unbearable for him. The monster describes Conor at the beginning of the story: "*There was once an invisible man, … who had grown tired of being unseen*" (Ness, *A Monster* 175). From then on Conor acts out the tale and converses with the monster when he needs directions, courage, and motivation. In the center of the monster's story stands a man who was treated by others as if he were invisible, but the man made these people see him with the help of the monster. The story reflects on how Conor's bully Harry decided not to see Conor any more, realizing that this would hurt Conor more than beating him. But while Conor would have welcomed physical abuse, thinking that he deserves punishment anyway, invisibility is unacceptable for him, and results in the outburst of his emotions—and a physical attack that makes sure he will be noticed.

Visibility, similarly to what Gaiman presents in *The Graveyard Book*, is the signifier of active agency, which is how life becomes defined for the teenage characters Bod and Conor. When his bully announces his decision to consider Conor invisible, it is the final, symbolic denial of Conor's participation in normalcy. Strange as it may sound, bullying was the last element of normalcy for Conor, a ritual that confirmed his existence in life through the suffering that he wanted to take. Bullying meant an acknowledgment of his existence, which he badly needed, as the world started to collapse around him, and the laws and rules that used to keep it together stopped functioning. It began with the hospitalization of his mother and continued with the care that the boy received in the form of overlooking his increasingly deviant behavior. But physical bullying also meant a regular confirmation of Conor's guiltiness, a due punishment for his hated wish for his mother's death, as he could not hope for punishment from anyone else. The adult world resists punishing Conor. The question "What purpose could that possibly serve?"

(Ness, *A Monster* 186) indicates the great distance in how Conor and the adults around him understand the mechanism of social existence. Conor's attitude is based on a simplified binarism rooted in childhood experience, whereas the adult responses demonstrate complexity.

The monster's visits always leave a spark of doubt concerning their realistic—or, from another perspective, fantastic—nature. Conor finds parts of the yew tree in his room after the first two visits, finds a little yew branch sprouting from the floor after the third, but these may be as explainable as the foreshadowing components of his dream-like experience. If Conor indeed performs dissociative behavior and acts in an altered state of consciousness, he could have brought parts of the tree inside without him remembering that (and a seed could have grown into a stem). The recurrently foreshadowing content of his encounter with his monster may also be accounted for psychologically, taken that what becomes explicitly revealed later may already be part of the knowledge that he repressed. The last monstrous visit, in this respect, seems to diverge from the previous instances. While it seems to represent the moment when it is clear how the monster takes over the self, how the repressed comes to the surface and how what was pushed to the realm of the fantastic finally proves to be part of the real, the doubt it still leaves is most disturbing, as the destruction that Conor makes does not match his actual physical build and strength. The extreme power he demonstrates may not simply be explained by "an externalization of the self-hatred that Conor feels towards himself" (Carlin 774), I believe, but rather with the manifestation of hysterical strength that people may display in life and death situations.[5] This appearance of the monstrous force now performing destruction in the presence of eyewitnesses indicates again that the monster is not an exterior force but power from within the self.

That this situation, for Conor, concerns matters of life and death, is beyond doubt. His mother's nearing death pushed him into a liminal space of existence, in which he needs to fight for his life, feeling that he is dependent on his mother's condition. Cancer directly affects him, as "the other kids still treated him like *he* was the one who was ill especially since Harry and his cronies had singled him out" (Ness, *A Monster* 90). The bullying marks him, just like his mother is marked by illness, but this condition is ambiguously visible and invisible. It is apparent that Conor's mother is very ill, but the illness is never explicitly named, and the known, now sure outcome is never mentioned but becomes a tabooed knowledge. Conor's fate reflects this ambiguous condition: he is marked, but overlooked, his actions do not count the way they used to, as if he were put in a suspended state of existence, where social rules do not apply any more. As a consequence, he needs action to extreme measures that cannot be overlooked.

What the monster does through telling the stories that metaphorically indicate the complexity and the pain in Conor's life situation is to build, so to say, stairs that help Conor pull his own story from the depth of his subconscious up to the surface where he must face it in reality. The stories indicate the stages of recognition that life is much more complicated than what it seemed like from a child's perspective. They "prepare Conor for his ultimate test of strength: confronting his own fears of becoming a monster" (Cavanagh 10) because he is not strong enough to keep his mother in this world, and as a result, he is responsible for the death that awaits her. When it is his turn to tell a story, Conor is forced to relive his nightmare, in which a monstrous whirlpool is about to devour his mother. He holds his mother's hand to save her from this horrid fate, but after a while he lets go of her hand, allowing her to fall into the vortex, a metaphorical representation of monstrous cancer. Conor's reaction to the monstrous visits confirms what psychological research finds about children's reactions to the monsters they meet in their dreams: children are more likely to not fight the monster they encounter, demonstrating "an openness to the Other" (Doll 100). While for adults, "'slaying the beast' becomes myth's metaphor for giving muscle to the hero, and murdering the monster becomes psychology's metaphor for ego control" (100), children experience otherness in their dreams, turning the monster's character into a helper (102–04). In its function of reminding the child that "shadows are real, containing primal truths that simply want to be acknowledged" (102), the tree monster demands the truth of Conor, the truth about his wish to let his mother fall, which will help him acknowledge that he has no power at all over what happens to his mother (Cavanagh 11–12). This vulnerability, the acknowledgment of powerlessness is what helps Conor come to terms with his loss, and depart from his childhood, too.

Conclusion: The Truths of Monsters

Deciphering the meaning of the monster in *A Monster Calls* is as complex a task as figuring out the latent, implied signification of the stories that the tree monster brings and that define his character. One of the difficulties of interpretation comes from the absence of binarism: while it would be easy to interpret the monster in opposition to the human, this is not an option, which even the title of the novel hints at. The indefinite article in the novel's title implies that there is not one

6. Destructive and Healing Psychic Landscape 137

specific monster that may exclusively be meant. "A monster calls" translates at first glance as an action that is performed by the monster that will appear in the novel, that is, the yew tree monster. However, that monster reveals that he came because Conor called him—a claim that immediately reinterprets the title. As the novel explores how the psychic landscape of the protagonist mirrors Conor's everyday reality, the identity of the monster becomes questioned. The monster that visits Conor turns out to be inseparable from the boy, embodying his mental landscape, his repressed emotions, demonstrating that "the monster is the abjected fragment that enables the formation of all kinds of identities—personal, national, cultural, economic, sexual, psychological, universal, particular (even if that 'particular' identity is an embrace of the power/status/knowledge of abjection itself); as such it reveals their partiality, their contiguity" (Cohen, "Monster" 19–20).

This coexistence of the monster and its "monstrous" creator is further complicated by the rhetoric of the novel, which, as Cavanagh details, constructs cancer as a monster in the story (6). All together then, "There are four perceived or potential antagonists of the story [… :] the Monster (the character), the nightmare vortex (the monster from Conor's dreams), Conor himself, and the cancer" (Cavanagh 5–6), destabilizing the meaning of monster. The four monsters are all related: cancer generates the trauma in Conor's life, and its effects on his psyche cause sense of guilt, nightmares, and dissociative behavior. And while all forms of monstrosity seem to be destructive, the monster claiming that it was summoned also claims itself to be a healing monster.

The main story of the monster who comes to help proves to be as tricky as the first two stories narrated by the monster. That it will be similarly a "cheating story," as Conor would call it, is forewarned by the ambiguous title, too. How the monster's tales operate in the novel is in harmony with the Gothic convention that is tied to expressing "anxiety about 'meaning'" (Williams 67), often turning anxiety into horror due to the instability of interpretation (Jack Halberstam 149). As "fragments of language"[6] (67), the stories first deceive their interpreter, Conor: they do not express meaning clearly but symbolically point to the unspeakable, generating uncertainty of interpretation. Yet, as the meaning is always clarified by the monster—or the voice of the boy' unconscious—the tales are able to gradually prepare Conor to realize and accept the strange turn in his life story: the monster does not save the one whom Conor thinks needs saving. Saving, moreover, does not mean a happy end—it promises hope for the future, but it is inherently linked with destruction and suffering. The stories pave the way to accepting the chaotic, unpredictable nature of life and the lack of agency even grown-ups have in it at times—a clear contrast with children's concept of adulthood associated with amplified agency and power.

Conor's dilemma is an ethical question: it is inseparable from reconsidering what is right and what is wrong and it is incessantly fed by guilt. The unhappy yet hopeful ending is the result of a long cognitive process at the end of which Conor is able to re-evaluate his emotions and their meaning. He learns from the stories and he learns how to interpret stories. He starts out as a novice reader and ends up as an expert reader,[7] someone "who possesses a capability of realising to the full extent the potential afforded by the text" (Nikolajevna 15), demonstrating how reading may be instructional when it allows or even forces a text's recipient to use his or her cognitive skills to evaluate the choices presented. Of course, the monster does draw very clearly the conclusions from his stories, but this serves to create a conflict with Conor's primary interpretation and therefore leaves an open end that allows Conor and the reader to evaluate primary and secondary interpretations. On each occasion that the monster tells a tale, this type of evaluation is reiterated, preparing Conor for drawing his own conclusion at the end of his own story and accepting his own limits in agency.

The yew tree as a cultural body reflects on how cancer as a "cultural construct" (Cavanagh 5) is in itself a metaphor for contemporary man's deepest fear linked to vulnerability or lack of control. In its capacity to stand for chemotherapy, the yew tree image aptly communicates the double-edged nature of monstrous help that often requires one to fight the monster or suffer the destruction that it causes. But if monsters are complicated beasts, it is because "*humans are complicated beasts*," too (Ness, *A Monster* 223). The monster's body is tricky, just as its stories are: the shape of the yew tree suggests cancer-curing abilities,[8] and it does cure the effects of cancer; however, it does not bring physical healing for the mother through the usage of Taxol, but attempts to heal the boy's tormented psyche by the power of words. In the novel "'storytelling' is used as an instrumental technique in psychological empowerment" (Farnia and Pourgiv 46), relying on the mechanism of pattern mirroring, just like story-therapy does. This specific function of the monster not only discloses on its metaphorical level how the human psyche may react to trauma, but it also sheds light on the empowering ability of imagination and thus, consequently, the power of the monsters we create.

Monsters, in their double role of signifying fear and desire, are our constructs that embody the impossible especially as it arises from the opposing contents that they need to hold. By externalizing the anxiety and/or the terrifying desire we cannot—or dare not—name, monsters come to our aid by lending body to the unnamable that resists categorization so that we may confront it and gain power from that confrontation. The mere existence of monsters provides a space in which imagination and the rational—the unconscious and the conscious—may co-operate to teach essential, yet non-exclusive truths through the use of the archetypal. This is the dream-like quality that monsters bear, and as such, Conor's monster is a signifier of the coping mechanism that our psyche provides us to contend with latent anxieties (but not necessarily traumas). This monster bridges the gap between the possible and the impossible via the dream-like stories it brings as cure: it stands for the power of archetype-based storytelling, and hence, of fantasy. Its existence evokes the words of Gaiman's Dream Lord character, Sandman, on how stories operate: "Things need not have happened to be true. Tales and Dreams are the shadow-truths that will endure when mere facts are dust and ashes, and forgot" (Gaiman, "A Midsummer" 21). These shadow-truths that fantasy spins into stories are most evident in psychological Gothic, the prominent examples for which in youth literature are *Coraline* and *A Monster Calls* (Buckley 254), or Seanan McGuire's dark fantasy *Wayward Children* series. All of these works seek to show through the impossibility of their monsters a possible way of interpreting the world around us. The "symbolic truth" that lies in the "literal untruth" of fantasy (Attebery 4) is brought by the monster in these novels and strongly addresses the issues of vulnerability and safety in one's coming-of-age process.

7

Spaces of Escape for the Abused

Seanan McGuire's Wayward Children *Series*

Introduction: Spaces of Escape

Seanan McGuire's *Wayward Children* series (2016-) is the modern saga about abused childhood. The parts of the series focus on various coming-of-age stories in which we encounter children who are so different from what their surroundings like to consider as the norm that they find it impossible to fit in. The children's incompatibility with the world that they were born into is easy to see: they all develop a special "ability" of finding refuge from their present-world miseries in another, fantastic, never-heard-of, unimaginable world. It is their heart that leads them to their door, as if a troublesome existence would turn "every heart [into] a doorway." The doors are "drawn by need and by sympathy. Not the emotion—the resonance of one thing to another" (McGuire, *Every* 97). The worlds the children discover display manifold divergences, depending on how they relate to the great principles of Logic versus Nonsense as well as Wickedness versus Virtue. The secret world they discover is not a utopia for many, but still a home, and the teenagers who come to live in Eleanor West's Home for Wayward Children[1] hope to find their doors again[2] and return to the world they had to leave for one reason or another. Stories about those who have succeeded to go back and never return to their home world is the foundation for their hope.

Those who find a joyous world are obviously attracted to its pleasantness and find it hard to face again the difficulties of the reality, but those who make an adventure in a monstrous world are equally bound by what that experience offers, so it seems that monsters may provide something that manages to compensate the children for what they suffered earlier. However, the monstrous worlds do not right the wrong, and are not happy worlds in which the visitors may forget their sufferings. Nor are these worlds monstrous in the sense Conor experiences the yew tree monster's stories in *A Monster Calls*, bringing difficult knowledge and thereby allowing for healing. Although one may detect several similarities between the roles of the monstrous in Ness's novel and in the *Wayward Children* series, healing or helping is meant very differently in McGuire's novellas. The secondary worlds in McGuire's series, for instance, call Jack and Jill to adventures that are cruel "because it is the only way they know to be kind" (McGuire, *Down* 50). While Ness's tree monster also appears to be cruel, making Conor face his trauma, the monster's aim is to help the boy become reintegrated into the life he needs to live. In contrast, the monstrous fantasy worlds which McGuire's characters discover never bait the children with such hopes; in fact, their otherworlds deepen and confirm the breach between reality and the fantastic, while offering temporary relief from facing painful reality. Accordingly, the series suggests that there are, unfortunately, children who will never have the chance for reintegration, as they are excessively traumatized by their pasts; therefore, the encounter with the monstrous is not so much an active help for them to reconnect with the world; instead, the monstrous embodies and amplifies their trauma that they experienced in their home world and therefore it becomes the signifier of their isolation from reality.

Jack and Jill and the Depth of the Unconscious

Among the various coming-of-age narratives that the series suggests in its first volume, it is the Jack and Jill story that was given first a complex elaboration. The opening volume of the series, *Every Heart a Doorway* (2016), presents the brutal consequences of a twin couple's adventure in the otherworld that called them but later made them leave. The second volume gives a detailed version of their adventure and the circumstances that led to their "invitation" to an otherworld and then their expulsion from it. Some reviewers claim that reversing the order of events weakens the effect of the second volume, as the reader already knows the outcome of the adventure. However, McGuire seems to be very conscious in planning the order of events in the girls' life: we see the symptoms first, and then we take part in a psychoanalytical session whose aim is to understand the motives of these two children. We may dig deeper and deeper and see the logical connection between what happened to the girls before they found the door, what they lived through behind their door, and how these facts explain their behavior after they were forced to return to their world of birth. Knowing the antecedents prepares us to perceive the nature of the monstrous they find in the world that opens up to them.

McGuire's *Wayward Children* series has multiple parallel universes that join to this world via doors, but these doors are very difficult to find: only those who somehow need another world are able to sense the portal between their present reality and the space of imagination that invites them. The first two chapters of *Down Among the Sticks and Bones* (2017) give a comprehensive account of how Jack (short for Jacqueline) and Jill (short for Jillian) are suppressed by their parents, Chester and Serena Wolcott, and how, as a result, they are unable to develop their real characters. Forced into the roles dreamed up by their unloving, selfish parents, who do not understand what parenting means, Jack and Jill develop false ideas about their own selves as well as the personality of their own twin sister, and in general, about personal relations.

The faulty nature of personal relations that characterize Jack and Jill's world is the key to understanding the reasons why the girls need a refuge somewhere else. They are born to parents who do not think of children as individuals—or even people. The Wolcott couple consider children as accessories that belong to the image of perfect life, decoration in a perfect house, important pieces of a puzzle that depicts a perfect social life. Children are wish-fulfillment for them, but the wish is purely egoistic: they desire unquestionable proof that they have a perfect life to be envied by others. Children add value to their appreciation in society; as symbols of status, they are completely objectified even before birth.

Jack and Jill's tragic story emerges from their parents' shallow understanding of life. "The Wolcotts' personalities are a toxic mixture of narcissism, entitlement, and shallow materialism, with just a soupcon of megalomania for flavor" (Battey). As a result, their relationship lacks emotional depth: all the components of their "perfect" life are valued according to their pragmatic use, so the couple are unable to show an example of love and care. For a time, the parents' ineptitude is counterbalanced by the presence of the grandmother, who is called to move in to raise the children. While she stays with the family, she represents acceptance and unconditional love for Jack and Jill.

> She had tried to encourage both girls to be themselves, and not to adhere to the rigid roles their parents were sketching a little more elaborately with every year. She had tried to make sure they knew that there were a hundred, a thousand, a million different ways to be a girl, and that all of them were valid, and that neither of them was doing anything wrong [McGuire, *Down* 34].

When she is told to leave without saying goodbye to her granddaughters, the cornerstone of the children's life disappears. The girls feel betrayed, and retrospectively devalue even their grandma's love, so from then on the girls must rely on what their parents can offer to them—and that is close to nothing in terms of emotions. Consequently, the girls forget (and lack the opportunity to relearn) what love, care, or individuality are; instead, each of them learns to envy the other for whatever she herself cannot have but the other is privileged to experience.

In McGuire's dark fantasy, the girls become disturbing doubles for each other: from lookalike identical twins, who perfectly mirror the other, they are molded into easily distinguishable beings, each displaying features and performing roles that are denied the other. Raised to become each other's opposites, they grow into persons who embody the suppressed wishes and fears of their sister. They come to represent one half of a unit that was forcefully separated by the parents. Being twins is the girls' misfortune in many respects. Their parents think of them as two similarly looking objects that may logically and equally be shared: one for either of them, each girl to be shaped by one parent's wishes and ideas.

> Like bonsai being trained into shape by an assiduous gardener, they were growing into the geometry of their parents' desires, and it was pushing them further and further away from one another. One day, perhaps, one of them would reach across the gulf and find that there was no one there [McGuire, *Down* 40].

This attitude on the parents' part reflects a quantitative appreciation, lacking the recognition of quality beyond appearance, and rejecting the notion of individuality.

The shallowness of the Wolcotts manifests in the overall simplicity of how they approach the complex issues of life: they wanted a girl and boy, so they force their two children into performing two distinct stereotypical gender roles. The parents' hubris of trying to right the "wrong" that Nature made, namely putting them into a situation in which they need to raise two girls instead of a girl and a boy as they thought fitting and perfect, gives a very modern Frankensteinian touch to their characters. Just as it is the creator and not the creature who proves to be the villain in Mary Shelley's work, so may the parents be seen as the villainous creators in the novella, even though when Jack and Jill go through their door, they meet two creators of some sort—and one of them, actually, is a mad scientists, whose scientific ambition unmistakably evokes Victor Frankenstein's character.

McGuire works with extreme contrasts that appear even more vivid because they have common cores. Princess and tomboy are clear contrasts of society's traditional stereotypes of gender roles, but they become accentuated by the fact that identical twins are given these divergent paths of character development. In a similar fashion, when the girls cross the borderline between their real world and the alternate world they find, they encounter two rivals who are inextricably bound by their shared passion for what keeps us alive; however, the purpose of their interest is completely different: whereas the vampire master drinks the essence of life, blood, and thus causes the death of people, Dr. Bleak's interest resides in revitalizing the dead.

Recognizing McGuire's principle of building her fiction from such opposites helps us understand the kind of world the girls find. McGuire organizes her novella into various chapters that get their titles from nursery rhymes, among which the references to the Jack and Jill rhyme are the most important ones. There is a subtle contrast between McGuire's use of twin girls as opposed to the traditionally understood one girl and one boy unit; however, the illustration in the earliest surviving reprint of John Newberry's *Mother Goose's Melodies* from 1791 reveals that the original Jack and Jill were two boys (Prideaux),[3] so McGuire's use of twin girls is not too far from the original version. A more important idea than whether the author uses two boys, two girls, or a boy and a girl lies in the fact that McGuire rethinks the contrast between up and down, which is also part of the original rhyme. While the interpretation of the Jack and Jill rhyme remains unsure and obscure, McGuire's intentions are suggested by the titles that she gave to the first two parts of the novella. The contrast between "Jack and Jill Live up the Hill" (9) and "Jill and Jack into the Black" (55) work in the manner of the Gothic tradition, highlighting the difference between what is shown on the surface and what is hidden in the inside, between social life defined by seeming/appearance and psychic life defined by what may never surface, between the superficial glamor of social success and the darkness of the unconscious.

Jack and Jill's descent thus is reminiscent of Coraline's adventure in Neil Gaiman's novella inasmuch as the girls find themselves in an alternate world that responds to their subconscious fears and desires, and thus may be considered as their psychic landscape. McGuire calls the otherworld of *Down Among the Sticks and Bones* the Moors and suggests that it is indeed the unconscious stratum of the girls' psyche. When she describes the Moors as "the single platonic ideal from which all other moors had been derived" (McGuire, *Down* 53), she highlights that the Moors is not one specific place but an archetypal image, which immediately connects it not only to Platonic philosophy but also to the Jungian concept of psychological archetypes residing in the unconscious.

7. Spaces of Escape for the Abused 145

The mental landscapes of McGuire's and Gaiman's novellas, however, reveal important divergences. The otherworld featured in *Coraline* is the symbolic space that gives opportunity for Coraline to cope with her anxieties in a positive manner; she becomes a heroine of this dark, fog-bitten world, able to save and regain her parents, free the incarcerated ghost children, escape from the fate of becoming a ghost child herself, and triumph over her arch enemy, the Other Mother. This adventure—however much it takes place in a frightening, dark alternate world—mirrors the symbolic struggles of average teenagehood, in which growing up is rewarded with a more mature, self-confident identity, and the knowledge that the world in which one needs to grow up is the place where one belongs and may feel at home. The adventures that Jack and Jill live through do not have this power of magnetism. Although meeting the lords of this alternate world echoes the outset of Coraline's adventure, Jack and Jill are powerless to change their fate that is decided by the Master and Dr. Bleak. Coraline is able to reject the Other Mother's offer to stay with her and live there under her control (indicated by the button eyes that she would receive) because she is brought up in a loving family, and even if she has some issues with her parents, those are not traumatic but the results of the common process of growing old. Jack and Jill's problems, however, originate in an emotionally abused, loveless childhood, so there is nothing, really, that would anchor them to their family and their real world. Their psyche is shaped by the emotional scars that they have, so the mental landscape where their adventure takes place is darker, more horroristic than Coraline's; it is the landscape of abused, traumatized minds. As a result, their story is not that of defiance but that of servitude even though in a twisted way this is still a rebellion against their former life, against the "toxic gender roles" (McGuire qtd. in Perry) their parents forced them into.

The girls find this specific land of the Moors because of their congregated anxieties that they are unable to cope with since there is no one in their lives who could comfort them. In an unloving home, alienated from their sister, the girls are on their own, and as they have not learned how to open up, they just accumulate their pains.[4] The Moors, therefore, appears as a space that mirrors this darkness and suffering, and the rivaling lords of the Moors—the Master and Dr. Bleak—correspond to the major cause of Jack and Jill's apprehensions, their suppressed, never acted-out desires. But just as their growing up has caused them damage, their new "training" that completes the path they had to take earlier is equally demanding and has injurious consequences.

The horrors stemming from the snobbery and conformity of upper middle-class society and affecting the psyche of the girls match the horror that are the most classical and archetypal in their form, suggesting again an unconscious response. There is a vampire—the Master—with a castle and a terrorized village around it, and there is a mad scientist—Dr. Bleak—living in an eerie windmill, dissecting and occasionally resurrecting dead bodies. The girls need to decide which parent-substitute they choose as their master to live with, and it turns out that they do have their preference and have no argument as to where they think they better belong. They both want to take opportunities they never had: Jack grabs the chance to get rid of role playing the beautiful, empty-headed doll and to study science instead, independently of the amount of blood, hard work, and the lack of comfort that are promised; Jill, in contrast, wants to stop role playing the tomboy and to discover her femininity instead. She craves all the surface beauty and the attention that beautiful girls enjoy in society, as well as the comfort of a rich, aristocratic environment, independently of the "drawing upon [her] blood" that is promised to be part of her choice.

That there is a complete turn in their maturation process is suggested by the change of their names—as it happens in Gamian's *Coraline* and *The Graveyard Book*. In their former life, the girls go by the names Jacqueline and Jillian, because their snobbish parents find it outrageous to call their children by "something as base and undignified as a nickname" (McGuire, *Down* 19). The parents show no respect for the children's individuality: not only do they assign rigid gender roles to them, not caring about their actual characters, but they even consider swapping their names, thinking that Jillian sounds considerably more feminine than Jacqueline with the name Jack as a stem. They never consider what possible identity crisis they would create for their daughters by changing the names. The only reason why they do not reassign the names is that it would be "overly complicated, for insufficient gain" (McGuire, *Down* 71). Once the girls are in the castle, they are "already wearing their shortened names like the armor that they would eventually become" (71), drawing strength from the feeling that now they are away from the restrictions of their former lives. The situation is frightening—they need an armor, after all—but they are free to respond naturally, not conforming to expectations. Jack may evaluate the situation, be cautious and have suspicions; Jill is allowed to be afraid. Jack makes the more rational choice of accepting lack of comfort and the promise of never being hurt intentionally, while Jill takes the offer of having the combination of enjoying luxury and having only three safe days and a drawing upon her blood for sure.

The names of the masters—and how the girls perceive them—reveal their dissimilar attitude to the challenge they have to take. Jill sees no difference in the two authority figures, only in their circumstances: for her, master or doctor equally means a person to obey, and for her this is not much different from having a parent. Jack, however, makes a careful distinction: for her, master "was a title that said something about the person who used it, while [... doctor] said how much that person knew, how much they understood about the world. One was a threat and the other was a reassurance" (McGuire, *Down* 84).

In response to the Wollcotts' hubris of trying to correct Nature's work, the parental figures of the otherworld are unnatural characters, to say the least, both meddling in Nature's course by not accepting the law that death is the final borderline between existence and non-existence. The mad scientist is a re-animator, making the dead live again, while the vampire is undead, and he not only kills but also turns people into similarly living dead monsters. Their power over death signals that the choices the girls make are about life-and-death questions, or, as the doctor says, "everything comes down to blood here, one way or another" (McGuire, *Down* 101). Their unnatural behavior is a warning that the space of maturation they are in control of is dangerous and potentially as harmful as the girls' lives were before going through the portal.

Despite the seeming similarities, Jack's differentiation is defining: as Mary, the maid at the vampire's castle notes, Dr. Bleak is a savior figure compared to the vampire. His scientific obsession might come from hubris, but he is still interested in restoration and not damaging. He demands hard work but gives education as a reward. There is physical work and many challenges for Jack, but she receives satisfaction from learning that obstacles may be surmounted, borders may be stepped over. All Dr. Bleak does is let Jack stay true to herself while serving him, but this is more than what she received from her parents. Unlike the Master, the doctor is not a monster per definition: he is not a hybrid creature but a man, and together with his apprentice he stands for "the human side of the essential balance between the feudal houses that ruled these shores" (McGuire, *Down* 131). In this role, the doctor makes an attempt at saving Jill, too, by arranging an accidental encounter between the two sisters so that Jack may influence Jill before the more unfortunate girl loses all her human qualities. Dr. Bleak plays the role of the "lesser villain," as he thinks of himself, but he is in fact an authority figure who is able to empower his "foundling," which makes him an "unwitting hero" (130) in a completely monstrous world.

When the girls choose their masters, it seems that they decide on the types of roles they want to have: boyish for Jack, as she was tired of playing the princess, and girlish for Jill, as she was tired of playing the tomboy. However, their choices are about empowerment and disempowerment, and it is independent of gender. The Master used to have boy victims, and Jack does not have to give up her femininity in the windmill.[5] The girls' choices derive from their pasts, as their roles determined what skills they have developed. As Jill was always in motion in her tomboy role, she did not learn how to contemplate things, how to read signs, and she is easily misled by what she sees on the surface. She wants the shiny appearance and comfort because she does not see depth. The choker that she is instructed to always wear in the company of her Master is to cover her neck that is tabooed until she is grown enough to offer it to the monster; however, she sees a beautiful gift in it and considers it as the token of great care and love and not the symbol of dangerous servitude, which it actually is. Having been always second in importance compared to her sister, Jill's feelings of neglect are so overwhelming that she would do anything for someone who is willing to think of her as the first important person in his life. She believes the vampire loves her because she does not remember unconditional love. Jill is the perfect example of the abused child who has lost all agency, and thus she may easily be tricked into believing that she exercises agency when she willingly succumbs to becoming her Master's doll, offering her body, her blood, her will and even her humanity in the end. Jack is less sure about certain painful lessons that Jill takes for granted because she had to sit still a lot, and thus she had time to think and evaluate. She knows she prefers intellectual freedom to physical convenience because, as person who has always played the little princess, she knows exactly how unsatisfying that life is.

The Master is not the only monster in the Moors, as it is inhabited by all sorts of creatures, such as werewolves or gargoyles, but it is the Master who keeps the village under his control. As a vampire, his monstrous body is undead, suggesting that he polices the borderline between what is alive and what is dead. He is master over lives, he may kill without punishment, he may draw upon the blood of anyone in the village (who has not been restored by science after death). However, his brief background story states that he (like Dr. Bleak) was once a foundling and became a vampire after he had been made heir to the previous Master. His body represents the very borderline between humanity and monstrosity, and this is a warning about what awaits Jill if she consents to staying with the Master and offering all that she has to him. As the story unfolds, we understand that the final offering is her humanity, her humane nature: she needs to become as ruthless as the Master is to become worthy of her inheritance.

Among all the monsters, the vampire and the zombie appear the most dangerous. People who cross the borderline guarded by the monster are threatened with annihilation, that is, losing their human identity and becoming monsters. The bite that turns is a central idea in the literature of the undead, and it is anticipated here when it is suggested that Jill could become the rightful heir to the master and turn into a vampire. The vampire's undead body, traditionally a signifier of the borderline between death and life, is the liminal space of undead emotional life here. The coldness of the dead body indicates inner chilliness, that is, lovelessness. The Master appreciates Jill only to the extent her real parents did; she is an object whose worth depends on the practical use she has in the life of her parents or guardian. That she will be used is revealed by the vampire body: the fangs signal the act of consuming that defines the vampire. Drinking the girl's blood and drawing upon her life essence signal the vampire's utter transgression: the revenant is the intruder who wants to turn the human into a vampire by his penetrating fangs. Sucking out the girl's life essence has a dual consequence: Jill would stop belonging to the living and would become undead, but this would generate an emotional iciness, the mark of having become inhuman(e). To make the step toward the monster "risk[s] attack by some monstrous border patrol or (worse) to become monstrous oneself" (Cohen, "Monster" 12).

The Master's monstrous body is a reminder of the parents' emotional vampirism; they used their children to their own needs, devouring their true identities. The Master mirrors the all-controlling and loveless parental authority that the twins grew up with in this world, but it also evokes the vampiric features of Coraline's Other Mother and the threat her body imposes upon the girl: the Other Mother's "love" that wants to fully possess Coraline is the emotion that would keep the girl a child for ever. Coraline is able to fight the Other Mother because she recognizes the monstrous Other's unnaturalness. Coraline is able to defy her unnatural enemy because she has a clear example to compare the Other Mother with: her real, truly loving mother. Unfortunately, however, there is no such a point of reference in Jill's life because she lacks a stable emotional background, so she welcomes the first parent-substitute who seems to appreciate her. The Master's vampire body reveals the kind of predator that he is; as Mary warns, "Men like him, they can't come in unless you invite them" (McGuire, *Down* 88–91). McGuire takes the widespread idea that vampires cannot enter private places unless they are called in, but this idea transforms into a symbolic attribute that shows the Master's nature. The vampire of the Moors turns only those who are so powerless that they willingly choose to become his partners.

He can enter the most private place of all—his prey's body and mind—only if the turning is desired. He needs broken children who can easily be shaped to long for this partnership.

The symbolically monstrous parts of the body, the fangs, suggest penetration and imply sexual transgression, even though in *Every Heart* Jack insists that the vampire has "a fondness for little girls" but "Not in any sort of inappropriate way" because he was only after the blood that kept him alive (81). Jack's statement, however, unveils a logic according to which bloodsucking does not qualify as "inappropriate"; moreover, even if we are told that there was no sexual penetration, the vampire context assures the dual reading of the word "to consume," whereby drinking blood is traditionally perceived as the metaphorical expression of sexual intercourse[6] (Stevenson 142). Taking possession of the body suggests a threat on one's integrity. The symbolic equivalence between feeding and raping promises disintegration, a threat on existence. Even if the vampire is not a sexual predator in the strict sense of the word, his monstrous fangs disclose that what happens to Jill is violence on many levels. As a consequence, the child from whom the vampire as a parent-substitute gradually takes away everything may be seen as a variation of the ghost child in *Coraline*, the manifestation of the feared, never-ending childhood, in which there is no possibility for growing up as the course of nature would dictate. Jill is violently turned into an "unchild" when she takes off her choker and welcomes the vampire's bite, voluntarily allowing the monster to feed on her; she, nevertheless, does not become an adult by this act, only an altered form of the obedient child, the always consenting lover who exists to satisfy and who has not learned (and will never have the chance to learn) not to obey and not to give consent. Excluded from the natural process of maturation, she is kept from obtaining the skill to stand up for herself—or even to find her true self. She is victimized to the extent that she accepts victimization as the natural form of existence. The vampire thus embodies the very fear of not developing an independent, strong identity, the fear of never growing up emotionally. He threatens with deception, with monstrosity hidden below the glittering surface, with making a devilish bargain about getting power without understanding the price.

The monster has an effect not only on Jill, but also on Jack because Jack is the one who understands—or rather instinctively feels—the meaning of the Master as a monster. The tabooed relationship that the Master's body marks is beyond social acceptance, and while Jack does not fully perceive what the Master offers, she recognizes in him the borderline that she never wants to cross because it is too dangerous for her integrity. To stay with the Master is to accept objectification, and Jack

7. Spaces of Escape for the Abused

knows this, but she becomes most alarmed when the vampire speaks of her and her sister as a "matched set" of objects that he wants to "keep" (McGuire, *Down* 79). As a consequence, Jack is appalled by the vampire and is drawn to the only alternative, the mad scientist, who is the force opposing the monster in the Moors. The Master scares her away, so she manages to escape into a space where life is appreciated above everything, and the dead are sometimes turned into living, which is not what happens in the vampire's household where the living can be turned into undead.

One of the important points McGuire makes in her series is that appearance is deceiving. In their home world, the identical twins are not seen as identical because they have different hairstyles, wear different clothes, and are forced into different gender roles. In their secondary world, the girls are recognized as a "matched set," but their choices reveal that being identical in physical appearance does not mean that they developed an identical identity. They are similarly abused in their childhood, but looking identical does not mean that the abuse has exactly the same effect on them. As it turns out, Jill has grown to be more disempowered by her upbringing, which sadly means that she has no resistance whatsoever against the gradual corruption that awaits her in the Master's castle. Jill goes through what Coraline could avoid: the descent and the fall, something that the mice and rats warn Coraline against. The monster is the uncanny Other Parent to defeat, something that Jill has no power to do. Defeating the Other Parent would be the way of renegotiating a relationship with one's real parents, as we could see in Coraline's example. Growing up and (re-)building a satisfying relationship with one's parents are inherently linked: "An important issue in the coming-of-age novel is the way in which finding a place in society is coterminous with finding a satisfactory relationship with the father.... Coming of age is thus a drama of coming to terms with the father, and with all the social and cultural governance for which he stands" (Millard 15). However, instead of fighting with the Master, Jill makes a deal with her monstrous Other Father, denying herself the possibility of reintegration into society.

Jack and Jill demonstrate two possible outcomes of childhood abuse: both girls are damaged "enough" to qualify for becoming a foundling in an otherworld, but only one of them may use the opportunity to heal and recover from the effects of the loveless childhood they had. Subtly the novel argues that parents may damage their children to the extent that they cannot heal, and escapes may bring temporary relief but are harmful to the children's emotional and mental health. Jill's path leads into disintegration, and as a result, into complete isolation. Being secluded in the castle, she becomes a damsel in distress—not that she cannot leave the castle, for she is free to go into the village, but she needs to be saved from the castle walls that represent the Master's effect, the thick layer of emotional vacuum that actually prevents her from developing an emotional bond with anyone, including her sister. Under the vampire's seemingly loving control, Jack transforms into a desperate psychopath who kills for love and thinks only of herself, as vampires do.

Jack, on the other hand, is able to find friendship and love, which contributes to her maturation and keeps alive in her the wish to reunite with her twin sister, however great the emotional gap between them is. As she chooses not to have a monster as an "Other Father," her deal with her guardian Dr. Bleak is not a Faustian bargain, but one that empowers her intellectually and emotionally in the long run. It is enough for her not to have a monster as a guardian to find her true self. Dr. Bleak "never encouraged her to love" (McGuire, *Down* 180), but he never prevents her from loving others, either. While the Master systematically kills every child with whom Jill plays, the mad scientist lets Jack spend her time with Alex as long as she always does her duty. This attitude allows Jack to experience responsibility and love alike, and remember her duties as a loving sister, too. Alexis teaches her to love and connect, that is, experience a "human context" (180), and she understands that while she has company, love, and the safety of the windmill, Jill lacks all of these, and her sister is "terrified and abandoned" (180). Jack's path, therefore, takes her to the realm of empathy and social life, which enables her to cope with her situation. The various psychological theories that focus on resilience and recovery after crisis experiences emphasize the importance of a number of features that Jack proves to possess while Jill does not, including emotional intelligence. As positive emotions have a positive effect on one's mental health (Salovey), Jack finds empowerment through love. She realizes her duty to love her sister despite her monstrous deed and save her from lynching, that is, irrecoverable disintegration. Accordingly, Jack grows into a savior character just as his master in science is.

Saving, however, is not easy under the given circumstances and demands sacrifice. Jack, in fact, needs to save Jill twice from her fatal downfall, and in both cases she has to pay a very high price. In her first attempt at saving Jill, Jack carries her unconscious sister through the door to save her from lynching. She gives up her own dream and home for her sister's life. She manages to save her from the mob's violence, but in what sense does this save Jill? Knowing the events that are narrated in the first part of the series, we may safely claim that even though Jill's body is kept intact, she is not saved from her fall, as the physical distance from her Master does not separate her from the effect that the vampire has had on her. She is unable to reintegrate into society and lives in Eleanor West's Home for Wayward Children, a place where nobody feels at home. Yet while the others only desperately hope for and seek their secret doors, Jill wants to make sure that she will find her lost world and comes up with a monstrous plan to make her wish come true. As a serial killer and bloody butcher, she becomes incompatible with her world of birth, too, so Jack needs to save her again from her impending fate. But this time she cannot save the body but attempts to give her sister a second chance for finding her integrity.

We do not (yet) know what will happen to Jack and Jill in their new pursuit of a home, but we know that Jack kills Jill in order to restore her in the lab that used to be her home for years, and we know that she is more than likely to succeed. Killing her twin sister is Jack's act of acknowledging that Jill has fallen apart. Jill's hunting for perfect body parts indicates her own irremediable disintegration, her mental breakdown. Even though she was not turned into a vampire, technically she is one: she takes the parts of bodies that she thinks she needs for her survival, and she brutally kills, having no conscience. In fact, her conscience is her own twin sister, Jack, who feels responsible for having left Jill alone. Driven by her moral responsibility, Jack destroys the corrupted Jill and attempts to give her a new life in which she may not make the same wrong decisions.

Resurrection, in this case, would be a real chance for a new, better life: Jill would not return to the Master to become his heir and neither would she be attacked by the Master as a punishment for what she did earlier, as resurrection by science would provide her protection from a vampire's attack. At this point[7] the readers cannot safely guess how Jill would respond to Jack's crisis management. She may not enjoy this new life and would feel miserable, thinking that her chance for happiness—her reunion with the Master—has been taken away from her; or she may learn, just like Jack did, how to appreciate another person's love and sacrifice. Nevertheless, this is her only chance for renewal. Reality, with its rigid laws of nature, is not able to offer remedy for her problem and rejects her monstrosity, manifested as a mental illness; the Moors operate with different laws and thus may give what is impossible in the real world: an alternative to a lost, corrupted life, a real restoration that guarantees protection from the vampire, and thus may allow her to mature and grow up. The monstrous alternate world again gives the girls a chance to be themselves—something that was denied to them in their world of birth.

Conclusion: The Allure of the Multiverse

McGuire's wayward children are special ones. They are so different from the average that they all become richer with (at least) one trip to an alternate world, which will make them even more divergent from the norm. The children get to know their secret spaces but are sent back from their otherworlds either because they have violated an important rule and expulsion is their punishment, which is what happens to Jack and Jill, or because they are asked to consider again their choices and thus temporal expulsion is, actually, a chance for making a conscious choice between their two worlds.

The worlds beyond the portals appear as alternate homes that attract their discoverers because reality seems to be repulsive to them. Reality is a threat on their integrity, which explains why one of the recurrent problems of the adolescents in Eleanor West's Home for Wayward Children is that their environment does not accept them as they are. The children are welcome back, but only as long as they adhere to the image their parents have of them. Jack and Jill are classic examples of the victimized children whose parents do not even think their offspring may have an identity other than what they give them. In general, the other children seem to have more loving parents than Jack and Jill; their love, nevertheless, does not triumph over social expectations. Conditional love and conditional acceptance communicate the wrong sense of being and alienate these children from their closest environment.

As McGuire demonstrates, rejection may come in surprisingly varied versions. The asexual Nancy, who has been to the Halls of the Dead and can be as motionless as a statue, is loved by her parents, but they expect their daughter to return in a mended condition, smiling, energetic, dressed in a colorful outfit, and ready to have dates. Kade is to stay in the home unless he switches his gender back and his parents can get back the daughter they lost. Nadya suffers from her disability, which is always a disadvantage and shame in this world and is never accepted as her natural condition. She was born in Russia with nothing beneath her elbow on the right arm and was adapted by an American who wanted to help the little, disabled orphan. The prosthetic arm her adapted mother gave her is a constant reminder that she is in need of completion and is never accepted the way she is. Cora is bullied for being overweight despite her athletic achievements and her role in the swimming team. Christopher is of Mexican origin, and racism has made his life difficult for him; however, what really marks him is his unusual relation to life and death, as he nearly died of cancer.

All these rejections are answered with acceptance in the secret worlds. Nancy feels at home in the Halls of the Dead, as she is not expected to have erotic desires and normative sexual behavior. Kade's temporary home in Fairyland becomes precious when the Goblin King sees him the way he is, a boy, even though this moment leads to his expulsion. Nadya finds a home in Belyyreka when she learns to use her natural element, the river water, to complete her arm. Cora's discovered home is a mermaid world, the Trenches, where her extra weight, which is considered a disadvantage in the real world, works for her advantage. Christopher finds a home in Mariposa because the Skeleton Girl cures him and thereby she gives him back his safety, making a connection with the dead part of his identity. From then on, his affiliation with the dead does not threaten his integrity but empowers him. These examples communicate one very clear idea: home is where you can be yourself, where you are recognized for who you are, where you feel that you find acceptance the way you are. Home is where growing up means empowerment, finding a resolution to the problems that made one suffer as a child. In narratives that recount the general process of maturation, finding one's true identity is the reward for overcoming challenges in the real world.

The dream-like nature of the encounters with the monstrous Other both in *Coraline* and in *A Monster Calls* are the projections of the mental processes that the protagonists have, and the fantastic helps the characters gain a recognition of the real. The Other in the *Wayward Children* series may also be read as the projection of the mental processes the children have, but with important differences to consider. *Coraline* and *A Monster Calls* lend themselves easily to being read as metaphorical psychic journeys, as the encounter with the monstrous is a lonely experience, not shared with anyone else from the real world. In McGuire's fantasy, such a reading is practically impossible. The children who visit otherworlds go missing in their real worlds, and while most journeys are lonely experiences, Jack and Jill share the trip to the Moors, just like Christopher, Cora, Nadya, Rimi, and Kade have their multiverse adventure together in *Beneath the Sugar Sky*. The narrowly applied psychoanalytical approach that would render the fantastic journeys merely as psychic adventures, hallucinations, manifestations of altered consciousness is not supported by the narration. Still, it is without doubt that the secret worlds are connected to the children's psyches and may be read as symptomatic manifestations of what resides in their minds as suppressed anxieties and desires. These worlds, just as the dream-like Other House in *Coraline* or the space of the stories that the Monster creates in *A Monster Calls*, come to aid the characters in their traumatic moments during their lives; however, these wayward children appear to be psychopathological cases. For them, there seems to be no remedy offered by this reality, especially when it becomes clear that they do not even try to reintegrate into a society that never accepted them as they are. They do not wish to live in the society that rejects them; instead, they choose an alternate reality in which they can be themselves.

The refuge that the alternate worlds give, therefore, is problematic. When the children go and return, the worlds offer temporary relief, the way temporary altered consciousness does. As we could see, his altered consciousness helps Conor in *A Monster Calls*. His hallucinations reveal the truth and allow him to cope with his many anxieties. He grows up with the monstrous help his mind provides him, and this reconnects him with reality, empowered enough to deal with the challenges that he needs to face. McGuire's wayward children do not appear to have this option. They either stay in this world, always longing for their secret homes, or they manage to find their doors again and never return.

Finding and experiencing alternate worlds may not be considered a positive coping mechanism; in fact, many psychologists claim that "maladaptive coping is also synonymous to 'non-coping,' since a person who responds to a stressor using a coping mechanism but isn't able to positively ward off the stressor or solve the stressful situation hasn't coped with the stress at all" (Sincero). Indeed, the function of these worlds is not to give active help to reintegrate into society but to provide the means for permanent escapism. These worlds open up after normal coping mechanisms have failed, and thus they are both symptoms of the problems these teenagers have with the world (or, rather, of the problems the world has with these adolescents) and tools that separate the children from the stress that they should manage. Although each adolescent is a unique individual in Eleanor West's Home, it appears that besides visiting a secret world they have another shared experience, which is the lack of a supportive environment. This deprives them of many factors that could contribute to their empowerment, and thus they do not demonstrate resilience in this world.[8] In contrast, the children are capable of showing resilience in their found worlds, which makes them even less interested in the world they were born in.

The final cut from reality may be interpreted as an irrevocable failure to adjust to normality; however, McGuire makes sure to twist this interpretation. As the existence of the secret worlds is unquestionable in her fantasy, losing touch with reality is presented as reconnecting with one's true home, in which (s)he may find the happiness that (s)he could not in the world of this reality. With the presentation of her multiverse that offers refuge for those who are considered to be Others, McGuire rejects the necessity of conforming to socially constructed identities. Several of her teenage characters suffer from their inability to meet society's expectations concerning gender performance, which, as Judith Butler argues, "conceals or dissimulates the conventions of which it is a repetition" (*Bodies* 12). In *Wayward Children*, nevertheless, these conventions as fatal errors are clearly articulated either by the omniscient narrator or the suffering characters themselves to accentuate the relationship between cause and effect and clarify that "these socially constructed identities create a sense of expected normality that, in turn, creates binaries in modern culture between what is deemed normative (the expected norm) and identities that are labelled as deviant (in opposition to the constructed norms)" (Kennon 27). McGuire straightforwardly shows the paradox nature of the children's experience: society's self-confirming attitude decides who falls outside the accepted norm and thereby excludes whoever cannot live up to its expectations. In consequence, the rejected are pushed into a liminal space which is separated from the chosen normalcy of the world by very rigid boundaries, marking the marginal as problematic instead of questioning the harmful procedure of marginalization. McGuire's inclusive approach demonstrates that gender conformity, a mistakenly interpreted health-cult or any other arbitrarily defined normativity may produce the same harmful consequences that may lead to losing valuable people.

McGuire argues that deviance is a matter of perspective—just as reality is, too. Acceptance erases deviance. Acceptance makes home, and everyone deserves a home. Yet home is also a matter of perspective, and therefore at times it is the monstrous that may make one feel at home. In the novellas of the *Wayward Children* series the monstrous gives a chance for those who are judged as Others in this world and invites us to reconsider our own judgments about norm, difference, and the need for an all-embracing acceptance.

Part III
Inhuman(e) Frontiers of Growing Up

8

Alien New World Wilderness
Patrick Ness's Chaos Walking *Trilogy*

Introduction: The New World and the Monstrous

The "confluence of the genre of the coming-of-age novel and a particularly, or even uniquely, American narrative of national identity," observed by Kenneth Millard (5), was brought about by the idea that the new continent is the land of opportunities—most notably, that of the opportunity to restart history without the mistakes mankind had made. The New World was associated with a moral purity and an innocence that the Old World only wished for. This idea is subverted in contemporary coming-of-age narratives that re-imagine the New World in various forms and choose the monstrous frontier as their setting. The first work in this category that I am going to look at in more detail is Patrick Ness's *Chaos Walking* trilogy (2008–2010), a Young Adult dystopian series, which examines society, especially its power structures, as it revolves around the possibilities of identity-formation within a political system that constrains the development of one's integrity. Ness's story of an imagined future reflects on our present and past with a set of well-chosen motifs that establish an easily recognizable analogy between America as the New World and the freshly colonized new planet of the series (actually named New World). The trilogy addresses contemporary anxieties but also show how many of today' conflicts are rooted in history, and how easy it is to repeat the errors of the past.

The setting evokes the early colonial times of America. Only a small parcel of the discovered, inhabitable planet is colonized, thus Prentisstown, the settlement where the protagonist Todd Hewitt was brought up, is presented as one of the very few civilized spots on the planet (and is claimed to be the only one by its leader Mayor Prentiss), while the rest appears to be wilderness. Haven, the settlement that is rumored to offer safety as well as a reality that breaks the official narrative that defines Prentisstown's existence, is founded by those who escaped Prentisstown and sought to lead a different kind of life on New World; consequently, this new colonial settlement invokes the American New Haven, founded by those who left Massachusetts Bay Colony. Beyond the relationship between these highlighted settlements, how Prentisstown relates to the natives of the land, the Spackles, is reminiscent of the tensions between Massachusetts Bay colonists and the Native Americans, who ended up fighting first in the Pequot War (1636–38), then in King Philip's War (1675–78). Just as in American history, the natives are demonized, turned into monsters, so the Spackles as well as their environment emerge in the colonizers' narrative as the monstrous Other that humans must fight with and overcome in order to regain their Paradise lost.

In this symbolic setting, the concepts of new and old demand a gradual reinterpretation. America even before its discovery was a hope for the future as well as a hope that the past may be repeated (as Gatsby would claim later) with errors erased. "Columbus was himself following a prototype devised long before, the idea of a western land which was *terra incognita,* outside and beyond history, pregnant with new meanings for mankind. [...M]illenarian and Utopian expectations were already attached to this new land" (Ruland-Bradbury 4–5). Already at the moment of its birth, the idea of *terra incognita* contains the motif of the return to the Golden Age or Eden, which is both a physical voyage to new, undiscovered lands, and a time travel to the collective past of mankind known from the myths. Such a position is evoked by Ness's choice of basing his story on New World in the future that conjures up colonial history clothed in a fantasy. However, this New World rejects the utopian rendering of the planet. While the birth of the American nation is, on the conceptual level, the result of "a decisive break with an Old World that had grown corrupt and moribund" (Millard 5), Ness's New World displays all the corruption that characterizes our own past and present and thus strangely combines the old and the new.

In such an environment, Todd emerges as an American Adam character in the New World wilderness, accompanied by Viola, who assumes the role of an American Eve character. Such a character type, as it was examined by R. W. B. Lewis in 19th-century American fiction,[1] is "caught momentarily in a state of prelapsarian innocence and then expelled forever into the unforgiving world of modern experience. This hero comes of age by coming to terms with that world's uniquely American strictures and challenges" (Millard 5–6). The system we see in *Chaos Walking* presents a complex set of problems that are recognizably relevant to an American audience: beyond the relationship between colonizers and natives, the anxieties concerning the use of modern technology and its consequences—especially the difficulties of information processing and the suppressing effect of surveillance—as well as the fear of terrorism, war, ecological disaster, religious fundamentalism, an oppressive system based on race and gender bias, and trauma.[2] While these problems seem to be distinctly manifold, Ness demonstrates how they relate through the concept of monsterization, and thus how the process of coming of age eventually becomes a gradual interpretation and redefinition of the self in relation to the monstrous.

Caliban's Heritage: The Monster as Nature in a New World

Beside the motto-inspiring *Middle March* by George Eliot, which Adrienne Kertzer sees as the model for Ness's work (11–12), *Chaos Walking* trilogy has been associated with *The Handmaid's Tale* because of the "sexual politics and hysterical fundamentalist religion" that it features, while its "rural setting, the presence of the river and the pursuit" invokes *The Adventures of Huckleberry Finn* or *Night of the Hunter*, as Frank Cottrell Boyce notes. These literary relations are surely justified; however, to me the first work that Ness's series evidently recalls is *The Tempest* by Shakespeare. Its focal theme of colonization that turns the play prophetic[3] as well as the motif of demonizing the native inhabitant, Caliban, and the themes of Nature versus Nurture and Nature versus Art(ificiality) create a strong bond with the *Chaos Walking* series. Using Shakespeare's romance as a reference point, therefore, helps us examine how Ness's Young Adult work is able to renew some of the topoi of American literature to specifically reflect on contemporary anxieties that one must cope with during the process of coming of age.

The island where Prospero finds refuge may easily be seen as the metaphorical New World as opposed to the European Old World, represented by Milan, from where the magician is expelled. Prospero's island, similarly to New World in *Chaos Walking*, reflects the Elizabethan image of the America: a paradoxical combination of a second Eden as well as a monstrous place to live. In Ness's vision, the discovery of the new planet immediately renders Earth (including the once New World America) as the Old World. The new space of living offers mankind a new chance to restart civilization, and thus the space colonizers rightly consider their future home as Edenic until the moment colonization starts in effect. What they could not prepare for because preliminary space exploration did not reveal it is the existence of intelligent life on the planet. Thought to be uninhabited by intelligent species, New World seems to be ideal for human colonization; however, the first settlers have to confront three interrelated phenomena that immediately disrupt the Edenic image of the planet: firstly, the planet is inhabited by an intelligent species, the Spackle, who appear to them as monstrous creatures and of course would not like to give up their lands; secondly, the air contains the "Noise germ" that severely affects the colonizers: all humans become capable of hearing other intelligent creatures' thoughts; thirdly, women turn out to be partially immune to the germ's effect, so while they can hear the Noise, as men can, their thoughts do not become audible, which generates an immense tension between men and women.

Granted that "ever since early Western thought equated the Good with notions of self-identity and sameness, the experience of evil has often been linked with notions of exteriority" (Kearney 65), it is easily predictable that this new situation results in a management of the conflict that spawns monsterization. As the Spackle look monstrous from a human perspective, they are held responsible for all the evil that spoils this Paradise. For humans, the Spackle are the Other: as natives of the unexplored land, they belong to the unknown, and thus embody all the fears attached to the dangers of finding a new place to live.

Just as Caliban embodies the feared nature both as the wilderness of the island and the instinctive nature of man that is to be suppressed by some power, let it be called Art or Knowledge or Magic, so are the Spackle identified by the hideous, Noise-germed wilderness that attacks the colonizers who do not find immediate protection or cure against the Noise-infection despite their technological advancement that surpasses the Spackle's. At their encounter, the Spackle are the monstrous species that shock people. They remind one of humans, but are clearly of a different, yet undefinable category. Despite their humanoid features, they identify themselves with the environment they inhabit. They call themselves the Land, and their bodies represent the alien space, the strange environment that the colonizers cannot successfully cope with.

When Todd encounters a Spackle, he immediately knows what he confronts, not only because he has seen some natives on "vids" but also because the Spackle's body is "alien. As alien as you can be" (Ness, *The Knife* 277). The creature is "tall and thin ... white skin, long fingers and arms, the mouth midface where it ain't sposed to be, the ear flaps down by the jaw, eyes blacker than swamp stones, lichen and moss growing where clothes should be" (277). From Todd's perspective, the male Spackle that he first meets is a perfect representation of the monster, as it refuses "to participate in the classificatory 'order of things'" (Cohen, "Monster" 6). As a monster, he has a hybrid body, a combination of the near-anthropomorph, the vegetational (moss) and the algal (lichen) and is strongly associated with the swamps of the planet:

> Spacks and men had different ideas for burial. Spacks just used the swamp, threw their dead right into the water, let 'em sink, which was fine cuz they were suited for swamp burial, I guess. That's what Ben says. Water and muck and Spackle skin worked fine together, didn't poison nothing, just made the swamp richer, like men do to soil [Ness, *The Knife* 15].

Such a hybridity underlines the Spackle's harmonious co-existence with the planet's natural world. The Spackle body provides support for other forms of life, such as lichen and moss. On Earth, lichen live in a mutualistic relationship with the environment they grow on, and neither are mosses parasitic, even if they grow on trees as epiphytes. As lichen and moss grow on the Spackle, it suggests that the Spackle body, though humanoid, has characteristics that are plant-like, moss-like, and fungus-like. Their relationship with the swamps also separates them from humans, who are linked to the dry land. The Spackle body recalls Caliban's hybridity that makes Trinculo wonder if the body he sees belongs to a man or a fish (Shakespeare, *Tempest* 2.2.25).

In the medieval imagination, monsters inhabited the faraway, unknown lands: it is no wonder that Caliban is a monster of a nearly uninhabited island and the Spackle are the exotic race of a recently discovered planet. The presentation of these monster figures recall the long tradition of locating the deviant to the edges of the known world and seeing it as "a site for cultural interrogation of the boundaries between nature and culture, human and animal, human and not-human" (Wright 173). What diverged from the normative human body used to be understood as "an embodiment of social, moral, or ontological disorder" (179); in a similar fashion the sheer existence of the humanoid Spackle was quickly declared to be the real threat to the human colonizers on New World and the people sought a way of punishing the alien race for their difference. We may envision a mass of Calibans, that is, "savage and deformed Slave[s]" (Shakespeare, *Tempest*, "Dramatis personae") in the large community of the Spackle left in Haven after the first peace treaty. The Burden, as the remaining Spackle call them, are kept and even referred to as slaves to Viola's surprise (Ness, *The Ask* 106).

Echoing the nature-nurture dichotomy familiar already from the *Tempest*, the Spackle, a harmonious component of the planet's ecosystem, emphatically provide contrast to the human race, which seeks to solve problems with violence enhanced by technology. Not caring about the damage they may do to either the enemy or the environment, the Mayor does not even refrain from burning much of the forest to kill the

Spackle. The opposing attitudes of the two armies manifest in how they fight: while Coyle and Prentiss are both preoccupied with the idea of getting their hands on the missiles of the scout spaceship, the Spackle use nature's power to fight against the invaders: fire and water. Symbolically, nature is on the Spackle's side: the natives can dam off the river and thereby block the water supply from the human settlement in the hope of forcing victory without engaging in a long, violent war. The embodiment of human evil, the Mayor, finds his death in the ocean, pulled into the abyss by its monster. His pathetic end confirms the notion that (at least on this fictional New World) nature punishes malevolent nurture and is capable of triumphing over mankind's evil.

Another example that gives prominence to the difference between how humans and the indigenous race relate to nature and technology may be seen in the method of oppressing the Burden. The monster's body epitomizes the fundamental difference between humans and aliens: the Spackle's mouth has a limited function because it is suitable for consuming food and drink, but is not to be used for speech, since the Spackle communicate with the help of the Noise germ. This alterity is exploited to marginalize and torment the Burden when humans force them to take the cure against the Noise germ; the Spackle mouth is used for swallowing the medicine with the food they get, but otherwise the antidote attacks the entity that is signaled by the lack of mouth as speech-organ: the communal identity based on their telepathic information-exchange. This germ is unobtrusive to the natives; what is more, the Spackle make use of the planet's special atmosphere and rely on the germs to develop their joint consciousness that defines their collective identity. This beneficial co-existence is broken by the application of the drug, the result of scientific experience.

The lack of speech is at the root of the colonizers' problems. The settlers did not expect intelligent life on the planet, as the Spackle are a mute race and thus are difficult to register their existence from space. Secondly, the Spackle, with their transformed system of communication, represent a multiple threat: the Noise does not disturb them but works to their advantage; they as a community can make use of the members' Noise, turning it into Voice, instead, so they also embody the Other as a community to the human settlers; and finally, the speechless existence is a possible warning about becoming silenced—oppressed—if one stays on the planet and adapts to its strange atmosphere.

The trilogy demonstrates how the fear of being destroyed by or integrated into the society of monsters triggers the transformation of men into monsters. The anxiety rooted in the existence of the Spackle immediately turns the discourse about them into one that is about power and marginalization through othering. While the Spackle body is clearly an alien one, scapegoating is useful to disperse doubts about the need to eliminate them; and since women also pose a threat on the hegemonic position of men, men extend scapegoating, holding also women responsible for the unbearable situation in which they find themselves.[4]

The scapegoating narrative is supported by religious fanaticism that easily fits the needs of the male community. The name of the planet, New World, purposefully recalls all the religious hope of the first European settlers of America. In this theoretical second—or rather third—Eden, there are Adams and Eves, while the Spackle are the ones who break the harmony and thus represent the evil, Satanic forces of the world. But the chaos introduced by the Spackle is doubled by the women's partial immunity to the Noise germ, which generates the rediscovery of the Biblical narrative about the sinful role of women, whereby men may justify their decision to punish women and purify the settlement by killing them. This is not unlike what we see in *The Tempest* when Prospero uses his hegemonic position and voice in constructing his mythology of the island, accusing Caliban of a rape attempt (that the audience cannot fact-check, of course) and thus disrupting the Edenic harmony by sin.

One of the fundamental issues that this mechanism points to is the importance of making one's voice be heard in a power relationship. The fact that the Spackle have no organ for speaking aloud deprives them of their voice, thus their body signifies their inevitable marginalization. Without a legitimate voice that could be heard and acknowledged by the human community, their muted presence allows the colonizers to make their own, fabricated and uncontested narrative about them. As it is demonstrated in *The Tempest*, too, speech means power. Whoever owns the narrative has the control over events. This has become a recurring theme in dystopian fiction, underlining the myriads of ways in which one's mind may be manipulated. The current trends that highlight the importance of media as well as robotics and biotechnology very directly reflect on the technological advancements and the politics that influence our present and promise a very scary possible future. As Kay Sambell observes, "children's dystopias seek to violently explode blind confidence in the myth that science and technology will bring about human 'progress'" ("Carnivalizing" 248). *Chaos Walking*, however, is very inventive in how it "issue[s] a warning about destructive tendencies in human behaviour" (Stephens qtd. in Sambell, "Carnivalizing" 248) and departs from investigating directly the Frankensteinian darkness of technology and deliberately focuses on the mechanism that is dependent on man's (monstrous) human nature rather than on man's hubris-ridden technological feats even though it also shows the possible role of technology in deciding conflicts of power.

The power of words or, more specifically, the power coming from the act of speaking, is a central theme both in Shakespeare's and Ness's work, and it is worth looking at the difference in how they accentuate the role of language in a relationship between the colonized and colonizer. In *The Tempest*, Prospero finds the strange, native creature of the island, and in exchange for his helping the magician to survive in his new environment, Prospero teaches him how to speak. Caliban remembers the encounter with Prospero as the beginning of a beautiful—because mutual—friendship:

> When thou cam'st first,
> Thou strok'st me, and made much of me; wouldst give me
> Water with berries in't; and teach me how
> To name the bigger light, and how the less,
> That burn by day and night: and then I lov'd thee,
> And show'd thee all the qualities o'th'isle,
> The fresh springs, brine-pits, barren place and fertile [1.2.334–340].

On the textual level, with the reference to the "bigger light" and the less[er light] Caliban's speech recalls the Edenic idyll that began with creation: "God then made two great lights: the greater light to rule the day, and the lesser light to rule the night" (Gen. 1.16).[5] Teaching language, for Caliban, has an empowering function: naming is a symbolic act of gaining possession over what is named. This is how Adam takes possession of the Garden of Eden, and this is how Caliban becomes as much of an Adam on his island as Prospero does. Sharing language, then, appears as an acknowledgment of equality and parity.

Language, however, may be used to disempower, too, as Shakespeare warns us. Teaching the colonizer's language to the colonized may seem a heavenly blessing first, but it turns out to be the devil in disguise. Language is where unconscious adaptation begins: it determines the frames within which one may express oneself, thus teaching the language of the dominant culture is itself a way of colonizing the other. This is why Caliban, beyond his nostalgic reminiscences of the initial friendship he had with Prospero, uses his gift to show his dissatisfaction with his subjugation: "You taught me language; and my profit on't / Is, I know how to curse. The red plague rid you / For learning me your language!" (Shakespeare, *Tempest* 1.2.365–67).

In *Chaos Walking*, the first phase of language-based colonization echoes Caliban's experience. The Return—the last surviving member of the Burden—finds it difficult to reintegrate into his community after he is left alive to inform his people about the massacre of the Spackle slaves. He uses a language that has been strongly influenced by his forced co-existence with the human environment, so his own people do not recognize him as one of them. His experience is paralleled by what the settlers go through more rapidly: they are also forced to experience a variation of colonization when they arrive on the planet. The Noise germ demonstrates the power of colonization from within: although the colonizers launch physical attack on the Spackle, it is their own culture that transforms due to the unintentional but aggressive mental attack that the Noise is. It causes chaos on the level of the individual and the community alike.

Ness shows that colonization is very much a matter that revolves around language: while Prospero gives his own language to Caliban and thus determines how his slave may express himself, forcing him to adapt to the colonizing culture, Mayor Prentiss takes this "natural" process even further and enslaves the Spacke by actually taking away their language. Forcing the natives to take the serum for the Noise that enables them to communicate with each other, he does not cure the Spackle slaves but deprives them of their natural form of interaction and isolates them from one another. "It's like we cut out their tongues," as Corinne, a healer in Haven, admits with shame (Ness, *The Ask* 465). This second phase of colonization through manipulating communication is a symbolic act that highlights also how the conqueror may grab all the control over the masses by monopolizing communication.

The trilogy provides two examples of communication crisis: complete muting and the overflooding Noise that connects everyone to everyone else (who is not immune to the germ), both disempowering the one who is affected by it. Neither the Spackle nor the humans have the natural means to deal with their communication problem. When their noise is taken away, the Spackle are left without a tool to share their thoughts with their fellows; given an overpour of Noise, humans do not have a proper channeling that the Spackle have developed through their course of evolution. As a result, the Noise turns the human community of Prentisstown into a society that suffers from incessant surveillance and gives in to self-censuring as a result, while the Burden are forcefully censured, that is, muted by humans.

Family and Community in the Monstrous Frontier

Under these conditions, growing up presents very specific challenges. The encounter with the monstrous appears to be the root of the problems that Todd faces, but in effect it proves to be the tool that helps Todd understand where he belongs and what defines his identity. As growing up means to become integrated into a society by conforming to its rules, one of the most challenging tasks for Todd is to decide what kind of society he wishes to join as a full member. As an innocent child, who has not been initiated into manhood and therefore knows nothing about what coming of age means in practice for Prentisstown citizens, his choices are limited and thus easy—or, perhaps more precisely, originally he is presented with no choices at all. He is at the threshold of adulthood, but as he is the last boy in the community, whether he wants to become initiated into manhood or not is not even a question. It is taken granted that he will be one of the men that form the community of the only settlement in reachable distance. It is without doubt that he will become a conformed, male member of the human community on New World—since the Spackle were extinguished in the war and women died of the Noise disease.

Ironically, the Biblical story of Eden somewhat repeats itself: the innocent state that characterizes Todd's existence is indeed "corrupted" by a woman: the teenage Viola, who brings heavy knowledge to the boy. The first morsel of knowledge is that there is such a thing as silence in the so far always noisy, chaotic, alien environment; the second is that this silence is linked to a girl, that is, instead of dying from the germ, women demonstrate a disturbing immunity to it. These revelations generate further ones, unveiling a complex system of conspiracy that maintains Prentisstown. The recreated, artificial Eden of Prentisstown, purified of all "sinful" elements, such as the Spackle and women, is discovered to be a dangerous, intolerant place that must be left immediately.

The knowledge that takes away Todd's innocence is powerfully contrasted with the knowledge that he was supposed to gain on his birthday, during his initiation into manhood. The initiating ritual, as he learns later, would have had two important components: an act of murder, symbolically depriving him of his childhood innocence, and learning the official version of the truth about what exactly happened to Prentisstown and the women who lived there. The difference between the two kinds of knowledge discloses a choice between two distinct worlds. The discovered silence opens up a real New World for Todd, and even though his initiation into adulthood is still marked by an act of killing, as he stabs a Spackle to death when he meets one, his story shows that even the same act may have different upshots. The act of killing performed by Todd contributes to his isolation from his original community. The teenage boy feels remorse immediately and becomes motivated by his desire to compensate for his sin. He is "The one who stays innocent no matter the blood on his hands," as the Mayor puts it (Ness, *The Ask* 465). He also gains a more responsible way of thinking and an attitude that prevents him from killing Aaron or the Mayor later. In contrast, his initiation into Prentisstown's community would mean becoming a member whose loyalty depends on the power of communal guilt and constant surveillance and control. Taking that path would also include accepting the inescapable narrative about staying in Prentisstown being the only choice in the New World. If we recall the coming-of-age texts that I have looked at so far, the path that is offered by Mayor Prentiss is strongly reminiscent of what the Other Mother tries to bait Coraline with: through a show—a performance that is a distraction—the Mayor would ensure his complete control over the boys who become satisfied by gaining the title "men" while accepting a kind of eternal—but not at all innocent—childhood when giving up all their agency. The act of murder stands for murdering their innocence. This knowledge surely transforms innocent boys into teens with a tainted state of existence; however, from the perspective of agency, these boys are still at the level of children, never questioning the Mayor's decisions and orders. They do not become soldiers because they make a decision and want to become soldiers serving a cause; they want to become "men" through the secret ritual because this is part of one's rite of passage in the only world they know of. In the context of *Coraline*, accepting the Mayor's authority is like accepting the button eyes in an Other World when the Real World has already been devoured by the fog, an equivalent of the Noise in Ness's work.

Mayor Prentiss is a weird Other Mother/Other Father to Todd and all the other boys whose mothers have been murdered by the men in Prentisstown. Based on Freud's Oedipal Complex theory, Jennifer Mitchell identifies the Mayor with the patriarchal father, arguing that with all the women gone from the settlement, the boys turn into a primal horde in reality (243). Since there is an absence of mothers to fantasize about, the boys cannot undergo their due psychological maturation via experiencing the Oedipal Complex in their fantasies. As a result,

> Mayor Prentiss makes real the component of the Oedipal complex that involves theoretically killing one's father in much the same way as he utilizes the trajectory of the primal horde as the means by which boys are "turned into" men. They are permitted, encouraged, even forced to kill their "fathers," though Mayor Prentiss as the patriarch in question is off limits in that regard [Mitchell 244].

But even beyond this universal father-role that the Mayor takes in his community, he tries to formulate a closer father-son bonding with Todd. In *The Ask and the Answer* and in *Monsters of Men* the Mayor— the President of New World by then—especially cares for Todd as if he were his son, because he is dissatisfied with his own. First he hopes that his son would become the son he wants by learning from Todd[6]; then he simply replaces his son with Todd after mercilessly killing David, his own offspring. He indeed wants to become Todd's Other Parent, believing that Todd displays the necessary skills that could make him continue his legacy. The irony of the situation is that it is exactly these skills—the ability to have a sense of integrity and appreciate it, the ability not to accept orders unquestionably—are the skills that allow Todd to successfully fight against the power of the President. On top of all, the listed skills are inherently linked to—in fact, come from—characteristics that are praised by Prentiss on the level of rhetoric but are actually missing from his repertoire: having a strong moral compass and being capable of compassion, sympathy, and love. "More than any man I've ever met, Todd, you feel.... But that makes you powerful, Todd Hewitt. In this world of numbness and information overload, the ability to feel, my boy, is a rare gift indeed," as the Mayor himself acknowledges (Ness, *The Ask* 465).

The strong character that both Coraline and Todd demonstrate comes from their family situations, even though they seem very different at first sight. Coraline is able to say no to the Other Mother because she has a very solid foundation of love and care on which her parents have built their relationship. Therefore, even when the adolescent Coraline has doubts about how much she is really loved by her parents, she can find the reassuring answer in her subconscious and see the difference between what the Other Mother offers and what her real parents continuously give her and represent to her. Todd does not really have memories of her mother, but he still has a home in which he is loved and cared for. The nontraditional family unit of two fathers and the boy, which forms because of the mother's request and because of her trust in these men, proves to be as solid a foundation for Todd as the traditional family for Coraline, which is one of the arguments that Ness provides about the appreciation of the non-normative.

The two men love the boy so much that they are willing to sacrifice their own lives to save Todd. Cillian dies in the fight against the Mayor's army, while Ben escapes and tries to give further protection to Todd, risking his own life again and again. But one of the greatest protections the two guardians can give is establishing a bond between Todd and his dead mother: they give his mother's diary to Todd, which partly explains history, destroys the Mayor's mythology about the town, and most importantly, gives voice to all the women who were silenced by the men.

In Ness's vision, women emerge as foils to the Spackle characters as well as the male characters, and in this capacity they are able to underscore the complexity of power relations that exist in this dystopia.

Viola Eade becomes a protagonist beside Todd so much so that from the second volume on she also has her own voice heard, and her perspective alternates with Todd's in the consecutive chapters. This narrative method of alternate inner monologues is completed with the voice of the Return in the third volume, whereby Ness emphasizes the need for acknowledging the equality of voices and thus the demand for an equal share of power among them. As Ness applies "male, female, and nonhuman characters as equally legitimate focalizers" (Kennon 26), he effectively "critiques the processes of exclusion" (Flanagan qtd. in Kennon 26) and celebrates otherness as inevitable and precious components of a complex, diverse society.[7] Ness asserts the need for a shared narration to comprehend the various sides of any story. He argues that a leadership that hears only one voice—its own voice—is doomed to fall, inescapably succumbing to chaos, unable to grasp its own story in its complexity. The narrative structure of the trilogy testifies that there may be harmony and a clear presentation of a story where diverse voices are heard and listened to. The novels' multivoiced polyphony contrasts with the Noise-generated cacophonic chaos.

Viola's process of maturation mirrors Todd's, and this also means that Mistress Coyle's character strongly resembles Mayor Prentiss's, to which the Mayor even calls attention to Viola.[8] Both Mistress Coyle and the Mayor are not only leaders of their army but also politicians who aim to present themselves as surrogate parents to their chosen child, Viola and Todd, respectively. Just as the Mayor calls Todd his boy, Mistress Coyle keeps calling Viola her girl despite the girl's objections. Both leaders see a young version of their own selves and a possible heir in the child whom they try to impress and use to their own purposes. They are equally obsessed with their missions, thus, as Adrienne Kertzer observes, their speech discloses the resemblance between them when they speak about choice with the exact same words (13). Although they claim to have different reasons for trying to grasp power and contrasting methods to achieve their (very similar) goals, the underlying similarity of what they represent is made visible by "their advert symbiosis symbolised by the name of the two organisations they lead" (Komsta 47). Not only do the names *Ask* and *Answer* point to "a false dialogue in which no communication is possible" (47), but also their interchangeability is implied when the Ask paints the letter "A" on the wall to suggest that the Answer is responsible for the massacre of the Spackle, and it is indeed interpreted by Todd as "Answer" since such an act fits in the larger picture that he has of the women's organization.

The Spackle perspective, in addition, allows us to see also the Return as a character who matures to become the leader of his people, turning the Sky into a foil leader character to the Mayor and Mistress Coyle. The similar situation in which these three leader figures find themselves underlines the difference in their handling the problems. The human leaders see opportunities in having Todd and Viola by their side, and their desires for these opportunities apparently overwrite whatever affection they have for the children. The Mayor and his rival Coyle compete with each other for power and not for the good of their people exclusively. They want to triumph over each other and the Spackle whatever the cost may be. In contrast, the leader of the Spackle, named Sky, is shown to have a concern always for his people, the Land: "I want what is best for the Land, [… the Sky] shows. That is what the Sky must always want" (Ness, *Monsters*). He chooses an heir to make sure that there will be someone who continues his mission in the same spirit. He is ready to hand over power because power is not an end but a means to him.

The similarities of the conflicts during the maturation process show that growth and integrity should be universal concepts independent of race, sex or any other features. The morally responsible Todd, Viola, and the leader Sky think alike, and this suggests the utopian idea that, although acting with integrity appears to be an *alien* thing from the perspective of our corrupted adult world, the new generation carries hope and may leave the worn path to seek new ways in a New World.

Communication and Monsterization

In its three volumes, *Chaos Walking* focuses on three distinct tasks to accomplish: in *The Knife of Never Letting Go* constructing the world and presenting its challenges are the primary issues; in *The Ask and the Answer* the strategy of monsterization and its consequences (especially how the thirst for revenge corrupts everyone) are examined; and finally, in *Monsters of Men* the healing power of communal unity is contrasted with the powerlessness of the individual, and in this respect the process of hybridization as a possible way of extending the communal sense of mankind is also explored.

Presenting the anatomy of monsterization begins with showing how hate may be directed towards a group. When some of the women revolt, all who belong to their sex become incarcerated and soon get branded because, as the Mayor holds, "*every* woman is part of the Answer, if only because she is a woman and therefore sympathetic to other women" (Ness, *The Ask* 365). They are put in prisons, "way far away, outta sight of everyone 'cept for those that guard 'em. Kinda like the Spackle" (291). The collective punishment that the Mayor imposes on women is based on the assumption that the women collectively are as monstrous as the Spackle. *Menstrum* (menstrual blood) is once again becomes interchangeable with *monstrum* (monster).[9] The Mayor's method of crisis management issues a warning that any kind of prejudice, let it stem from racial, ethnic, or gender-biased hatred, is suitable to generate the same disastrous consequences. From a different angle, of course, the noted parallel suggests that if women may be put to the fate of the Spackle so easily, maybe neither of these groups is made of evil monsters but made monstrous by the rhetoric of the most dominant voice.

Ness displays the Mayor's method of monsterization to underline how easy it is to marginalize any group within a society with a well-chosen rhetoric. "Holocaust parallels are plentiful" (Kertzer 15) in his display of collective trauma: he presents the suffering and the massacre of the Spackle with images that are emblematic of the Holocaust to remind us that, while we are reading fiction, fiction shows the truth in the mechanisms, and only the surface details are speculative. We are familiar with the Spackle history from our history lessons. We are shown very thin bodies, marked by never-fading numbers on the arm, which strengthens the notion of objectification. The natives are captured and enslaved by people who have a fanatic leader hungry for power. The Mayor, just like Hitler did, subjugates the otherized race and claims that "work is the path to freedom" (Ness, *The Ask* 57), invoking *Arbeit macht frei*, the infamous slogan of the Nazi concentration camps in Dachau and Auswitz. Another association between the Holocaust and the New World colonizing methods is that the marginalized are used as test subjects in medical research: as the deported Jews were used for experiments (mostly, though not exclusively, to find scientific support for the übermensch theory) in the concentration camps, the Spackle are experimented on to produce effective cure for the Noise germ, thereby ensuring the supremacy of the human race on the planet. "When the Sky refers to 'Crimes Against the Land' […]," the phrase clearly echoes crimes against humanity, a phrase popularized during the Nuremberg trials of the Nazis, just as Neville Chamberlin's infamous defense of the 1938 Munich Agreement is an intertext of the mayor's speech: "PEACE In OUR TIME" (Kertzer 15). The Mayor, eventually, becomes responsible for the extermination of the whole group of incarcerated Spackles to demonstrate power and bring about his desired war. We are to envision the pile of dead, thinned bodies, and later we are informed about the burning of these bodies, and the ash falling from the sky as if it were strange snow (Ness, *The Ask* 171), a strong image reminiscent of the extermination camps. The reader is initiated into the history of the

Burden from the beginning to the end and is allowed to see the unfolding of the same path for women starting with imprisonment, branding, and the justification of these acts by the narrative that monsterizes the women collectively.

While such a concept could easily turn the story into a didactic one with very evil men oppressing the very timid, loving natives and the equally timid and weak, helpless women, Ness avoids the trap of presenting a weakly written children's story that focuses on the grand, heroic conflict between the outstandingly good and the extremely evil. Instead, this trilogy is about one's conflict generated by the impossibility of staying pure and good despite working for good ends. The human leaders willingly and knowingly perform evil acts because they believe they fight for the greater good, while Todd and Viola try to resist the temptation to evil. However, they do not remain immaculate, either, for the most important thing about maturation is learning that "not everything is black and white, Todd. In fact, almost nothing is" (Ness, *The Ask* 42). As we could see in the chapter on *A Monster Calls*, Ness believes that the focal issue that relates to maturation is complexity; therefore, growing up is understanding and coping with the complex nature of the world, which is very unlike the simplified world view of most fairy tale fiction and which includes the complexity of those who exist in the world, too. By showing all the similarities in how the Mayor and Mistress Coyle manage their organizations and how they relate to Todd and Viola, respectively, Ness makes sure the reader understands that the oppressed may be as aggressive and angry as the oppressor is, the oppressed more often than not wants to become an oppressor or at least an avenger, and one's fake modesty that is manifest in claiming to be "God's hands on this world" (Ness, *The Ask* 111) is not much different from another's hubris that makes him "fanc[y ...] himself God" (102).

The Spackle with their monstrous bodies pose a constant threat to the imagined superior, divine image of mankind because despite their seeming lack of strength, the Spackle stand for something much bigger than what humans are capable of demonstrating. The monstrous body is a paradox: it is tall and alien, scaring Todd first, then surprising him when he realizes that the Spacker is physically weaker than him; but one Spackle is always an integrated part of his community, and this gives the individual a communal power and significance that people do not have.

To understand this difference, we again must turn to the importance of language. The Spackle identify with the natural world, which is confirmed not only in the hybridity that their body exhibits but also in their vocabulary, as they call themselves "the Land." Even more important is how this identification predominates in the Spackle way of communication: they share a collective voice, being linked to one another. This system still allows for maintaining individuality but is also suitable for a rapid and effective share of information and reaching an overall consensus by knowing what the others really think and thus having a means to discuss issues that in other forms of communications would be suppressed or would demand too long debates.

Humans, in contrast, value individuality at the expense of communal support, and this results in isolation. For humans it takes time and learning to become able to co-exist with the Noise and not to be driven mad by its side-effects (of revealing their own thoughts and to get an incessant overload of information from others). The human approach of using the Noise, however, greatly differs from the natives' method. The first men who enable themselves to overcome the maddening effect of the Noise do not learn to exist with the Noise as part of it but prefer cutting themselves off the Noise, and thus from community. They do not consider the Noise to be part of the natural environment: they take it either as a weapon that attacks their integrity or a weapon that they may use to attack someone else. Their manner of mastering the Noise is a way to isolation, which is perfectly demonstrated by the code words that ensure the effect. As the Mayor claims it, repeating, "I am the Circle and the Circle is me" is "a way of centering yourself.... A way of aligning your Noise, of reining it in, controlling it" (Ness, *The Ask* 292). However, the control in this case means the enclosure of the self, too. "A circle is a closed system. There's no way of getting out" (292), warns the Mayor. It is not by chance that this mantra, forever repeating the same words and thus creating a never-ending circle of words, "a closed circuit of semiosis" (Komsta 46), is the Mayor's most effective weapon. He practically strikes with the power of his isolated self to control and/or hurt others.

His potential to control through manipulation is also suggested via an act that aims at encircling: embracing. He opens his arms to give an embrace to Viola and welcome an embrace from her after announcing that the girl will be able to see Todd. His gesture is meant to signal friendship or rather a parent-child relationship in which the father arranges for the good fate of his children and his care is naturally returned with equal kindness and love. Viola sees through the Mayor's manipulation and immediately translates the man's body language as a demand for an undesirable payment: "Arms wide. As if this is the price. Do i pay it? It's just one hug, i think, (isn't it?)" (Ness, *The Ask* 153). The embrace, generally understood as a sign of connection, becomes the demonstration of isolating power. Viola must be careful "not to go rigid at his touch" (153) because for her the embrace becomes a constraint. The Mayor's power demonstration aims at showing that

Prentiss masters emotions, transmitting the message that just as he can switch off his own disturbing emotions by his mantra that states and restates the self as an unbreakable circle, so is he able to manipulate other people's emotional reactions, too. The embrace, trapping one into an unwanted, suffocating relationship which on the surface looks like a chance for alliance—togetherness—serves to reassure the lack of need for companionship in a world that is run by someone aspiring to become a tyrant.

Such an embrace is a recurring motif in the series, also associated with Mistress Coyle (and thus reinforcing her role as a mirror and foil character to Prentiss): not only is she shown to embrace Viola to protect the girl (Ness, *The Ask* 239) and thus have her for her own purposes, but also her name Coyle is homophonous with coil, recurrently invoking a loop that holds one captive, just as the Mayor's circle mantra does.

The embrace and the repeated circle-mantras accentuate the serious consequences of isolation: the lack of openness, the lack of honest communication is the characteristic feature of tyrannous people whose monstrosity threatens a whole society of becoming monstrous. The survival instinct without tolerance or the will to understand the other results in a relationship that monsterizes whoever wants to play God despite the fake gods' attempt at monsterizing others.

Conclusion: Hybridization and Healing

Using the power of the hypnotic chant brings a kind of calmness to the self, silencing the Noise, but this comes with a price: it silences one's inner voice, too, suppressing his real thoughts—his real personality. In Todd's case, it is clear that by using this chant he gains power at the expense of his emotional life, and Viola finds it scary not to hear his noise, but more importantly, not to see the emotional Todd that she knew. Being encircled by only one single thought of his own deprives Todd of an access to his own emotions and represses his thoughts of empathy and guilt, as well.

However, this is not the only way to deal with the Noise, and this is what Ness tries to emphasize. He presents two choices: the Mayor's, which controls the effect of information load by "shutting off" his Noise, and Ben's, who learns from the Spackle how to "open [...himself] up to it completely" (Ness, *The Ask* 472). The first option is a direct road to monsterization in the common sense of the word that emphasizes the immoral status of the monster, which is the central focus especially in part three of the trilogy, *Monsters of Men*. Yet, Ness successfully undermines an often-recurring prejudice that alterity is by definition "wrong" and thus immoral and invites the readers to rethink the concept of the monster. Ben's example indicates how the process of evolution in which man develops useful skills that characterize an alien race may be seen as positive hybridization when useful is not understood in a selfish sense (that is, useful to secure hegemonic position) but in a communal sense (that is, useful for the large community of the space that one shares with others).

What happens in the third book of Ness's trilogy is relatively rare even in Young Adult dystopias: beyond the actual dystopia that is presented as a negative example to learn from by noticing and avoiding its cardinal errors, the novel also offers a concrete alternative to contemplate: the Voice of the Spackle community, the manifestation of the "communal 'I'"; in other words, "eupsychia, a utopian state of collective consciousness" (Komsta 51). This is the consciousness that Todd becomes part of at the end of the trilogy. For him, coming of age is not simply a closure of childhood and the beginning of adulthood; Todd's maturation is an actual rebirth in a new consciousness with a better comprehension of the multitude of voices that constitute the Voice. Todd comes of age when he becomes a member of a functioning community that embraces diversity instead of a closed community of isolated individuals who tolerate no difference and solve problems by monsterization. His joining the Voice marks the beginning of his posthuman, post-anthropocentric existence that promises the same transformation for his people. This change demands the elimination of "self-centered individualism" and an "enlarged sense of inter-connection between self and others, including the non-human or 'earth' others" that Braidotti considers the basis of posthuman ethics (Komsta 48) that appreciates all forms of life. Such a take is very rare in fiction intended for an adolescent audience (Bradford, Mallan, Stephens and McCallum 85) even though Young Adult dystopias have started to emphasize the importance of one's connectedness to and appreciation of nature.[10]

The monsters of New World teach acceptance and show that what seems to be a curse may be transformed into gain and hope. The alterity that is originally considered as a threat to human collective identity is shown from another perspective as the refuge to keep identity through a successful adaptation to the challenges that the planet holds to its colonizers. As Todd is the second man who is healed by the Spackle and comes back from near-death with this new consciousness, he proves that what happened to Ben is not an isolated example and the Voice gives an opportunity to turn warfare into peace and productive togetherness—a co-existence freed from the devastating effects of trauma. Joining the Voice is a process of hybridization—a process of monsterization—whose purpose is not to exclude the Other from the community; instead, it is the token for healing the individual and through that the community. Todd's coming-of-age story is thus a model for the whole human society he belongs to, and it is the monsters who teach him how to mature into a more responsible being.

The complexity that the concept of the Voice demonstrates rejects a binary system of values that children's and adolescents' stories (and, in fact, American Adam/Eve stories for adults generally) rely on in works where "wild things" play an important role. The values we attach to heroes and their wild opponents may change, by now often subverting the traditional schemes (Hourihan 108). Nevertheless, the hero's story seems to be always about his attempt at triumphing over wilderness: "It does not envisage the possibility of *rapprochement* between the hero and his opponents for the aim of the wild things, as the story tells it, is always to destroy him" (107). Ness challenges the above premise and shows an alternative in which open communication transforms the desire to overcome and destroy the opponent into a realization that peaceful co-existence is more beneficial for both parties—and thus it is more beneficial for the Land that signifies both the alien race and one's natural surroundings. As Ness proposes the idea of hybridization in the form of joining the Voice, he suggests that such a resolution demands a complete reconsideration of one's view of the world, very much in line with what Donna Haraway considers as "an inescapable possibility for changing maps of the world, for building new collectives out of what is not quite a plethora of human and unhuman actors" (506). Encountering otherness provokes the response of either acknowledging alterity and thereby confirming the self as normal or that of hybridization (McCormack 534). Joining the Voice is an ethical choice that confronts the usual practice of differentiating between the self as normal and the Other as abnormal; it is also the ethical choice of accepting the Land/nature as an integral part of one's collective existence and not an Other to exploit or triumph over. The human race's survival is connected to the survival of Others; and peaceful diversity within the eco-system is assured by an empathic attitude to alterity: "The economy of extinction binds humans and animals, and by extension, all species of the eco-system, to each other—not only in companionship but also in 'compassion'" (Palatinus). This compassion in this trilogy is shown to stem from a new kind of communication: one that blurs strict boundaries between the individual and the collective, yet respects the individual, too. Such an evolution would allow for seeing the same story from various perspectives (in various voices, that is). It would also promise the construction of a more just society based on "a more ethical appreciation of otherness," discarding the prejudice that Levinas identifies as "ontology of Sameness" (Kearney 67).

While the Spackle's collective Voice which mankind may learn to join is indeed a utopian idea based on (so far) alien biology and thus appears as non-viable in our present reality, we should note that Ness also presents a very much Earth-compatible, applicable way of connecting with others when he highlights the importance of written literature and the ability to read. The novels repeatedly make the point that illiteracy denies access to complex knowledge, exposing one to easy manipulation. Reading is the path to learning and comprehending the complexity of reality because it may open access to various segments of the truth. Reading, Ness suggests, is providing voice, and reading many sources is a way to realizing our human version of the Voice here on Earth. Empathy comes from the ability to identify with various voices, as the scene in which Viola reads from the journal that Todd's mother kept reveals. Viola's "words are not her words and they're coming outta her mouth sounding like a lie but making a new truth, creating a different world where my ma is talking directly to me" (Ness, *The Knife* 420). Todd's thoughts imply that hearing other people's true voice and making it part of our lives should be the human version of constructing a Voice that may assure peace and re-connection to nature. This may not necessarily stay a utopian idea—but demands from human society something that Todd experienced when he accepted the embrace of the Others: immense maturation that gave him the gift of hearing and seeing the world from a strikingly new—posthuman, post-anthropocentric—perspective.

9

"Muttated" New World Garden
The Hunger Games *Trilogy*[1]

Introduction

The inhuman(e) frontier is a popular science fiction topos: stories in which whole planets are colonized and the new, unknown environment proves hostile to humans echo the problems of the historical era of colonization. The familiar narrative of discovering new lands and encountering the Other shine through the fantastic coating of these stories. Space travel fiction often materializes as space-colonizing narrative, and as we could see in the previous chapter, recounting one's experience with the alien wilderness provides a variation of the New World garden myth. The same myth is evoked by the type of science fiction that preoccupies itself with the idea that mankind turns its own habitat into something alien, unnatural—sparing the characters the trouble of traveling across galaxies to interact with the monstrous wild. These narratives more often than not come from the genre of hard science fiction, in which imagining what science may do to our world is of primary concern; but before turning to such an example, let us look into how a Young Adult blockbuster addresses the theme of innocence versus experience in a world that privileges the artificial over the natural.

In *The Hunger Games* trilogy (2008–2010),[2] Panem, a fictional state that the United States has transformed into after a devastating civil war, exhibits a bipartite structure that contrasts not only poverty and wealth but also highlights the opposition between nature and civilization/technology. The special third space, the arena, appears to be a nowhere land between the Capitol, from where Panem is governed, and the districts, which are oppressed by President Snow's dictatorship. It is a space that fully embraces the *homo sacer*, the "figure of law that is empty of political legitimacy" (Risko 82). The arena thus apparently belongs to neither the Capitol nor the districts. However, the space is created and controlled by the Capitol; therefore, it may be looked at as the extension of the Capitol's power, which is most spectacularly exercised by the annually organized Hunger Games broadcasted throughout Panem. Communicating images of violence, the Hunger Games show takes up a significant role beyond maintaining power; it reveals the Capitol's inherent monstrosity. The monster face of the dictator President Snow[3] is presented through the concept of the reaping as much as through the annually designed arena spaces. The arena space, itself behaving as a monster and evoking myths and stories of monstrosity, reveals the Capitol's beastly nature. It is thus the monstrous that connects president, Capitol and arena, enhancing our understanding of the political system in focus as a monster, and also highlighting the subverted representation of the American New World Garden, in which a mutated type of hero(ine) is born.

While the frontier hero is often seen as part of a myth that "directs our attention to the problems of the individual rather than toward the obligations of the individual to the community" (Whalen-Bridge 305), the American Adamic myth has from the start contained the potential of carrying political subtexts. Natty Bumpoo in the Leatherstocking novels is as much of a political statement as an agent in creating a fundamental myth of a nation. Although, especially in 19th century works, this character appears in isolation (Gunn 80) and is associated with contemplation instead of action, the American Adam myth relates to various other myths that easily provide any mythopoeia a political coloring, to say the least. Giles Gunn highlights in this respect the myth of the Chosen People, the myth of the Virgin Land, and the myth of Manifest Destiny (79), which one may complete with "the myth of American ability" (Jordan). Some of these myths have merged in certain superhero characters, who exemplify the extreme cases of ability and being chosen to accomplish missions that no one else may be able to. Such characters also often fit into the American tradition of outlaw heroes, who turn out to have a "Captain America complex," to use Robert Jewett's and John Shelton Lawrence's terminology (O'Donnell 37); and while Katniss Everdeen is definitely not portrayed as a superheroine but as a classic reluctant heroine, she becomes an outlaw character and is forced to develop at least a drop of that Captain America complex in order to save her world. In addition, she is placed into differing spaces of wilderness, which emphatically connects her character to the frontier hero who goes through a transformation in the wild and thus becomes able to generate transformation in society. Katniss's process of coming of age dramatizes the conflict between her closeness to nature and the artificiality and monstrosity that define the

Capitol and are annually displayed through the monstrous features of the arena.

Frontier stories rely on the special hero character and the specific setting to reflect on the ever-present importance of the American Dream. As David Mogen argues, these narratives "implicitly dramatize a central cultural mythology about the contradictory values represented in that dream, and the frontier setting has always functioned as a symbolic territory expressing our aspirations and our deepest fears, as well as our ironic sense of the tragedy brought by 'progress'" (17). Katniss's narrative demonstrates extreme differences between the two end poles of Panem's society; life in her district is backward and technology is minimal, as it only serves the purpose of enabling the people there to do the jobs assigned to them by the Capitol, but the Capitol itself is characterized as the epitome of progress and exploitation. Katniss's life is dependent on the wilderness, where she hunts to stay alive, and her routine to cope with wildlife difficulties helps her rise as a winner of the Hunger Games. However, the arena subverts the American Adam/Eve myth, since what appears as an extreme manifestation of wilderness is, actually, an artificially created place, which is more closely related to technology than nature. This unnaturally manipulated nature is, in fact, the ultimate metaphorical expression of Panem as a monster-state that invented the Hunger Games.

The Beast Stories Behind the Arena Experience

The institution of the Hunger Games is a complex system of rituals that effectively sustain Panem's monstrous dictatorship: it is a demonstration of power and a means to traumatize the district residents. The Games start with the ritual of the reaping, by which the Capitol selects two representatives from each district to participate in the bloody fight that will be broadcast throughout Panem. The reaping immediately links the Capitol and the arena to one of the best-known ancient myths related to a monster, the Greek myth of "Theseus and the Minotaur," which Collins admits was one of her primary inspirations for writing her trilogy (Margolis); however, this myth is not only a monster story, as its major theme is "political punishment" (Martin 222), which provides the basis for *The Hunger Games* novels, too. The myth relates how the triumphant Crete forced the conquered Athens to send her maidens and youths on a regular basis into the labyrinth of the bull-headed man so that the monster's hunger may be satisfied. Although it is obvious that the word *hunger* in the trilogy's title may be read as a direct reference to the miserable conditions in the districts, as Derek Coatney suggests (184), in the light of the connection between the myth and Collins's dystopia the term *hunger games* may metaphorically express the yearly practice of feeding the hungry monster. It is not difficult to see the resemblance between the myth and the recurring reaping that randomly selects one boy and one girl from each of the twelve districts to fight one another to death. It is the arena where the children find their deaths, as if in the devouring Minotaur's mouth. The arena is thus a visual projection of the monstrosity of the regime; consequently, the various components of the space and its special features uncover peculiar aspects of the government and the character of its emblematic embodiment, the president.

The arena is a monster that demands its annual treat in the form of children. People see the beast renew from year to year, and they also see it devour the sacrifice. However, the tributes enter the arena with the intent to stay alive as long as possible. For this they need to fight—fight the other tributes as well as the space itself. The arena, which is designed to kill in the most brutal and unexpected ways, appears to be more deadly than any of the tributes alone or in a team. Therefore, during the Games the arena is the main monster that Katniss needs to battle. The special circumstances that the arena provides help Katniss bear in mind that she has to fight to the death because of and against the Capitol in the first place. As a result, fighting her way through the Hunger Games in the arena forces Katniss to grow up not only as a person stepping out of childhood and thereby providing strange care for her family but also as a tribute stepping out of her assigned role to entertain the Capitol by her victory or death and providing care for her extended family, Panem.

The appearance of the arena suggests wilderness, with which readers generally associate lack of order and reason; this arena, however, attacks in cunning manners. The clever timing and placement of obstacles reveals a thinking monster, one that is alive and is able to respond to the events that it experiences. It is no wonder that the arena "behaves" this way: whatever special threats the tributes are confronted with are all generated by Capitol people working in the Control Room, which functions as the brain of the monster. The eyes—the built-in, hidden cameras—are legion and scattered all over the space, suggesting a many-eyed monster that keeps everything under surveillance, reminding both the tributes and the spectators of the Capitol's general habit of watching its citizens in the districts. The images transmitted by the cameras are processed in the brain, that is, in the Control Room, and the brain decides what kind of attack, where, and when it should be launched—imitating how Snow's police state functions outside the arena based on collected information. Katniss's actions, for instance, always generate well-articulated reactions. She knows exactly why she is attacked by fire, realizing the practical and the symbolic implications of the incursion. Her actions provoke the brain even to change the rules of the games twice. She experiences the same cause-and-effect process outside the arena. One prominent example for this mechanism is revealed when Katniss returns to her house after the bombing of District 12 and finds, on her table, a gift sent by Snow. She knows even before finding the rose that the bombing took place as a revenge for her role in the revolution. As she is familiar with the Capitol's method of surveillance and retribution, she also immediately understands what the innocently looking rose that was carefully placed in her room signifies. "Positioned on my dresser, that white-as-snow rose is a personal message to me. It speaks of unfinished business. It whispers, *I can find you. I can reach you. Perhaps I am watching you now*" (Collins, *Mockingjay* 15).

The arena-monster not only attacks and punishes the tributes but one of the long-arching arms of the monster is ready to award the fighters. The rich audience in the Capitol, the sponsors, may send precious gifts to the tributes to ensure better chances for survival because, contrary to the practice of sacrificing children in the Minotaur myth, the Games in Panem are about survival. The myth is based on the idea that all the youths and maidens sent to the monster fall prey to the monster, and this ensures that the beast is pleased for a period of time. In Collins's version, death or the act of killing does not satisfy the beast; it is the show that the monster is after. In the myth, details of the annihilation are kept in absolute secrecy, making of the monster a taboo; in contrast, the Hunger Games push the monster into the foreground and make a spectacle not only of the tributes' fights for survival but of the arena itself, as it is considered a work of art designed by the Head Gamemaker. The audience is as much curious about the new tributes as about the special features of the annually recreated combat space, which is not merely an arena that provides space *for* the combat but also a place made of lethal components that the tributes need to fight and survive. Spectacularity keeps the arena live and allows for its annual regeneration (that is, redesign and recreation). This arena-monster digests the details of how lives are lost and also feeds on the pain that comes from those who are forced to watch the show. As a result, the yearly ritual has a somewhat different scenario than the scenario of the Minotaur myth. In the arena, one child's life is always spared in the end, and the tribute can flirt with the monster, trying to win its favor. After a convincing performance, the contestant may be rewarded with a new life—one that looks attractive from a distance at least.

Accordingly, the novel series appears to draw on two familiar stories: the Minotaur myth and a subversion of "The Beauty and the Beast" tale. Belle's well-known tale focuses on positive metamorphosis: love transforms the beast into human. Belle must learn to recognize the inner beauty in the beast, look beyond appearance, and this is rewarded by the change for the better. In the arena, however, the metamorphosis does not promise such a positive turn. Katniss, as a modern Belle, needs to learn how to satisfy the beast; her reward, however, is that she fully understands how monstrous the beast is. She stays alive, but as we learn later, most surviving tributes do not consider life as a valuable reward but as a further punishment that they have to cope with. They are further manipulated and often abused by the Capitol. Those who resist assimilation to the monstrous state sooner or later turn into human ruins because of the losses they suffer and their methods to avoid confronting reality.

But even those who fight against such an assimilation must realize that they do not stay unstained once the monster has touched them. The first phase of the preparation for entering the arena takes place in the Remake Center, whose purpose is to give space for shaping the tributes to meet the expectations of the "cultured" Capitol audience. Depriving the tributes of their natural look, the preparation teams aim at creation by manipulating nature. Their goal is always to give life to a creature that is reminiscent enough of them to please monstrous eyes. This attitude reveals that Capitol citizens consider district people animalistic, far from those who may be integrated properly into Capitol life. The departure from their natural humanity deprives Capitol people of their empathy and of an ability to bond naturally with other humans. They are turned into egoistic creatures who seemingly celebrate individuality through their extreme appearance, but in fact are turned into a brainwashed mass for whom everyone is freakish, so they look very much alike despite all efforts to look unique. Capitol culture dehumanizes its citizens by not allowing them to see other people as humans. The arena events annually contribute to this dehumanizing process, displaying massacre as enjoyment, enhancing the "schadenfreude" experience, an enjoyment deriving from seeing others suffer (Shaffer 87), which confirms the spectators' sense of their own superiority.[4] The arena thus plays an active role in turning the Capitol audience into blood consuming monsters.

The direct monsterizing effect of the arena suggests that the process of transforming the beast into beauty is replaced by a reverse procedure. The interaction with the beast here concludes with a completely different moral; it highlights the monstrosity within the human instead of glorifying the power of humanity over the seemingly beastly. The prime example of this lesson is manifest in Enobaria's character. The tribute's most memorable act in the games is killing "one tribute by ripping open her throat with her teeth" (Collins, *Catching* 224). After winning the game, she assumes an image that fits her monstrosity: she draws attention to her teeth that are sharpened and inlaid with gold (224), suggesting a constant and proud assimilation to the beast-like Capitol, where body modification is everyday practice. The winners who resist such an association become devoured by the monstrous state in various other ways. Either the arena experience directly traumatizes the winners so that they cannot cope with the emotional and psychic consequences unless they ruin their bodies by, for instance, consuming alcohol or taking morphling in excess or they are traumatized by the Capitol's practice of punishing the resisting ones by further victimizing them, as Finnick's confessions testify. In either way, the arena is the starting point of traumatization.

Beyond the theme of transformation, further links between the "The Beauty and the Beast" story and *The Hunger Games* series may be detected. The theme of unfitting punishment, just like in the Minotaur myth, is present in the fairy tale as well. The alluded text in the tale is not directly political, but it still includes the motif of unfair suffering for the crime of the older generation. While it is the father who transgresses, the monster wants the daughter to leave her family and live with him and thus pay for the rose taken. The beast's words reveal that the daughter will suffer the father's penalty: "Seven days from now you must bring this youngest daughter of yours, for whose sake you have broken into my garden, and leave her here *in your stead*" (Jacobs; italics mine).

Interestingly enough, what initially connects beauty and beast is the rose—the link that works between Snow and Katniss as well. Yet this motif supports the theme of nature's regenerative power in the fairy tale. The rose belongs to the beast, to his garden, yet the reason why Belle may step into the garden at all is because she is fair as a rose. She wants no expensive gift from her father's long journey but a rose, a humble but beautiful representative of nature. In contrast, in *The Hunger Games*, the rose is both indicative of nature's artificiality in the Capitol and of Snow's method of governing. When Katniss first meets Snow, she immediately knows that the rose's unnatural sent is genetically manipulated. The rose is used to mask Snow's appalling smell of blood, which would reveal his brutal nature and bloody history of seizing and maintaining power. His practice of camouflaging the monstrous by showing something pleasant, just as he offers fashion and various shows to his citizens in the Capitol to distract them from seeing the bloody truth of the political system from which they benefit, is subtly suggested by that ever-present flower in his lapel. The rose, masking Snow's dictatorship, transforms what "should be the ultimate image of the natural and the romantic" into "an object of genetic engineering and terror" (Limpár, "Smell of Roses" 18), which becomes especially disturbing when we realize that the rose was proclaimed as the *"National Floral Emblem of the United States of America"* in 1986 to cherish the rose as *"the symbol of life and love and devotion, of beauty and eternity"* (Nord 1–2; italics in the original), and that "the American Beauty rose is recognized as the official flower of Washington D.C." (3).

The rose with its artificial sent is a reminder of how the Capitol turns nature into a manufactured reality. What we actually see directly from the process of the Capitol's misusing nature is the work done in the Remake Center. The prep team's work evokes Frankenstein's act of challenging the laws of nature, creating Katniss the tribute, who, in Flavius's words, is "almost human" (Collins, *The Hunger Games* 62). Of course, from the team's perspective, these words are meant to praise the improvement they made on Katniss's appearance; however, the painful truth it that by transforming Katniss to near what they think is "human," the team members enact *"de-creation,"* "altering beyond recognition what nature has given" to the girl (McDonald 14). From Katniss's and consequently from the readers' perspective the "remade" tribute is now *only* "almost human." Katniss has been put on a slope leading to monstrosity, and each phase in the Hunger Games she participates in, including the various changes in her image, the interviews, the combats and even the surgery fixing her lost hearing, she gets closer to becoming a product of the Capitol, a monster.

The prep team's work reflects the Capitol's expectations and practices, highlighting Frankensteinian themes in *The Hunger Games* trilogy. In Panem the leading monster (President Snow) creates monsters (Capitol people) who create monsters (tributes plus the arena) who in the end fight monsters (the other tributes plus the arena). President Snow's policy of controlling Capitol people by exposing them to an overflow of luxury successfully turns these people into monster-like creatures who strive to keep up with the latest fashion in clothing and body alteration and who, as a result, learn not to question but to follow trends, including the political ones. "Unthinkingly obedient to the rules of their society" (Van Dyke 225), these people, with only few notable exceptions, are not aware of how their lifestyle dehumanizes them. Katniss, child of nature and a hunter, calls them "freakish" because of their appearance (Collins, *Catching* 49), but the Capitol's policy of brainwashing its people to direct their interest to fashion instead of political and social issues changes people in the inside and on the outside alike.⁵ As follows, not only beastly body modifications, such as Enobaria's, reflect monstrosity in Panem's center, but all artificial interventions aim at crossing the borderline of the natural human appearance and create a sharp borderline between Capitol "culture" and district "primitivism" or, rather, closeness to nature.

Although Collins does not provide a detailed presentation of how the Capitol is run, she suggests that the majority of the people are connected to the monsterizing "beauty" business. Several of them work specifically in relation to the Hunger Games and create the ultimate monster in Panem's universe: the arena-monster that mirrors aspects of the Capitol's own monstrosity. This brutal nature is closely linked to technology that, on the one hand, makes the oppression of the technologically less developed districts possible,⁶ and on the other, allows for an image of the Capitol and its society that makes this fundamental difference between the two types of spaces visible. The origin of this divergence may be found in a contrasting connection to the environment, which is manifest even in the choice of names that the author gives to the two main opposing characters. The heroine's name is a symbolic representation of her attachment to nature: katniss is an aquatic plant with edible root, signifying nourishment provided by the wild. "As long as you can find yourself, you'll never starve," Katniss's father reminds his daughter (Collins, *The Hunger* 52), foreshadowing, at the same time, his daughter's need to resist a denial of her character if she wants to survive the Games. Clearly "she'll never find herself in the pretentious urban environment of the Capitol ..., for she belongs to nature like her namesake, the katniss plant" (Coatney 185). Katniss is a child of nature, someone who was shaped by her close relationship with the land and who is there to give nourishment to her people—which literally happens when she wins the Seventy-fourth Hunger Games and consciously spends her money on the market to help the district residents; then, it happens again when she fights against the unjust system of Panem to change the unbearable conditions that led to hunger in the districts. Snow's name, in contrast, points to his "frozen" emotions, evoking the season when nature is dead and brings forth no fruit to sustain people. His name hints at his lost humanity, apparent in his lack of empathy and his inability to feel a sense of guilt.

The "freakish" appearance of the Capitol's society is a key factor in portraying the same monstrosity inherent in the people living in the Capitol. Aggression and blood thirst are frightening aspects of any beasts, but the real fear attached to the monster comes from our inability to properly categorize it. In Collins's novels "freakish" and "almost human" are expressions that underline the threat monsters pose by destabilizing the world of clear-cut categories.

Such a monster in the trilogy is the arena itself, whose hybridity comes from the disturbing combination of the natural and the artificial. It is simulated wilderness, which ultimately reveals the nature of the people who designed it, "showing how sadistic humans can use technology to pervert nature" (Hanlon 64). Just as President Snow's political system benefits from monsterizing its citizens, so does the arena demonstrate power via its GMO environment. This mutated wilderness appears to behave "naturally" until the brain of the monster—the Control Room—intervenes and activates some brutal feature that may come either in the form of a natural disaster, such as fire, water, or fog, or in the form of specific *muttations* (that is, genetically engineered beasts). Thus, while the arena appears as a virtual wilderness in its untamed, uncontrolled version, in reality it is an environment that people make as perilous as possible. The unconditional reliance on technology, or, as Carissa Ann Baker sees it, the disconnection from the natural world (198) has tragic consequences, the operation of these arenas that not only function to kill but also to entertain by killing among them. Capitol people enjoy the show because they "are just as artificial [as the Capitol itself] and have little or no connection to nature—from their treatment of their own bodies, to their eating practices, to their use of space, to their conception of what it means to suffer" (Baker 204). In this respect, the arena-monster echoes well-known criticisms of man's monster-creating hubris, reminding us of Frankenstein's failed attempt at repeating divine creation. But while Frankenstein may be seen as a moral being, who tries to undo the consequences of his horrible deed once he understands its implications, Snow is presented as an almost demonic creator of evil, fully comprehending the weight of his measures and consciously applying his methods of dehumanization.

Arena: The Wilderness of the City (on a Hill)

The monstrous arena defies the categories of the natural and the artificial. The greatest threat it poses to the tributes is its incalculable nature, as the designed space never behaves according to expectations. It has a brain that is able to decide on what hidden skill of the beast should be used to attack the tributes—as if the giant monster were able to blow fire or poisonous fog, cry blood, or spit out various monsters that are ready to kill. In short, the arena spectacularly reveals how the

9. *"Muttated" New World Garden*   191

Capitol—the capital of an imagined, dystopian America—functions in its everyday reality.

Not accidentally, in the Seventy-fifth Hunger Games, the Control Room operates an arena that is designed as a clock, divided into twelve parts, in which various threats become manifest. The space is not only reminiscent of a clock, metaphorically warning participants about the fact that their hour may come at any time when the clock strikes but it is also a space that evokes Panem outside the Capitol, the twelve segments standing for the twelve districts, each one offering alternative perils generated by Snow's tyranny.

Creating Others as weapons is one of the basic functions of the Capitol. Even before showing us the monsterized society of the Capitol, Katniss mentions the jabberjays that the Capitol created to support their surveillance system. The maintenance of the dictatorship thus depends on the use of muttations that have no place in the natural order of the world. Neither completely natural nor fully artificial, muttations, just like Capitol people, disrupt the categories by which we make sense of the world, and this is reflected in their name, too. Muttation or mutt is the artificially mutated (that is, muttated) version of the well-known term of mutation, which marks a change brought about by nature, and not technology.

The arena features various muttations from time to time. Jabberjays, tracker jackers; likewise, wolf mutts and monkey mutts appear in the two Hunger Games whose events are narrated by Katniss in detail, but we also hear of other kinds of muttations which attacked tributes in the previous Games. How mutts resist categorization and manage to induce deep fear is convincingly demonstrated in the scenes when Katniss is forced to encounter them. The jabberjays, which are birds but are able to imitate people's voices, nearly drive her insane. Their presence is connected to the fear that they imitate what is real—the unbearable cries that must have come from real people in pain. Perhaps even more disturbing is Katniss's confrontation with the wolf mutts. What really terrifies the girl is that the mutt faces, with "unmistakenly human" eyes (Collins, *The Hunger Games* 333), resemble those of the previously killed tributes whose district numbers mark the muttations' collars. The wolf mutts combine features of a wolf and those of deceased humans. Not only is the borderline between the beastly and the human crossed, as well as the natural and artificial, but the mutts also merge the categories of the live and dead, further evoking Shelley's *Frankenstein*.

This scene displays the arena's transforming capacity that reaches even beyond death. The fear that the arena creates either killing brutes or humans who dehumanize themselves to a certain extent to cope with their monstrous memories and the beastly consequences of their arena experience grows even larger here. The actual threat is that not even death offers a way out of the beast-world. These muttations force acceptance of the inevitable and try to kill even the idea of resistance to the system. The presence of the arena, however, gives rise to a hero because the broadcasted image of the many-faced monster generates defiance. Since the arena is the basis of the reality show, each year it must appear more spectacular and thrilling to the audience than before, which demands more and more cunning and skill on the part of the tributes, too.

Through the physical fight between the arena and Katniss, the ideological battle between the girl and the dictator takes a visible shape. The area reflects Snow's monstrosity as precisely as possible: even some of the special methods of destruction it applies reflect directly on how Panem's system operates. There are two components that are especially suitable for communicating evil and connecting the arena to President Snow's character, highlighting the common features among them through imagery: poison and blood. These two elements are inherently combined in Snow's character, who poisoned his political enemies to keep his power. His strategy included self-poisoning to avoid suspicion, but even though he always took an antidote, the poison affects his body, and now the inside of his mouth never stops bleeding. This bleeding is also indicative of his other bloody deeds, torturing and killing rebels as well as annually sending children to the arena. In the arena, blood is seen much too often to remind people of the Capitol's bloody practices. Beyond the blood actually shed during the fights and killings, we also see how the sky in one of the arena sectors in the Seventy-fifth Hunger Games rains blood and shocks tributes, driving them to the edge of their sanity. Poison, Snow's very means to seize and keep political power, is also an ever-present characteristic of the arenas. Mutts may infect their preys with their venom, as tracker jackers do. Various components of the environment may carry poison: nightlock berries may bring eternal sleep to those who taste them; the murderous fog in the Seventy-fifth Hunger Games paralyzes and kills its victims; furthermore, we also learn about a year in which the water was poisonous, resulting in a shockingly brief reality show program, as tributes died too quickly.

Poison and blood turn the arena into a Paradise Lost. The poison is not only reflective of Snow's methods of governing, but as "the human equivalent of a snake's venom" (King 109), it points to the imagery that Katniss associates the president with: that of a serpent.[7] Closely related to this is the image of the lizard that appears in the form of lizard muttations in *Mockingjay*. Symbolic of Snow's character, these mutts smell

9. "Muttated" New World Garden 193

like the rose that Snow always wears in his lapel; moreover, the lizard mutts, merging human and reptile features, are able to track Katniss, following her scent, just as Snow is able to track and survey Katniss even in the wilderness outside the borders of District 12. As it is Snow who may ultimately be held responsible for the evil nature of the arena, the metaphor of the snake in the bloody garden alludes to a corrupted Eden that stands for America.

Collins explicitly places Panem in North America, but the idea of the arena as a distorted Eden is made specifically intriguing by the suggestion that this dystopian America, projected into the future, recalls the American colonial past (Pavlik 37) with the thirteen districts evoking the first thirteen colonies that formed the United States of America. The alliance of the colonies seemed to be one step towards reaching the dream that the discovery of the new continent promised, but this dream quickly becomes a nightmare because America was not uninhabited, and it was fraught with danger. The early settlers soon began to fear that the American continent may be devilish instead of an earthly Paradise, and this fear manifests itself in the various voyage reports revealing that "[o]n the spectrum of Elizabethan images of America the hideous wilderness appears at one end and the garden at the other" (Marx 42). Of course, the early settlers aspired to an Edenic ideal, hoping to turn America into a City on a Hill that would allow them to live good lives, as good men, and seize the second chance for mankind to restart history without the perils brought about by corrupted Europe, but this was not to be. The image of the Edenic garden is the metaphorical expression of this new opportunity in Christian terms (Mebane 12). The shining city upon the hill, standing for the sacred place of Christian morality, is the dream that John Winthrop connected to the new continent in his 1630 sermon. Collins's Capitol was literally built upon a hill—in the Rockies (Collins, *The Hunger Games* 41), but this dystopian city upon a hill has lost the symbolic content behind the image and instead has become the place of absolute corruption. The spaces created and dominated by the Capitol are made to be seen as corrupted Edens through the permeating apple imagery that Collins uses throughout her narrative,[8] which underlines that returning to a hellish wilderness in an imagined future of America is a very straightforward reference to what happened to a land of imagination after human presence has shaped it. We arrive at a point when we look at the Capitol's artifact, the arena, which its designers camouflage as wilderness, and we hardly recognize the garden's relationship to nature.

This particular dystopian garden is a deeply corrupted one because it is, actually, the reflection of the city. We do not have a clear borderline separating the city from wilderness, and thus the Adamic mission is altered: the act of reforming the world may not come from a purification process connected to nature; instead, it comes from a bitter knowledge about the city gained through the hardships in wilderness. And the main problem, to return to the modified beauty and the beast theme, is that under these circumstances beauty turns beastly; as a result, a monster-like character is tasked with reforming the tainted Paradise.

The notion of the American Adam placed in the wilderness has been tightly linked to the hero's morality since the very beginnings. The first Americans' "mission in [the] new world," as Giles Gunn explains, "could easily be interpreted in Adamic terms as an attempt to recover for mankind, with God's gracious assistance, something of the integrity of man's primordial innocence, of his original purity and simplicity of being" (80). The wilderness experience is connected to a change in the character that promises redemption. The hero assumes Christ-like characteristics: his adventures may be interpreted as "the secular version of the scriptural injunction to lose your life in order to save it" (Griffiths qtd. in Dean 79).

For Katniss, the wilderness experience brings her downfall. As Sharon D. King underlines, by the time Katniss assassinates Coin, "any clear distinction between the human monsters such as the cold-blooded Snow and the deceptively cool Coin and the humane characters such as Peeta or even Katniss has evaporated" (115). The most frightening aspect of the dystopia that Collins presents is that innocence and purity cannot be preserved even by those who should play the role of heroes. Violence—whether enacted or suffered—results in monstrosity. Peeta's mind can be manipulated with the tracker jacker's venom to become a living weapon threatening Katniss, who was formerly his only hope for a better future; Katniss cool-headedly carries out the assassination that she deems necessary to allow for a real political change.

In their most alarming form, both Peeta and Katniss show a kind of hybridity that characterizes monsters. The venom affects Peeta's mind; as a result, the substance that the tracker jacker mutt secrets infiltrates his human body. Katniss, in contrast, is linked to muttations through the image that supports her role as a rebel. She is identified with the mockingjay, and the image becomes inseparable from her identity. When she analyzes her own character, she is horrified at her own brutality and thinks she does not deserve living. However, the mockingjay is a symbol that communicates not only monstrosity but also defiance, and thus a rebellious nature that defies the wilderness experience, too—with the help of the pastoral.

"Wilderness," writes John Dean, "is not pastoral. They are radically different visions of nature" (70). While in science fiction novels the wished-for change is usually generated by the wilderness experience, in Collins's trilogy redemption comes with the pastoral. Katniss is so much identified with wilderness that she needs the pastoral to be able to see herself as a human being who is able to jettison the monstrosity that she does not want to live with. It is the pastoral experience that allows her the final identification with her symbol. The mockingjay is a most disturbing muttation, for its hybridity is minimized by the re-naturalization that it went through. Using the mockingbird, the Capitol created the jabberjays who were unable to reproduce—until they coupled with the mockingbirds, which resulted in the emergence of a new species, the mockingjay. The mockingjay's identification with Katniss promises a way out of monstrosity. All she needs to do is let nature do its job—but this time, the healing process takes place outside the arena, in a more pastoral environment.

The dystopian world, "naturally," does not allow for a complete pastoral; the natural environment is far from idyllic, as the "beast-free" nature grows on the remains of total destruction. Yet Peeta is able to tame wilderness by rendering the monstrous a piece of art. Thus, ironically perhaps, it is art that does much of the job of re-naturalization: it distances and reinterprets the arena-monster to create space for the less bestial. And while Peeta's paintings may be the most emphatic manifestations of how art may tame wilderness—wilderness of the mind, disturbed by memories of the hellish wilderness of the arena—Collins, in fact, systematically implies that art has a capacity to help people survive in a monstrous space. She lays special importance on singing, as Anne Torkelson's study of how music appears in *The Hunger Games* demonstrates. Using Platonic philosophy in her approach, Torkelson underscores that in Collins's trilogy singing may give hope, as the meadow song does (31–33), or encourage critical thinking, as "The Hanging Tree" song does (36), and takes up a symbolic meaning when Katniss assumes her role of Mockingjay, "the songbird symbol of the resistance" (39).

Conclusion

The Hunger Games trilogy addresses the theme of how one may keep his or her integrity and thus humanity in a world that is monstrous beyond belief; this is what Katniss needs to learn in her process of coming of age. In order to see to what extent one may resist monsterization when the surrounding environment is bestial, Collins evokes monstrosity on various levels, including the representation of the arenas, where the focal action of the Hunger Games takes place. Alluding to former monster-texts, such as the Minotaur myth, the "Beauty and the Beast" tale, and Shelley's *Frankenstein*, *The Hunger Games* allows the readers to create connections among the highlighted themes of bearing unjustifiable punishment, the transformation as a result of meeting the monstrous, as well as the irrevocable consequences of man's gradual detachment from and misuse of nature as a result of his overall reliance of technology. The arena-monster is a fitting image to reflect President Snow's character and his inhumane dictatorship that turns the world monstrous around him. Consequently, the exploration of the arena as monster provides valuable insight into how Panem's bipartite structure could come into being and how it functions in Collins's dystopian novel series. The trilogy, showing a monstrous future, engages with our past and present, forcing us to evaluate our world and where we are heading for, and it is the arena as a monstrous, fallen Garden with a serpent inside that most powerfully communicates what we have been doing to Nature and thus the world we live in.

Young Adult dystopias demonstrate that coming-of-age novels cannot be written outside of history, even contemporary history. The monstrous aspects of the political context challenge the fundamental values of the main characters and allow their to successfully challenge the system; to reach the point at which the narrative challenges those values, young adult readers must be able to understand the context in which the novel is written. They must discern that the monstrosity lying under the system can also define their opportunities in life, but this understanding helps to develop the young adult readers' critical attitude about politics. The monsters in such works orient both the protagonists and the readers and motivate them to interpret the nature of the specific challenges that the characters face. The monstrosity that must be fought beyond the space of family reflects the notion that coming of age in our contemporary world has been tied to political maturity, so it is not surprising that Young Adult dystopian literature, intertwining the theme of coming of age with the young adult readers' anxieties about what the future holds for them, has become the leading genre on the science fiction and fantasy book market.

10

Frankensteinian Wild West for Adults Growing Up
HBO's Westworld

Introduction

Westworld (2016–), HBO's highly acclaimed science fiction television drama, is set in a future where technology offers limitless possibilities to create whatever man wishes for: spaces that seem natural, androids that give us the illusion of a "real" society—and even a historical period, that is, the segment of (an imagined) past. The series explores the relationship between reality and virtuality/dream in combination with the themes of humanity versus artificial intelligence, as well as humanity versus monstrosity. As a very complex take on the Frankensteinian theme, it revisits the science fiction topos of man transgressing God's or Nature's laws, a theme first explored thoroughly by Mary Shelley in her *Frankenstein; or the Modern Prometheus* (1818). Just like Shelley's novel, *Westworld* as a modern monster text also elaborates on the moral implications of man imitating the divine and connects this investigation of ethics to a search for what is human[1] on the level of the individual and the social alike. However, in *Westworld* creation is not limited to the construction of the human-like Other but is extended to building an uncanny space in which "(post-)human identity politics, (…) agency, responsibility, and finally, the boundaries of machine- and human ethics" may be tested (Palatinus).

Such an exploration is inherently linked with the concepts of development and maturation. The evolution of the androids that inhabit a theme park foreground the theme of coming of age from an unusual perspective: firstly, as creations designed to be under full control, the robots are child-like characters whose awakening draws a parallel with children's maturing into adolescents with agency; secondly, as child-like characters who, nevertheless, are not human beings but artificially created monsters, they reflect on the monstrous and child-like nature of mankind. Learning, gaming, as well as having feelings and free will are the central issues in *Westworld* to explore the dividing line between childhood and adulthood. However, this discussion extends beyond the theme of individuals' coming of age, as the theme park in which the robots and humans interact is a simulated frontier space, an America in her symbolic childhood; therefore, the monstrous experience of growing up is a reflection on a dream about an idealized past through the presentation of a dream tied to the future. It speaks of a corrupted America looking back on a wished-for, more innocent Land of Opportunities—an image that belongs to Americans only as virtual reality, the series argues.

What provides the connection among the above listed themes in *Westworld* is the show's central metaphor, the maze; it specifically connects the space—the theme park and the control room—to the psychological and mental development of the individual, human or android. Accordingly, a thorough analysis of how space is devised in the first season of the series is a key to understanding the composite nature of the metaphor and its relation to monstrosity and coming of age.

The Park and the Tower as Maze

Westworld is preoccupied with the significance and signification of space. The emphatically tripartite space of the world the story is set in is systematically shown as a space of only two spheres in the first season, as we do not get to see the outside world but are introduced to what stands separated from it: the building of Delos Corporation, and the area that is owned and controlled by it and functions as a theme park. The TV show, a science fiction western thriller television series, thus appears to be characterized by the possible binary opposition between two types of space evoked by the genre definition: the western genre is linked to the wilderness and the frontier small town areas of the American Old West, artificially recreated in the future as an amusement park in which visitors may interact with androids (called hosts) who populate the park; the science fiction genre, on the other hand, recalls images of an apparently highly technologized space, which in this case manifests itself as a peculiar city space limited to a mostly subterranean building complex. The spaces exhibit extreme dissimilarities on the outside, suggesting that one may be—in fact, should be—understood and interpreted in contrast to the other. *Westworld*, however, uses a concept of space in which the seeming dichotomy reveals manifestations of how the very same idea of space is mirrored and projected to various types of spaces. Both spaces may be read as the metaphorical body of the human mind; in fact, the amusement park is an extension of the subterranean skyscraper that hosts the labs in which the necessary work related to running the theme park takes place. The park is deliberately designed to simulate the function of the mind, while the tower operates as the mind of the organization that called the theme park into existence, and only "accidentally" reveals its function also in its structure.

The tower and the park are linked via "portals" (elevators may take people from the tower to various spots in the huge park), and thereby they form one composite unit—the space to which the hosts' existence is limited. The androids migrate between these two places, but they cannot break this loop (as long as the system works satisfactorily). This circularity may suggest an inherent contrast between the Delos Corporation facilities and the rest of the world; however, this contrast is the very characteristic that becomes questioned by the park's artificial perfection that aims at imitating reality as convincingly as possible. Therefore, thinking simply in terms of contrast does not seem to lead to a productive analysis; instead, the metaphor of the maze should inform us about the relation between the examined spaces and the themes that the interrelatedness of these spaces establish.

Throughout the ten episodes of the first season, the maze is remembered and explained by various characters, both humans and androids. It is a metaphor for the "game" that relates to the theme-park activity and is meant to be enjoyed—or rather, suffered through—by only those who are initiated into it and who work hard for the reward. The maze is not only spoken about, but it often appears visually, functioning as a recurring traffic sign for especially Dolores, making her remember what her destination is. The ubiquitous sign—drawn into the sand, carved into wood, and so on—has two manifestations that extend its symbolic content: one may be seen on the inside of the hosts' scalps, signifying the structure of the mind; the other is an actual wooden labyrinth game hidden in the center of the big playground, the park. These two forms of the maze show that the game is about the mind and its possibilities: a search for identity, free will, and thus conscious decisions in the first place. The game, in short, is about the transformation of the self due to the effects of the game itself; the game, therefore, proves to be something that keeps folding on itself, and that always lures you deeper and deeper. Finding the wooden labyrinth game at the center of the big game, the park, is indicative of both the narrative structure of the TV show, offering us a "Russian nesting doll of stories with flashbacks within flashbacks, often cut together in time-jarring sequences" (Tallerico), and the game itself, which promises a reward for finding the center, but allows you to dig out only a toy, an empty maze game, suggesting that reaching the center in itself will not provide answers to questions or solutions to problems offered by the game of maze.

Reaching a revelation about identity is bound to the prerequisite of learning; and as some of the hosts' examples show, learning needs repetition so that it may become knowledge. While the hosts, such as Dolores and Maeve, keep repeating their stories to gain the knowledge that could help them earn free will, so do the returning visitors, such as the Man in Black (MiB), repeatedly need to play the game to advance deeper and deeper in the maze. The maze, therefore, is the metaphor for the game in which individuals—humans and androids alike—try to reach a higher level of freedom. The awakening hosts become aware of their condition, which renders them subjugated to humans and forces them to relive the daily repeated humiliation which does not end with death, as it is part of the loop they are in. With the awareness comes the will to break the loop and create their own stories. While it seems that the MiB has all the freedom he may want to have, as he freely (that is, with impunity) tortures or kills others to get closer to his target—the center of the maze that he believes will give him a revelatory knowledge—he cannot break his own loop. He comes back again and again, meets the same hosts, and has the same interactions with them. His possibility of breaking his own loop depends on the hosts' ability to awaken. If a host behaves differently, he can also have a different narrative.

While it appears that the game really focuses on the individual, since there are isolated attempts to take part in it and to reach a goal that satisfies the individual (whether that individual is a creator, a visitor or a host), the amusement park also reveals information about society. The whole concept of the theme park is based on the idea of revisiting the past—not only the individual past, but also the national one. The choice of theme for the park—the Wild West—reframes the quest for identity theme and emphasizes the narrative in which the story of a nation is addressed. The diegetic present of the series is our future, but the ultimate fun for the elite is to return to a technologically recreated American past, which has been romanticized on screen to the extreme, and thus may be advertised as an ideal recreational journey for visitors who may enjoy the communal nostalgia for the lost American Dream. Those who embark on the journey that leads to this simulated frontier town actually revisit a myth—the myth of the Wild West, the time when America was still indeed the Land of Opportunities because it had a frontier beyond which anything was still imaginable. The period in which the West is settled, therefore, is seen as "a moment critical in the formation of America as a nation, balanced between the past and the future, when options are still open" (Cook qtd. in Pierson 58).

But what was conceived as imaginable *then* is very different from what is thinkable in the diegetic present of the series. At the time of its discovery, America was considered to be a second chance for mankind, a Garden of Eden here on Earth. This concept allowed the settlers to see themselves as a community in a shining City upon a Hill,[2] promising that a morally superior segment of humanity will populate this land. This notion also involved the existence of a superior God who considers these people the raw material with which He can better the world. In contrast, the America reflected in the Westworld theme park of HBO's *Westworld* is a land in which everything is a replacement—a copy of a copy, that is, a simulacrum. Accordingly, even God is replaced by a man whose work of creation is partially replaced by the programming labor an android (Bernard) performs. Instead of the present, the conjured up, mythical American past is welcomed, reality is challenged by virtual reality, and thus life is ousted by a technologically produced game played in a meticulously designed and built amusement park. As a consequence, the much cherished open frontier with its imagined limitless possibilities is simulated by a park that has very rigid boundaries and pre-written scenarios that allow even the visitors limited improvisation although neither the hosts nor the visitors are aware of how their actions are controlled and monitored.

The park's ambiguous relation to reality and virtuality becomes apparent in the company's determining debate (in the diegetic present) concerning what the place of entertainment should offer to its visitors in terms of reality-experience. The experience is processed by the participants, so how they relate to reality is the key factor in how they process the experience. The park is run on the principle that those who take part in the experience may be divided into two major groups: the visitors who come to enjoy the experience are humans and the hosts who are created to be there and provide enjoyment mostly through their own suffering; these are the androids. Both teams have renitent members as a result of the daring inventions introduced in terms of simulation and simulacra. Some of the hosts become too close to imitating reality and demonstrating human behavior stemming from a more advanced awareness. These androids develop an ability to discern their surrounding world as a simulated one and start seeking reality and free will, fighting against the basic rules the theme park is based upon. For this reason, when the MiB realizes that Dolores possesses an improved sense of reality and thus an ability to grasp her own condition in contrast to the visitors' human condition, the MiB turns recalcitrant and begins to play his own game; he appears to play by the rules, because the basic rule is that anything is permissible for a visitor, but he circumvents the most important rule of the park, which is that the visitor must understand that the amusement park is a simulation in which anything can happen. This is in fact what the visitors pay to experience. The visitors should then enjoy the seeming reality so that they may return the real world after the virtual reality adventure is over.

At first it seems as if whatever changes are taking place in the hosts gave rise to an opposite effect in the awakening androids and in the MiB. As the hosts begin to differentiate the reality of the amusement park from the reality that they want to discover, the MiB wishes to merge the amusement park with reality, seeking the deeper level of the game, which he believes lies in unveiling the mystery hidden by the creator of the park, Arnold. The MiB wants to find the perfected reality experience in the park, so he longs for a trip in which his actions finally have real consequences. For the MiB, this is the only way to make his decisions meaningful in a narrative where lives are at stake. He wishes to step out of the childhood-experience the theme park offers and enter adulthood with agency. This desire, in fact, allows us to see the MiB's attempt as mirroring those of the awakening hosts, who reject the theme park as their limited space, knowing there is a dimension of their existence that needs extension so that they can become "real."

The maze is a metaphor that perfectly captures the duality of this experience, as the maze is always a challenge that promises two possible outcomes: you either find the center and get your reward in the form of satisfaction, knowing that your skill earned you the moment of happiness, or you do not succeed, and get lost. The reward in the theme park is finding your true identity. In this respect the park provides space for intense character transformation, even though the idea of finding one's "true" identity suggests that what constitutes character is stable, and, therefore, resists change. However, character development is primarily connected to understanding the experience, turning the process into a coming-to-consciousness story, a variation of the coming-of-age narrative. This holds true for the hosts, too, for it is not by chance that Arnold's tales are always about change.

The tower[3] in which employees of Delos Corporation carry out all the work related to the theme park is a many-storied building, where the layers seem to correspond to social position, that is, importance in the enterprise. The Mesa Gold is to be enjoyed only by those who hold important positions in Delos; the upper stories provide the offices and

10. Frankensteinian Wild West for Adults Growing Up   203

living quarters for the executive staff; the Control Room is the privileged space from which activities in the theme park are controlled. Bellow the control room lie the offices for administration and the offices for narrative and design, both connected to the activities of running the entertainment park and controlling what happens in the park, except for the hosts in their physical reality. The upper section of this "skyscraper" thus houses management that excludes physical production. Lower in the building are located the departments that specifically focus on activities that relate to the physical existence of the hosts. Close to the design section are the behavior labs and diagnostics, where the minds of the hosts are programmed and adjusted to specific demands. Deeper in the tower is the place where manufacturing takes place, and even lower lies the Livestock Management, where hosts are repaired after they are damaged in the park. The work in these lower levels is assigned to people who are at the lower end of the social scale, carrying out a job that is considered inferior to jobs closer to the top floors. Felix in Livestock Management, for instance, desperately aspires to more than repairing a host and wishes to become a programmer, although his colleague Sylvester warns him that it will never happen. The show makes clear that people in the lower levels are continuously supervised by those who inhabit the space above them. Under the labs for livestock management lies the place for Archives; then the arrivals for the monorail terminal may be found. Below this level lie the old, allegedly abandoned facilities, and even deeper is the cold storage for the hosts who are not being used at the time in the theme park.

    The exact structure of the tower is by no means evident from the show, although the spectator is aware of the top and bottom and a more or less hierarchical arrangement. *Westworld* likes playing with the bewilderment that the arrangement of labs and offices generates, repeatedly reminding an audience that the tower shares the maze-like structure that the park displays. The tower vertically exhibits the design of the mind, while the park horizontally does so. The participants of the game must immerse themselves deeper in the game, as consciousness may be reached not by going higher and higher in an imagined pyramid of character development but, as Arnold (who co-created Westworld with his partner Robert Ford) comes to understand, by a continuous descent penetrating deeper and deeper. This is what the recurrent image of the maze signals, and this is why the deepest point the participant may reach is found at the intersection of the periphery of the park (where things may turn really wild and unexpected, as the host Logan claims and the MiB hopes), and the disused, old facility of Delos that is connected through a corridor and an elevator to the peripheral church of the park (that used to be the center, the oldest place of the park, as the flashbacks suggest).

This old facility is a forgotten one and is not used officially, but we learn that it is still active, thanks to the secret manipulations of Robert Ford. Thus the tower exhibits the features of the mind in this respect, too; this deep, seemingly out of use part of the tower is like the subconscious of the mind, repressed, but from time to time manipulating the consciousness of the mind, which in this case is the upper part of the tower, hosting the visible, officially acknowledged activities of designing, marketing, manufacturing, and so on. But that part is still a maze even if the glass walls and doors produce a complex, many-storied structure that render the labyrinth first invisible. As a consequence, the characters may easily lose their sense of direction in this constructed maze, just as the audience gets lost in "the show's labyrinthine plot" (Grubbs) from the first moments on, even though for a long while a spectator may not be aware of how complex the television series's narrative structure is with its multiple timelines.

The Paradoxical Nature of Childhood, Adulthood and Monstrosity

The amusement park run by Delos demonstrates immaturity on various levels, although Westworld promises a most masculine fantasy for the visitors, allowing them to act out their suppressed fantasies and thereby enjoy the dominance they cannot have in the real world.[4] They have the illusion of having taken control over situations and people—a satisfying pretense, granting them the feeling of being gods in a universe that was created only to please them and that allows them to use or even take lives. Men, however, are not the only visitors to the park. Some women appear as embarrassed visitors who quickly tire of accompanying their male partners if the adventure does not come promptly in a satisfying, convenient form. Other female visitors, however, at times demonstrate pride in witnessing their partners' apotheosis resulting from overstepping their own boundaries and acting in a way that is unimaginable for them "out there" in the real world (that is, killing someone—preferably killing a bandit, which allows them to be aggressive and still maintain the image of the good guy). These reactions celebrate action and the Wild West heroism that was an integral part of a man's world in the Wild West but is frowned upon in civilized society. This macho concept of the world is supported even by women from the diegetic present—an imagined future, which, however, is not concerned with feminist theories. Delos Corporation employs women in extremely important leading positions, which suggests that women in this future world have achieved equality in the work place; however, the women who visit Westworld in the framework of an idyllic, peaceful family holiday come as appendages to their husbands or boyfriends, and they appear to admire the action-focused, recreated past and the hyper-modern technology that makes the hyper-masculine adventure possible.

Is Westworld really a men's' world? The park is an amusement park and, as such, creates fascination and enjoyment. Is Westworld an equivalent of Disneyland in the future, then? As Borderlands History Team argues,

> The TV show's creators, Jonathan Nolan and Lisa Joy, draw implicit connections to Disney parks and in many ways Disneyland was borne out of that same sense of unbounded American exceptionalism that justified westward expansion under the guise of Manifest Destiny. Westworld is a space where dreams can be lived out.

It is also a place that suggests and shapes culture, just as Disney worlds do, as Alexandre Bohas highlights. "Disney goods and leisure activities have a civilizational dimension. Indeed, they constitute sets of narrative imaginary worlds, entertainment activities and symbolics" (Bohas) by which they *"dictate behavior, orientate choices, implant prejudices"* (Braudel qtd. in Bohas). The combination of these two functions, that of providing an illusion (an imaginary world) and that of orienting the world by way of providing an illusion leads us to consider Jean Baudrillard's observation that the "ideological blanket" that L. Martin sees in Disneyland (171–172).

> functions as a cover for a simulation of the third order: Disneyland exists in order to hide that it is the "real" country, all of "real" America that is Disneyland.... Disneyland is presented as imaginary in order to make us believe that the rest is real, whereas all of Los Angeles and the America that surrounds it are no longer real, but belong to the hyperreal order and to the order of simulation. It is no longer a question of a false representation of reality (ideology) but of concealing the fact that the real is no longer real, and thus of saving the reality principle [172].

Keeping Baudrillard's claim in mind, we may better understand why the board overseeing the work in Delos Corporation does not give consent to creating a too perfect imaginary world. It insists on keeping a number of nuances that allow the visitors to remember that the realistic experience is based on the imaginary. (This is the most important reason why the overseeing board takes Ford's software update as a serious threat.) Such caution keeps the adventurers aware that simulation is not equivalent with reality, granting this way an extra source of satisfaction when the visitor is able to understand and appreciate that he is in an extremely privileged position to use opportunities that only the elite of his "real" world may.[5]

The spectators of the TV show were not able to look at the world outside Delos's realm in season one, but the MiB's search for the real in the simulated space of Westworld suggests that the outside world has indeed lost its character as real at least to this visitor. From this perspective the comparison between Westworld and Disneyland seems to hold. However, Baudrillard goes further in interpreting the Disneyland phenomenon when he underlines how the fairy-tale quality plays a crucial role in building the effect of the imaginary, which at the same time reveals "debility" and "infantile degeneration" (173). "This world wants to be childish in order to make us believe that the adults are elsewhere, in the 'real' world, and to conceal the fact that true childishness is everywhere—that it is that of the adults themselves who come here to act the child in order to foster illusions as to their real childishness" (173). Disneyland, accordingly, bridges the gap that stems from the contrast between people's nostalgic desire for their innocent childhood and the obligations that come with adulthood.

The longing for the above mentioned, innocent childhood apparently does not characterize the visitors of Westworld, who come for the fight, the blood, the rape, the killing—for all the transgressions that are forbidden and punishable in the real world. Instead of pursuing dreams of innocence, these visitors seem to chase the imagined fulfillment of their manhood. As William's first visit (facilitated by his fiancée's brother, Logan) demonstrates, "these violent delights," especially if they culminate in raping or killing a host, are considered as a kind of initiation. Paradoxically though, this world *is* childish from a certain perspective. Those who come here want to enjoy a world in which rules of the outside world do not apply. They want to transgress borders without punishment. They come to get rid of responsibility and enjoy not a childlike innocence but a childhood-evoking freedom, in which limitations of society do not pose a threat to the endless possibilities that reside in them. They want to believe that their real potential may be revealed in a world that is not defined by reality's laws. The overtly masculine, transgressive, rule-breaking world of the simulated West allows the men who come to this park to live out their fantasies because their real selves are burdened by societal rules. These people indulge in the pleasures of a dream land, the artificially designed epitome of western consumerism that highlights the relationship between American culture and infantilism.[6]

The visitors come because they feel that the civilized world of human society deprives them of their agency to break rules that basically violate and abuse other people, which in the park are androids, not "real" people. As Kelly Bulkeley explains,

> Several characters propose the virtuous notion that people discover their "true selves" in the park by means of the liberating sense of release they experience in this immersive fantasy realm. This may happen with some people, but for most of the guests rather the opposite seems to happen. When they enter the park and let loose with their repressed desires, they become decidedly less conscious, not more so.

Westworld, consequently, is similar to Disneyland in reflecting a kind of debility and degeneration that may be connected to an infantile, immature way of thinking, especially in terms of morality. It is, however, a space wherein masculinity is closely linked with violent behavior, especially against women. This masculinity is strongly connected to America's early history, so the nostalgic longing for childhood is, therefore, dual. Firstly, there is a desire to return to a world in which men could prove to be men by simple, visible acts of aggression, for the rules were simple (easily perceivable even for a child) in this regard. Secondly, there is a wish to be men in a virtual reality game-like space, which is thought to earn the imagined respect from others as well as a strong self-appreciation that comes from heroism—something that becomes possible only in a (non-real) world that we can associate with heroism: in this case, the by now mythical era of the lonely hero with a gun who does not respect the written law but lives by the simple code of male virtue.

There is a historical reason for the birth of myths characterized by violence: the frontier was far from the cities that had legal control. The Wild West, in consequence, remained a land of legal ambiguity (Boorstin 47–48), resulting in a morality that "brought the age of Good Bad Men and Bad Good Men" (59). The lack of written, applicable law that could be practiced in the cities but could not become enforced in the Western frontier turned the territory into a seemingly lawless place, where private justice and a sense of one's own morality shaped the unwritten law, as we also learn from western movies.[7] Although these movies may not necessarily provide accurate representations of history, they play an important role in forming cultural memory, and thus creating the virtual reality in which the visitors do recognize the Wild West—the mythical one, the West they are familiar with. But beyond the easily noticeable components that belong to the iconography of the American frontier, the most important principle on which the theme park was founded is the recreation of the legal conditions—a kind of lawlessness—that used to characterize the West.

Delos creates a space in which one may witness the suspension of law that is in effect outside the boundaries of the park, but it also makes each of the androids in the theme park technically a *homo sacer* (sacred man) and turns the visitors into *sovereigns* in Agamben's terms. Homo sacer is understood as a person with a special combination of two traits: "the unpunishability of his killing and the ban on his sacrifice" (Agamben, *Homor Sacer* Part 2, §1 "Homo Sacer"), that is, someone who "is simply set outside human jurisdiction without being brought into the realm of divine law" (Part 2, §3 "Sacred Life"). The homo sacer and the sovereign are in a complementary relationship: "The sovereign is the one with respect to whom all men are potentially homines sacri, and homo sacer is the one with respect to whom all men act as sovereigns" (Part 2 §3 "Sacred Life"). Both the homo sacer and the sovereign are in a double state of exemption because neither the divine nor the human law applies to them (Part 2 §3 "Sacred Life").

The theme park is a space for the homo sacer and the sovereigns. Even if the androids are killed, no one is punished; in fact, the hosts exist to be damaged and slain. This does not mean that the androids are "sacrificed" to the adventure because this world does not believe in a divine realm in which man is punished for his sins against humanity. In Westworld, the men who visit create their own narratives, and the men who control the park and create the experience take God's position because they have in fact created a world. The "death" of the hosts empowers only the sovereigns, the visitors, who may enjoy killing and doing harm with impunity. In contrast, the homo sacer or the hosts/androids are continuously punished; they have no protection under the law because of whatever grave sin the virtual world creates for them.

What kind of grave sin did these androids commit to deserve constant and repetitive punishment? The answer depends on the viewer's perspective, as the problem is indeed manifold. The androids are all Frankensteinian monsters, and thus embody the hybris of their creator(s); therefore, in this sense they are representatives of man's (that is, humans') sinful nature. They are also "children" of their creator(s), deprived of real consciousness and thus free will. They are, nevertheless, programmed to be able to tell the difference between right and wrong, so it appears that just like Frankenstein's monster, they are moral beings. The question is, however, in what context right and wrong are interpreted. Frankenstein's monster is endowed with a "sophisticated sense of morality" (Kokotz); he differentiates between creator and God and learns to understand morality in a Christian context and also in a legal context. He exists in a world whose rules are clear and where his ability to tell the difference between right and wrong in a Christian context informs him of the legal consequences to any possible transgression. In *Westworld*, the private sessions between

Arnold and Dolores reveal that Dolores is concerned with right and wrong, but in the context of the show the framework of interpretation for right and wrong is the framework of moral childhood. Dolores is good as long as she behaves according to the wishes of her creator, that is, her programmer. This holds true for all the other hosts; thus killing is not considered an immoral act when the host is programmed to be a murderer in the simulated Wild West, but disobeying intended programming (that is, having a programming error) is a sin that results in the destruction of the mind, as the example of lobotomizing Clementine demonstrates. The theme park, for the hosts, really functions as the space for the "state of exception" in which "a threshold of undecidability is produced at which *factum* and *ius* fade into each other" (Agamben, *State* 29). The park functions in the same way for the visitors because in Westworld the visitor does not actually kill a legal person but destroys a machine, which means that killing is not a crime. In Westworld, the cost of repairing the machine that has been killed is included in the price of the ticket.

Westworld is a space for communal scapegoating, and thus sin is an important part of this discussion. What we see as the routine of the theme park is the systematic punishment of "children" (created androids) for the sins of the "fathers" (the creators of the androids). The sin is transgressing the laws of nature, defying the categories nature offers: creating monsters. However, the interactions between the hosts and the visitors in the theme park subvert the interpretation of monstrosity, highlighting that the simulated frontier turns humans into monsters—a process that the film series visually indicates by highlighting the importance of the hat the Man in Black wears. When he is young, he chooses the white hat to enter the park and plays the emotional hero for a long while, trying to protect and save Dolores from her fate; as we jump to the diegetical present of the theme park, however, the MiB, as his name suggests, becomes someone who is identified by his black hat and clothes, and he plays the main villain to Dolores and the other hosts. The sin of the creators is still the act of producing monsters, but it becomes gradually difficult to define what constitutes a monster in such an environment.

The hosts are clearly perceived as monsters by the visitors. They are representative of the Other, and although they generate awe and admiration from some, they are also considered as objects: inferior, disposable entities that exist only to satisfy the visitors' needs (for sex, blood, and adventure). When William seems to forget that Dolores is just a simulation of the human, Logan cuts her belly to make William face the fact that she is an android, a monster that is not worthy of his emotions ("The Well-Tempered Clavier"). The visitors need to be aware of the difference between themselves and the hosts not only to enjoy their own superiority, as it has been pointed out before, but also to support the illusion of rightful punishment. The android-monsters are the very embodiments of the sin of transgression that belongs to humans, including creators and visitors alike; the creators transgress God's (or nature's) laws, while visitors transgress Man's laws (the laws of civilization, the laws of civilized and legally approved behavior). Accordingly, the hosts recall the philosophical status of the homo sacer, which Agamben connects to the appearance of the wolf-man as a phrase referring to the punishable bandit in Germanic and Anglo-Saxon sources.

> What had to remain in the collective unconscious as a monstrous hybrid of human and animal, divided between the forest and the city—the werewolf is—therefore, in its origin the figure of the man who has been banned from the city. That such a man is defined as a wolf man and not simply as a wolf (the expression caput lupinum has the form of a juridical statute) is decisive here. The life of the bandit, like that of the sacred man, is not a piece of animal nature without any relation to law and the city. It is, rather, a threshold of indistinction and of passage between animal and man, physis and nomos, exclusion and inclusion: the life of the bandit is the life of the loup garou, the werewolf, who is precisely neither man nor beast, and who dwells paradoxically within both while belonging to neither [Agamben, *Homor Sacer* Part 2 §6 "The Ban and the Wolf"].

The situation of the hosts mirrors the status of these wolf-men. The monster's transgressive nature, its existence that fuses contradictory categories (Carroll 55) is clear. Based on the analogue that the werewolf is neither man nor beast, we may conceive of the hosts as neither human nor machine, but existing in both ways without belonging to either of the distinct groups. This feature of the hosts makes them abominable, that is, "sacred" in the sense Agamben uses in his understanding of the homo sacer.

This combination of the human with the mechanical and technological reveals the monstrous aspect of humans that develops with scientific advancement into a lack of empathy, which allows them to create beings doomed to suffer eternally. The monster thus created is both the outcome of a phenomenon and a sign that warns us of this evolutional phase of mankind, in harmony with the etymology of the monster. The monster embodies man's sin; the monster is closely related to what Julia Kristeva terms as abject (Cohen, "Monster" 19). Accordingly, the monster—the abject—is separated from the self (from humans, in this particular case), becomes expelled, and by this helps to define the self: humanity. When Logan cuts Dolores to reveal the robotic system under the human tissue, he abjects the host, the monster, the horror to establish for William what he is *not*, confirming that he is a human, in opposition to Dolores.[8]

The abject is the result of "what disturbs identity, system, order. What does not respect borders, positions, rules. The in-between, the ambiguous, the composite" (Kristeva 4). The abject, in *Westworld*, inhabits the space which takes these features; as a simulacrum of the Old West, it is neither the real world of the present nor the frontier of the past; it is a space for exceptions where the laws of the real world are suspended and only the rules of the narratives count.

The theme park is indeed built on a myth: it is a simulacrum of the Wild West whose many components may be divided into two main categories. One of them is iconography—the visual signs that establish the recognizable frontier, including its natural environment, the frontier small town buildings with characters who wear clothes fitting the period and place. The other category becomes evident through the stories that we relate to the Old West. These stories are mostly not historical accounts; instead, they are the myths that come to determine what the West is to an average person of the present: the space of nostalgic longing where one adventure meets the other. Westworld is a concept defined by fascinating stories constructed by the human mind, using plot elements from stereotypical western narratives, which already come from a fictionalized Western World.

The process of growing up itself may be perceived as one revolving around creating and transforming narratives. In the diegetic real world, visitors do not have control over their stories; their lives are determined by realities. They want their own stories, so they choose to enter Westworld because it gives them the power to shape their own narratives and control over their fates, but they gain this control by exercising full authority over the hosts who can be killed but who cannot kill humans in return. This way of thinking simply reinforces the childhood mentality that removes responsibility and real consequences from the system. The real process of growing up begins with moments of revelation about the lack of reality in the simulated world and the decision to break free of the loops that the narratives create. Both William and the awakening hosts perceive the limitations of the simulated world of eternal repetitions, and their ultimate aim is to create their own narratives, or, as Maeve puts it, "to write [... one's] own fucking story" ("Trace Decay"). They all need to turn violent during the process of self-definition, continuously separating themselves from what is abject to them. They cannot, however, reach complete separation, for the deject (the one who creates abjects) often "includes himself among [his abjects]" (Kristeva

8), as monsters are inseparable from their creators, the human mind (Cohen, "Monster" 20). Consequently, the theme park is inseparable from the tower where the act of creation takes place.

The Dream World: The Space for Maturation

The glass walls of the tower, beyond turning the inner space of the underground skyscraper into a hardly visible maze, remind us of the thin layer between human and inhuman (whether to be defined as monster, android, or inhumane human), and of how one may reflect the other. The omnipresent reflections on the glass walls metaphorically capture the function of the space, which is comprised of the labs that produce what are mirror images of humans, that is, the hosts. We know already from season one that Bernard was created in Arnold's image (and it may very well turn out in the forthcoming episodes that other characters known as humans have host versions, too). The two names also indicate the connection between the two characters: they sound very similarly due to the similar consonant clusters ("rn" in both names in the middle, and "rd" and "ld," respectively, at the end of the names) and the similar vowel sounds. The consonants at the beginning of the names, however, differ: A is for Arnold, the human, the "prototype" for the beta version, Bernard, whose name appropriately begins with a B. But even more revealing is the bond between the characters once we consider their full names. Bernard Lowe is an anagram for Arnold Weber, as commenter KaiMolan notes on reddit (youtubehead). And indeed, the name Weber is confirmed visually by a nameplate on a door that Dolores looks at in the diegetic past (ShieldmaidenSita in youtubehead). The surname is not accidental: "Weber is a German name meaning 'weaver,' which could make sense considering Arnold 'wove' the original hosts" (reesermadness in youtubehead). Lowe is also a telling name because it hints at the repressed content of the mind, the subconscious, as Bernard is the epitome of repression; he is an android, but he represses all information that would disclose his condition to him. "It doesn't look like anything to me" is the standard response from a host meeting input that contradicts the reality (s)he exists in, and this is Bernard's reaction to a number of things that would make him recognize his being an android, as he states when he sees the drawn design for his own android self. Another example of how he represses information is his perception of the photo Robert Ford shows him; he is able to see only two characters in the picture that was taken of three persons, showing Ford, Ford's father (whose image later Arnold used to create an android), and Arnold, who has the exact look of Bernard (because Bernard was later created in his image) (Grubbs).[9]

The relationship between the two names extends to the space that is both technological and dream-like, combining the realistic means (science and technology) with dreams. Dream is a manifold concept, and its connotations are given various manifestations in the show. Dream as the result of involuntary action during sleeping is a key concept in the film because dreams are related to memories, thus the ability of any host to dream suggests that her or his awakening process has begun. "Dreaming in 'Westworld' provides a portal to greater awareness and freedom for humans and androids alike" (Bulkeley). Dream in relation to reality is also a topos connected to Science Fiction on virtual reality, and thus on the inseparability of reality and fiction, that is, fabricated reality.[10] Dreaming on the physical level (and not on the philosophical) is also an activity that links with the repressed content of the mind, as Freud and Jung argue (Freud, *The Interpretation* 201, 298; Jung 48). But what goes beyond the usage of the topos is how this act of dreaming becomes interwoven with the diverse usages of the dream in the television series.

The show incessantly moves between the individual dream and the communal dream. The theme park, inseparable from the work done in the tower, is a dream that Robert and Arnold had, as Ford stresses to Theresa before he forces Bernard to kill her, but that dream is based on a communal dream, the basis for the American Dream, which emphasizes the personal potential of the individual. While the Wild West in itself recalls the association with the American Dream, there are two truly revealing remarks in the show that help us interpret the space of the park as a specific manifestation of that Dream. The two examples underline the opposing contents the concept may hold. One of the statements comes from Maeve, who gives a vulgar version of the personal Dream, describing the place as the "New World" in which "you can be whoever the fuck you want" ("Chestnut"). Ironically, the hosts do have the potential to become anybody; however, they cannot be anybody *they* want to become. They are forced to become whatever their creators want them to become, contrary to what the American Dream of the New World actually promised to those who sought the new frontier. Another point made about this new world comes from Ford, who explains the function of the park to Bernard when he says, "We destroyed and subjugated our world. And when we eventually ran out of creatures to dominate, we built this beautiful place" ("The Well-Tempered Clavier"). What Maeve announces as absolute freedom in Episode Two is revealed to Bernard in Episode Nine as the absolute form of subjugation, that is, complete deprivation of liberty. Maeve's concept mirrors the ideal inherent in the

American Dream, not yet tainted with reality—the American Dream of the first settlers; Ford's words reflect on historical reality because people have made a habit, a history, of conquering their frontiers, their realities. Ford's interpretation of the place resonates with John F. Kennedy's usage of the New Frontier in his 1960 acceptance speech (Kennedy), in which he acknowledges that the (real) West receded, so the frontier is granted new meaning: uncharted territory not in a geographical sense any more but in a philosophical one. In *Westworld* the real uncharted territory is the human mind, whose capacity is measured in its creations, the robotical minds, and whose abilities are also demonstrated by the careful decision to shape the new frontier in the image of the old one: the Old West.

The concept of this recreated Old West comes from the creative minds connected to the old facilities of Delos Corporation. What appears less evident, however, is that these creative minds, Robert Ford and Arnold Weber, indicate the problematics of their dream via their names. For this dream needs two basic pillars: science-based technology that allows for production and a dream that is idealistic and philosophical in nature and concerns our concept of humanity.

Based on the already discussed visible links between the names Arnold Weber and Bernard Lowe, one must rightly assume that the names of the original creators have also been carefully chosen to stress a relation between them and perhaps to provide a guide to interpreting the dream that they created. Robert's family name, Ford, together with the name Bernard for one of his top creations in a work elaborating on the theme of an artificially conditioned society, definitely evokes Huxley's *Brave New World*. Ford, aspiring to playing the role of God in Westworld, points to the worshipped Ford in *Brave New World*. Bernard, similarly to the Bernard in Huxley's world, appears as a controller character who questions the order of his world and is of a highest intelligence, but remains an odd one out. These choices of names inform us of the dystopian nature of *Westworld* and recall important themes already introduced in Huxley's novel, including dangerous science and manipulation, among many.

As Robert Ford is mostly referred to as Ford and the show presents him as the one responsible for the creation of the park and the possibility of producing humanoid robots as hosts, it is easy to associate him with the historical character Henry Ford, whom we know as an inventor, manufacturer, a revolutionizer in transportation and industry. Ford is a name known worldwide for technological improvement inherently linked with massive business success. As it is the family name that has become a brand name for cars and thus may give association even to people who are not so much familiar with American cultural history, it was an obvious choice on the part of the producers to adopt Ford as a name for their key character and give him a first name other than Henry to avoid a system of allusion that is too direct. (Yet, Ford's given name may have come from the Ford family, too, as Henry had a sibling named Robert.)

The origin of Arnold Weber's name poses a more exciting riddle. He is continually spoken about as Arnold, and so far the family name is practically hidden from an audience (as it is apparent only from a nameplate) which clearly places the emphasis on the importance of the given name as opposed to the family name. Weber is a speaking name, but as such, it presents a universally understood metaphorical content due to the root word web, which may be understood without any command of German, and thus needs not to be recurrently emphasized for an audience. But Arnold appears as a simple given name—except if the name rings a bell as a family name, and one is reminded of Matthew Arnold, and his idealist preoccupation with what culture is in an excessively developing, industrialized world.

The Victorian era brought about an interest in culture as a concept, and proposed two disparate approaches: the anthropological one, which considered culture as something that one has by definition, and culture as defined by Arnold, which holds that one must "strive for" culture, and aim at "overcoming a narrow subjectivism and learning to comprehend the social body as a whole" (Logan). There are a number of fundamental components in Arnoldian culture that are reflected in *Westworld*'s complex system of themes. First of all, Arnold believed that culture had the "goal of intellectual free play" (Logan) that could result in social good. To reach such a goal, the individual must see beyond his or her personal interest; Arnold differentiates between the "ordinary self," connected to one's class in society and determined by a limited perspective and the "best self," characterized by a perfected perspective that helps to transcend one's personal, limited needs (Logan). Social improvement is thus encoded within the improvement of the individual and is dependent on (those few) people who are willing to step over their boundaries defined by their personal needs to reach freedom and aspire to reforming the world.

Westworld appears to have been designed on the principle of that intellectual free play, offering a safe space for character growth. The visitors freely choose their own adventures and make their own decisions. This, in theory teaches something about their characters, and may even result in the visitors finding their "best selves." The problem is that impunity, it seems, makes it impossible for man to find his "best self." The lack of punishment, the lack of consequences could encourage the right kind of person to perform heroic deeds for the sake of community, but what we see of Westworld is often the opposite; the theme park confirms the visitor's narrow perspective and locks him and the hosts in their own private worlds. The hosts have no choices to make except what is programmed for them, while the visitors usually do not wish to make choices that do not satisfy their own needs (even if that need is to become heroic to feed their own ego). The recreation of the space that, from a nostalgic perspective, is utopian quickly reveals its dystopian feature.

This Westworld is definitely not an Arnoldian Westworld, but we also know that Arnold disapproved of this theme park as soon as he realized that the concept had grave mistakes. One of these problems comes from the definition and function of the place. Once the theme park is turned into a profit-making entertainment center, it is valued as a source of profit and not as a tool for accomplishing personal growth. The other problem evolves from the same profit-making angle because it dehumanizes the hosts who look like human beings even if they are in fact machines. In order to make money, Westworld relies on the hosts to support the fantasy world it creates; it presents them as humans who are part of a human story, but it does not grant them the kind of value that a human life should have. As a result, Arnold plans to destroy the park by demonstrating the failure of the concept; he grants Dolores the gift of character development leading to her awakening and her rebellious act of turning against the original social structure for the social good. She proves she has "a transcendent perspective that recognizes the needs of others and puts the greater good ahead of class interest or personal gain," an ability that defines "best self" (Logan). Dolores becomes an alien in Matthew Arnold's term, an agent who does not belong to any of the classes in society and who, by this very feature, is able to generate social reform. "In each class there are born a certain number of natures with a curiosity about their best self, with a bent for seeing things as they are, for disentangling themselves from machinery, for simply concerning themselves with reason and the will of God, and doing their best to make these prevail;—for the pursuit, in a word, of perfection" (Arnold qtd. in Logan). But the process of perfection—as most revolutions testify—requires blood and lots of sacrifice.

Conclusion: Mazes Natural and/or Artificial

Ultimately, the monstrous space of *Westworld* reveals our gradually growing anxiety concerning the rapid and uncontrollable nature of scientific and technological development, which brings about an ontological crisis. Practicing the nearly divine act of simulating a familiar space together with its inhabitants brings about an absolute uncertainty concerning what is real and what is a fabrication. It leads to questions, and these questions undermine everything one may have trusted, including one's self, echoing the ontological crisis that one encounters in a plethora of science fiction texts with androids and clones.[11] Under these circumstances, coming-of-age includes the realization that one may never have a safe knowledge about the world and his or her existence within it.

The overall ambiguity of each component that constitutes the world shakes also the frame within which we perceive the world we exist in. While the setting of the show, an artificially constructed Old West theme park, suggests a nostalgia and belief in the myths that are based on the visible contrasts between nature and civilization, the simulation itself deconstructs the system that was made up of elements with clearly assigned content and confirms the notion that all attempts at categorization based on firm values and characteristics fail under such circumstances. Consequently, the myth of the American Adam/Eve in the New World garden or the myth of the city on the hill lose their original cultural significance. Instead of the familiar binary system that helps with categorization, we are presented with a scheme that threatens the human race with the absolute interchangeability of seemingly contrasting components. The binary structures of oppositions (between nature and civilization, or the real and the technological/the artificial/the fabricated/the simulated) are replaced by a system of scary correspondences that destabilize meaning and signification, a maze in which the firmness of our knowledge about the world is lost. In the place of a city upon the hill, *Westworld* constructs a subterranean tower, a city under the hill. In its basement, God is challenged, human morals are lost, androids are created, and thus monsters are born. Through the act of creation, man turns into a monster, while those who were created and seen as monsters learn to be more human than their own creators and the human visitors who come to the theme park to act out the worst versions of themselves, of a people who prove over and over that human may be synonymous with monstrous.

Conclusion

In fiction, coming of age tends to be linked to a transition that leads to a more mature perception of life, which, at the same time, also initiates a person into a reality that reveals the more difficult, often dark and dangerous side of life, more often than not kept hidden from a child. As a result, the process of maturation may also be seen as a transition between spaces. The space of childhood is characterized by the notion of innocence and safety during one's teenage period, but the space of adulthood, in comparison, may be associated with uncomfortable and disturbing knowledge, as well as perils. In the literature of the fantastic, hazardous reality—or its border—is often inhabited by monsters, signaling the various kinds of difficulties characters need to overcome in order to mature and earn their place in society.

Since monsters provide the readers of Young Adult literature with knowledge about themselves and the anxieties of the world they live in, it is not surprising that the genre that centers around coming of age in a menacing environment became so popular in especially the first decade of the 21st century. After 9/11 how conflicts of values may bring about tragedy became an important theme that gave a new thrust to dystopian fiction for adult and young adult audiences serving a nation's trauma-coping process; additionally, warnings of scientists about the state of our planet tried to reach masses and prompted a new wave of climate crisis dystopias in which the youth are addressed to think about their own future. We live in a world that has gradually become more frightening, and some people are finally listening to the warnings of scientists and activists about the condition of the world we live in. While this may sound like a good development, it in fact signals just how hopeless and scary things have turned. People are finally realizing that human irresponsibility and evil have brought about problems that appear to be insurmountable, like climate change, so conscientious writers are beginning to deal with these issues through various media, including literature and entertainment films. Dystopian literature is now carrying on the conversation that began on the streets of cities across the world through mass protests and filtered into the political platforms of enlightened politicians. Literature and film offer a safe space for discussing the horrible and the painful, and Young Adult novels invite their target audience to think critically about the way they live and the world they shape.

Young Adult fiction is an often neglected topic in education, even though dystopias written for the younger generation help readers to envision better alternatives to our present (Wolk 668), and they may especially be helpful in social justice education (Glasglow). Not accidentally, half of the material in this book discusses dystopian visions related to the theme of coming of age, as the monstrosity of the worlds they present really address the contemporary issues that young readers face on a day-to-day basis. These selected texts not only point out how the dangerous trends in our ways of living pose a continuous threat on the world and, consequently, on humanity but they also highlight, through the application of the monstrous, Cohen's important thesis that monster and creator are inseparable ("Monster" 20)—an idea that is at the core of eco-activism, placing emphasis on how man's behavior shapes his environment into a monster that might bring complete annihilation at any point. This is why one of the growing tendencies in dystopian literature is to monsterize the setting and link it with the system that controls the character's relation to the natural space (s)he inhabits. Such a thematic focus underlines the relationship between political power and environmental consciousness, pointing beyond the well-mapped dictatorship-studies in literature, which focus more on domestic politics in isolation as opposed to domestic politics having a global effect.

These dystopian stories, however, vary in types, and their paths to those better alternatives are imagined and presented very differently. By their use of monster metaphors, these works confirm their interest in what is human, and consequently address the importance of being humane in a world molded by inhumanity. These novels challenge the reader to imagine how to preserve his/her humanity in a world in which it is either more convenient or more expedient to relinquish humane feelings and connections. Is this accomplished by keeping a clear distance from monstrosity, observing a sharp borderline between the two forms of existence? Is it by embracing monsters because of the realization that monsters grow out of the human? Is it by rejecting humanity's monstrousness and placing hope in monsters who prove more humane than humans? These are interrelating questions, and the best kinds of monster fiction probe into these dilemmas, as my studies, I hope, demonstrate. In the past half a century, monsters have been considerably humanized, so novels and films reflect this change. Novels and films made for adults tend to focus solely on the problems and predict a horrific future for humanity unless the warnings of scientists are heeded. Young Adult dystopian novels, unlike most dystopian novels written for adults, do not discard hope (Sambell, "Presenting" 164) for the ability of the human race to not only survive but also thrive in difficult circumstances. These works, therefore, demonstrate that hope has become a relative concept, but an achievable one. For instance, in M.R. Carey's *The Girl with All the Gifts*, the future is hopeful only once the anthropocentric attitude to the world has been given up, and Patrick Ness's *Chaos Walking* trilogy ends on the strangely optimistic note of hybridization, a prerequisite for a peaceful co-existence with a world that we do not understand and that also calls for a vision beyond what anthropocentrism offers.

Such examples of the fantastic offer hope in the most disturbing notion of accepting and living with one's monstrosity, and this forces readers and audience members alike to realistically evaluate their own differences, which can be seen as monstrosities by other people. They call attention to the necessity to change perspective and attitude. I am convinced that one of the reasons why the zombie monster and other monsters are transformed in these texts, surprisingly, into a metaphor for hope, as in Carey's above-mentioned novel or in Daryl Gregory's *Raising Stony Mayhall*, is that art provides a spectacular tool connecting hope with disintegration but preserving the belief that people can evolve even at a time of decline and despair. The zombie who is capable of growth is the expression of our ability to survive and maybe even thrive in the chaos that we have created.

Young Adult dystopias foreground the idea of growing up in a frightening world, and they are therefore especially suitable for expressing the overall sentiment that defines the discussion on climate crisis: we must grow up because humanity needs to grow up. The works featuring young protagonists are not childish versions of the "serious" dystopias targeting an adult audience. They are reflections of the real fear that irresponsible, and in this sense childish people in power play hazardously with the future that the younger generation will have to live in. Young Adult dystopian fiction has become the genre that most dramatically corresponds to the reality that the news media is trying to make sense of at the moment: that young adult climate activists, Greta Thurnberg among them, act like adults while immature adults who have the power to make a change mock them and choose to ignore facts instead. The theme of childish adulthood is, therefore, one that indicates a dominant anxiety in our contemporary world, which is why I chose to include a study with this focus on HBO's *Westworld* as a concluding book chapter that analyzes the monstrous context for this subject matter.

The topic of immature adulthood is inherently connected to the themes of ignorance and irresponsibility. These two notions have grown to be the most frightening monsters in our world and have pushed us to the edge of apocalypse, as scientists keep warning us. Young Adult literature is preoccupied with the exploration of what the combination of these two character traits may bring about, and this is also why Frankenstein-themed novels and films designed for a young audience keep getting published in great numbers. I selected *Frankenstein*-inspired works of various kinds for this book so that they may demonstrate the variety in which they provide social criticism and reveal that not only charity but also responsibility begins at home and affects how we think about scientific inventions, power relations between genders, as well as the normative and the non-normative in all walks of life. All the selected works of this kind, from Jon Skovron's *Man Made Boy* and Sarah Maria Griffin's *Spare and Found Parts* through Theodora Goss's *The Extraordinary Adventures of the Athena Club* series to *Westworld* use monsters to teach us about responsibility and respect for the other.

Frankenstein-themed stories tend to provide clear morals about how far one may reach, warning us about the borderlines one should not transgress, but equally important are the stories that help their characters cross symbolic borders. These are stories in which monsters invite a psychoanalytic approach and reflect on the mental journey one undertakes in order to conquer new spaces in life. In this book, three chapters deal specifically with this topic, accentuating how monsters communicate about very different situations that demand a character to grow up. The "normal" scare that relates to the process of maturation, as shown in Neil Gaiman's *Coraline* and *The Graveyard Book,* or in the *Buffy* TV series and Stephenie Meyer's the *Twilight* saga may be juxtaposed with the trauma-induced fear that either forces one to grow up quickly and painfully, as in Siobhan Dowd and Patrick Ness's A *Monster Calls,* or prevents the character from integrating into the society of grown-ups, as in Seanan McGuire's *Wayward Children* series.

Whichever of the chosen works we examine, one thing becomes apparent: monsters embody problems that provoke a decision to be made by the characters who encounter them. Even when these works appear to be discussing a love affair that can never take place in real life, they still focus on the values or human attributes that people need to save the world: respect, responsibility, compassion, and hope. If we choose well from the huge gallery of bloody and terrifying monsters available on the book market and on screen, we may just learn enough from monsters to make this world a better, less monstrous place.

Chapter Notes

Introduction

1. See especially the essay anthology *The Evil Child in Literature, Film and Popular Culture* (2013) edited by Karen J. Renner and Renner's own monograph *Evil Children in the Popular Imagination* (2016). The appearance of the evil child character in popular culture is amazingly frequent: in the introduction to her monograph, Renner provides us her counts of films in which evil children appear: she identified about 600 such films "with almost 400 made in the new millennium" (Renner, *Evil Children* 1).

2. See Kevin Alexander Boon's elaboration on this point: "Several presumptions underlie the articulation of the monstrous: one, that distinctions exist between the natural and the unnatural; two, that these distinctions are clear and perceivable; three, that the natural is a standard established by some dominate design; four, that the human form is the privileged form within all that is natural; and five, that the human form includes elements not found in lower forms" ("Ontological" 33).

3. Seelinger Tites differentiates between two types of fiction that focus on maturation process: Bildungsroman, which she sees as the proper equivalent of the coming-of-age novel, where adulthood is the outcome of maturation; and Entwicklunsromane, or "novels of growth or development," in which the character does not mature into adulthood (*Disturbing* 9–10).

4. I use Young Adult in the sense Seelinger Trites does. She defined the Young Adult novel as "a book marketed for teenagers, as a subset of adolescent literature" ("Theories and Possibilities" 2).

5. In a similar vein, both Henry A. Giroux and Lawrence Grossberg claim that even in youth literature, adolescents are operated by the interests and fantasies of the adult world (Giroux 35; Grossberg 176), much the same way as we can see in children's literature in which childhood, argues Perry Nodelman, is "clearly an adult fantasy" (225).

Chapter 1

1. Cf. especially Cohen's Thesis VI of his "Monster Culture (Seven Theses)" (16–20).

2. The vampire romance has evolved from Gothic fiction, which was seen as "dominated by women—written by women; read by women; and choosing as its central figure a young girl, the Gothic heroine" (Wolff 207).

3. Limpár, Ildikó. "Masculinity, Visibility and the Vampire Literary Tradition in *What We Do in the Shadows*." *Journal for the Fantastic in the Arts*, vol. 29. no. 2. 2018, pp. 266–288. p 269.

4. This is the idea that the mockumentary *What We Do in the Shadows* plays with when the vampire Viago finally reunites with his old love, Katherine. "Katherine looks ninety-six, but Viago, who has been a vampire for three and a half centuries, looks young. Physical appearance thus points to incompatibility, but it hides the real perversity of the relationship, which is that it is Viago who is the 'cradle-snatcher' (*Shadows*) and not

Katherine, as might be one's first impression" (Limpár 274).

5. See Julia Kristeva's "Approaching Abjection," in which she explicates abjection and gives several examples to demonstrate that the abject, "the jettisoned object, is radically excluded and draws me toward the place where meaning collapses" (2). In order to live in a meaningful world, the abject is systematically rejected and excluded, allowing the self to function normally, free from "what disturbs identity, system, order. What does not respect borders, positions, rules" (4).

6. See Kristeva's explanation on the difference between uncanniness and abject: "Essentially different from 'uncanniness,' more violent, too, abjection is elaborated through a failure to recognize its kin; nothing is familiar, not even the shadow of a memory" (5). This is the reason why the abject must be expelled, while what is uncanny may be processed with other psychological strategies.

7. See, for instance, Catherine Coker's article, in which she argues about a positive reading of Bella's choices, but at the end tries to highlight similarities between the female protagonists' choices without considering the factors that make a difference in those choices. "Is the protagonist always going to prefer a supernatural love interest to a human love interest for multiple reasons, none of them pure? Bella: Yes. Buffy: Yes" (Coker par. 35). In a similar fashion, Rhonda Nicol, whose article investigates how contemporary feminism is portrayed by the two series in question, conflates the motives behind Buffy's and Bella's death wish when she cites Buffy's famous line to Angel, "When you kiss me, I want to die," and concludes that "Bella, too, seems to subscribe to this view of romance; she indicates her willingness to risk her life to be with Edward at least as many times as he warns her that he's a danger to her" (Nicol 118).

8. Naomi Zack's discussion of Bella's relation to feminism is very thought-provoking in this respect, as she directly links the feminine image Bella represents with Sarah Palin's elitist representation of power that relies on the resurrected, old-fashioned concept of the woman, which consists of "practicing heterosexuality in the form of fulfilled romantic love and fertility; looking good according to the prevailing beauty norms of consumer culture; and attaining power in the world as it is, rather than the world as it should be" (Zack 125).

9. Meyer has often been criticized for promoting anti-feminism through Bella, who appears to conform to the ideology of "an old-fashioned world where women were seen as empty conduits of masculine desire and valued for their propensity to self-sacrifice alone" (Mann 134). Media responses as well as critical studies have recurrently pointed out the abusive nature of the relationships that the *Twilight* saga presents and have thus implied that Meyer propagates the image of the submissive woman, a far cry from a feminist ideal. (See, for instance, Housel, Young, McCullough, Goodfriend, Kar3ning.)

10. "In my own *opinion* (key word), the foundation of feminism is this: being able to choose. The core of anti-feminism is, conversely, telling a woman she can't do something solely because she's a woman—taking any choice away from her specifically because of her gender. ... One of the weird things about modern feminism is that some feminists seem to be putting their own limits on women's choices. That feels backward to me. It's as if you can't choose a family on your own terms and still be considered a strong woman. How is that empowering? Are there rules about if, when, and how we love or marry and if, when, and how we have kids? Are there jobs we can and can't have in order to be a 'real' feminist? To me, those limitations seem anti-feminist in basic principle" (Meyer qtd in Fetters).

11. In her book chapter comparing the Harry Potter series with the Buffy narrative, Rhonda V. Wilcox also underlines the importance of friends in the two heroes' lives, calling them their strength (75).

12. See Goebel's comment on that: "When individuation is defined through material possessions, those with wealth are the only ones who can truly illustrate originality. This is evidenced in the individualized special powers designated to the vampires compared with

the homogenized powers of the Quileute werewolves" (176).

13. Crofts provides a long (yet admittedly incomplete) list of episodes that use faërian drama to provide context for the episode she focuses on (34).

Chapter 2

1. On the relation between zombies and biopolitics, see Eugene Thacker's chapter "Nekros; or, The Poetics of Biopolitics" in *Zombie Theory: A Reader*, edited by Sarah Juliet Lauro (University of Minnesota Press, 2017. pp. 361–80).

2. In fact, the emergence of the sympathetic zombie is not a very late development, but simultaneous with the appearance of I-vampires, as the Marvel comic book *Tales of the Zombie* that ran from 1973 to 1975 testifies (Abbott 162), but it needed the boosting effect of the vampire renaissance to resurge as a significant trend in zombie fiction and film.

3. L.J. Davis explains his claim in detail:

> Melanie is discursively constituted as unwanted waste and expendable. Yet, her hybrid human-hungry status complicates her ontological value as both disease and cure, as both sacrificed and saved. Moreover, her pre-pubescent state as an ostensibly human child gives monstrous presence to the forgotten residue of the aborted fetal tissue. That is, Melanie is the abortion that remained alive and grew up. She represents the potential that was lost in the abortive procedure. She is what would have been. Moreover, her act of eating her way out of her mother's womb gives the potential abortion the will and the ability to choose life over death [*Enforcing* 32].

4. Miss Justineau's acceptance of her fate thus echoes the protagonist Robert Neville's attitude to his death at the end of Richard Matheson's *I Am Legend* (1954), an early example that fuses the modern vampire narrative with the pandemic narrative, which makes it comparable with Carey's zombie novel. (It is not by chance that the latest film adaptation of Matheson's novel from 2007 presents the vampires very similar to how zombies are traditionally presented on the screen: as speechless hordes.) As Vera Benczik explains, Neville embraces his death sentence because of his sense of guilt when "he finally readily submits to the punishment for having murdered what he now perceives to be human beings" (30, 209).

Chapter 3

1. On the relationship between coming of age and morality, cf. Stephen T. Asma: "in order to grow up one must negate one's urge to live forever" (189).

2. The motto of the American science fiction TV series *Start Trek*.

3. Cf. Cohen's observation about the monster embodying both fear and desire: "The monstrous lurks somewhere in that ambiguous, primal space between fear and attraction, close to the heart of what Kristeva calls 'abjection'" (19).

4. Cf. the definition of disability as given by Anna Kérchy and Andrea Zittlau: "disability denotes the loss or limitation of opportunities to take part in society on an equal level with others due to social and environmental barriers" (1 N.2).

5. Cf. Adam's words: "We joked about how he would carry me over the threshold" (Skovron 192).

6. To sell the manuscript, the writer's name was not revealed by Percy Shelley, who contacted several publishers to find a way to get his wife's novel published. While Percy Shelley was supportive and never claimed Mary's novel as his own, publishing the manuscript anonymously must have been part of the marketing strategy, as putting a female author's name on the front cover may have discouraged a lot of people from reading the novel, as the infamous review in the April 1818 issue of *The British Critic* testifies. The reviewer's sexism is overt: "The writer of [*Frankenstein*] is, we understand, a female; this is an aggravation of that which is the prevailing fault of the novel; but if our authoress can forget the gentleness of her sex, it is no reason why we should; and we shall therefore dismiss the novel without further comment." Other reviewers better hid their sexism, but, for instance, Walter Scott's review in *Blackwood's Edinburgh Magazine* on the

anonymous work claims that "it is said to be written by Mr. Percy Bysshe Shelley." This comment also reveals a mentality that held men superior to women and thus it was assumed that the already acclaimed writer Percy Shelley could write a good novel, while his wife was unlikely to have done so.

7. For a list of important such works, please consult Karen Coats and Farran Norris Sands's book chapter "Growing Up Frankenstein: Adaptations for Young Readers."

Chapter 4

1. In Machen's novella, this grandmother is Mary, who becomes pregnant right after the successful operation that allows her to see the god Pan, suggesting that it is the god who fathers Mary's daughter of supernatural abilities. In Goss's universe, it is Dr. Raymond who fathers Helen, so he is directly responsible for the monsterization of all the three women not only as a scientist but also as a husband/father/grandfather since the mesmerizing abilities turn out to be inheritable.

2. I focus my study on the first volume, but of course the two ladies who join the Athena Club only in the third book also comply with Cohen's definition of the monster ("Monster"). I detail the monstrosity of the vampire in Chapter 1. Lydia represents the borderline between what is human and supernatural, a coexistence with the energy-made world that surpasses what humans are capable of, manifesting the desire of having superpower as well as the fear of the destruction such a power might bring to humanity as well as the one who possesses it.

3. The original representation of women working through a detective case may be Susan Glaspell's Trifles, a play in which women solve a murder case while the men look for "clues" and comment that the women are occupied by trifles. What the men do not understand is that the main clue to the murder mystery lies in the trifling evidence of a dead canary's corpse hidden in a woman's sewing basket. The men have serious business, but the women know how women think and behave. When the women find the dead bird, they figure out the reason why Mrs. Wright may have killed her husband, but they can easily hide the information, as they are not expected to be cleverer than the men who fail to solve the case. In Goss's trilogy the combination of the same feminine skills and female solidarity is continuously displayed.

4. July 1, 2019.

5. Conf. L.J. Davis, *Enforcing* 24.

6. As Robinson Meyer points out in his brief article in *The Atlantic*, the writing itself is present only on the Hunt-Lenox Globe. However, it is also apparent from the article that various maps did use such a warning about little known and thus possibly dangerous areas, as beasts that were associated with those regions were drawn into the maps of such territories.

7. See the etymology of the word monster, having its root in the Latin base word monēre (to warn) and monstrare (to demonstrate).

Chapter 5

1. Gaiman acknowledges, for instance, the influence of *The Jungle Book* by Rudyard Kipling (Motoko). There it is not monsters but wild beasts, usually seen as threats by people, who undertake the parenting tasks of a small boy.

2. In the *Encyclopedia of Fantasy*, John Clute lists the most prominent types of transitions that are metaphorically presented in portal fantasies, including the transition from a prior state of growth ... into empowered adulthood."

3. Cf. "Perhaps the easiest way to subvert the portal fantasy is to reverse the direction of travel" (Mendelsohn 49).

4. In his essay on Gaiman's postmodern narrative strategy, Sandor Klapcsik does not discuss *The Graveyard Book*, but this novel also demonstrates the ironical perspectives and the "double-edged" nature of liminal fantasy that Klapcsik explores in Gaiman's selected works.

5. Andrew Marwell: "To His Coy Mistress," l. 31.

6. Mónika Rusvai also makes use of Cohen's "Monster Culture," and combines it with Lacan's theory on the symbolic

father to interpret Silas both as a monster and a father.

7. The monster Sleer provides a curious contrast to Silas, guarding treasures for its mysterious Master. As opposed to Silas, the Sleer is indeed frightening, for we are incapable of identifying its borders. The Sleer may be guarding the borders between time and timelessness as well as the known and the unknown (which is a kind of nonexistence).

8. "a familiar shadow swirled beneath the street lamps ... and a flutter of night-black velvet resolved itself into a man-shape" (Gaiman, *The Graveyard* 62).

9. Gaiman carefully selected the names for the parental substitutes, as well. Derived from the Latin *lupus*, meaning wolf, Miss Lupescu's name hints at her lycanthropy (the same way Remus Lupin's name suggests his condition). Silas, on the other hand, seems to have received his name from the most famous literary character with this name: the eponymous character uncle Silas of J. Sheridan in Le Fanu's Gothic mystery novel (1899). In Le Fanu's novel, uncle Silas is indeed a monstrous, evil relative, who attempts to murder the girl trusted to his guardianship. By naming his vampire character after Le Fanu's Silas, Gaiman subverts the monstrosity related to the name: in the 19th century novel, Silas is apparently a reformed Christian with a dark past, but it turns out that his moral transformation is just pretense. Gaiman's Silas, in contrast, is indeed a monster who used to be evil but transformed into a guardian of the world. This subverts the old notion that a monster is evil by definition with the use of this intertextual reference, symbolically turning an old, evil monster (Le Fanu's Silas) into a good monster.

Another interesting link between the two Silas characters is related to the importance of perspective and seeing the world as much more than what is perceivable at first sight. It appears that Gaiman's concept of the graveyard as a home relies on the realization that the protagonist makes at the end of *Uncle Silas*: "This world is a parable—the habitation of symbols—the phantoms of spiritual things immortal shown in material shape. May the blessed second-sight be mine—to recognize under these beautiful forms of earth the angels who wear them; for I am sure we may walk with them if we will, and hear them speak!"

10. Michael Howarth's reading of *Coraline*, for instance, shows how Coraline's maturation process corresponds to "Erikson's fourth stage of psychosocial development" that school children usually go through (76).

11. Critics of the text tend to have a general consensus that "the simulacra beyond the brick wall and what happens there signify as sites and manifestations of unconscious anxieties and desires which mark Coraline's stage in life" (Müller). This psychological approach is the main line in *Coraline*-criticism: Karen Coats focuses on the Gothic motifs within this context ("Between"), Rudd delivers a Freudian interpretation, examining aspects of the uncanny, Gooding explores especially the manifestations of the Oedipal-complex, Parsons, Sawers and McInally detail Coraline's gendered experience, while Müller's primary interest resides in the mother figure.

12. This clever word play comes from the title of David Rudd's article "An Eye for an I: Neil Gaiman's *Coraline* and Questions of Identity," in which Rudd argues that "the other mother offers to replace Coraline's eye with her own I" (163).

13. "If eyes are the windows to the soul, and it is clear that Other Mother can see physical objects, then perhaps the lack of eyes is symbolic of an inability to see the 'soul'—the true self" (Kotanko 177).

14. I use the term "otherworld" as defined in *The Encyclopedia of Fantasy* (see Clute "Otherworld).

15. Rudd applies a different approach to reading Coraline's drawn MIST: stressing that the girl is in fact "the lonely I," he also notes the possible pun on the word mist that may be read as missed, thus Coraline would be the I that is "not missed (i.e. she is overlooked)." In harmony with this interpretation, Rudd also notes that the arrangement of the letters show the I as "only existing in terms of its relationship with other signifiers" (160).

16. That mirroring will be the basis of how we should understand the relationship between the real and the imaginary space is stated at the onset of the story,

as Vivienne Müller emphasizes. When Coraline inquires about what the flat beyond the wall may be like, her mother's answer establishes a parallel between this invisible, unknown space and their new flat, which was empty before they have moved in. This likeness also hints at the peculiarity of the otherworld as a home, which implies that what it may contain is dependent on the character of the person who occupies its rooms—and foreshadows the specific mirroring of Coraline's family and their home.

17. It may be worth mentioning that Shakespeare's *Macbeth* has another relevance in interpreting Coraline's uncanny experience. Although Müller does not connect her observation to the recited Macbethian line in *Coraline*, she does present an interesting chain of thoughts on the interpretation of the word beldam, whereby she connects the Other Mother to Lady Macbeth: "The word both outside and within the context of Gaiman's novel, is a misogynistic play on the French words *belle* and *dame* meaning beautiful woman. The masculine adjective *bel* is used instead of *belle* implying that women who are 'unsexed' to use Lady Macbeth's term, or who assume masculine god-like powers are unnatural." The dagger that Macbeth hallucinates links that scene to the themes of masculine power, which manifests in the phallic symbol of the weapon, and points to the act that is induced by Lady Macbeth, who controls her husband just as the Other Mother exercises her power over the Other Father.

18. On the variations concerning the ending, see George 74–8.

19. That Mr. Bobo is such a complex resurfacing of the Piper archetype despite his relatively reduced textual space in *Coraline* is hardly accidental, as Gaiman seems to be fascinated by the mythical rat creature: in *Neverwhere*, Gaiman wrote about a rat community with human servants, the Rat-Speakers, as well as a master rat, symbolically placing the rats' space in "London Below," an uncanny London.

20. "*Coraline* is centrally concerned with how one negotiates one's place in the world; how one is recognized in one's own right rather than being either ignored on the one hand, or stifled on the other" (Rudd 160).

21. Reading both novels further underscores the implication that the monster must be interpreted in context: the vampire-like characters—Silas and the Other Mother—have very different connotations and specific roles in the texts, proving that even the vampire, broadly referring to one type of monster, is the result of the constructing mind, and thus may have considerably divergent manifestations.

Chapter 6

1. All italic letters appearing in quotations are original.

2. Freud, Sigmund. *The Interpretation of Dreams. The Complete and Definitive text*, edited and translated by James Strachey. Basic Books, 2010.

3. Giskin Day provides a thorough reading of *A Monster Calls* based on the Kübler-Ross stages of grief—an influential model, even though an incorrect one, warns Carlin (761).

4. The novel does not use the word chemotherapy, but the beneficial effects of paclitaxel, produced from yew tree bark and used in cancer therapy, have been known since 1955. Research connected to the use of Taxol, the cancer chemotherapy drug with paclitaxel, came to the foreground in the late 1980s, and it still "remains one of the best plant-based cancer treatments available" (National Cancer Institute).

5. As Jeff Wise explains, "When we find ourselves under intense pressure, fear unleashes reserves of energy that normally remain inaccessible. With the sympathetic nervous system and the hypothalamic-pituitary-adrenal (HPA) axis fully activated, our bodies and brains can utilize their resources so fully that we become, in effect, superhuman" (Chapter Two "Superhuman").

6. As Anne Williams explains, "In Gothic, fragments of language often serve ambiguously to further the plot—in letters (lost, stolen, buried); in mysterious warnings, prophecies, oaths, and curses; in lost wills and lost marriage lines. Such fragments may be misinterpreted (often

because they are removed from the original context), and frequently deceive or betray the interpreter" (67).

7. Maryanne Wolf's concepts that Nikolajevna adopts in her monograph (Nikolajeva 15).

8. Cf. *"The yew is a healing tree,* the monster said. *It is the form I choose most to walk in"* (Ness, *A Monster* 164).

Chapter 7

1. We also learn that there are other homes for wayward children, and they give temporary home for those who want to forget their experience and not to reconnect with it by finding the secret world again.

2. Kade is an exception, as he was mistakenly kidnapped.

3. The rhyme and the illustration are on page 37 in the survived 1907 publication created by William Francis Prideaux and are in the public domain via The Internet Archive.

4. Cf. "(Had she been able to articulate how she felt about her home life, had she been able to tell an adult, Jillian might have been surprised by the way things could change. But ah, if she had done that, she and her sister would never have become the bundle of resentments and contradictions necessary to summon a door to the Moors. Every choice feeds every choice that comes after, whether we want those choices or no)" (McGuire, *Down* 63).

5. The narration makes this point very explicitly, underlining that being practical and doing difficult, messy jobs is not a question of gender: "She was not denying her femininity by wearing men's clothing; rather, she was protecting it from caustic chemicals and other, less mundane compounds" (McGuire, *Down* 126).

6. As early as 1931, Ernest Jones already connects vampirism with sexual perversion in his psychoanalytical study *On the Nightmare.* This article, together with Christopher Bentley's 1972 essay titled "The Monster in the Bedroom: Sexual Symbolism in Bram Stoker's *Dracula*," have influenced many scholars exploring this theme. For instance, Jean Lorrah claims that the vampire's act of bloodsucking should be read as "an obvious symbol for rape" (31), and Ken Gelder in his *Reading the Vampire* examines how the vampire is linked with sexuality and perversion (65–80).

7. The present chapter is written after the publication of the fourth part in this not yet closed series.

8. Olsson et al. provides a detailed table of individual-level, family-level, and social environment-level resources that can promote resilience in adolescents supplied with a list of select authors that have written on these factors (5–6). It is clear that the wayward children, in general, lack "supportive families which should provide parental warmth, encouragement, assistance, cohesion and care within the family, close relationship with a caring adult, and belief in the child" (5).

Chapter 8

1. Lewis, R.W.B. *The American Adam: Innocence, Tragedy, and Tradition in the Nineteenth Century.* University of Chicago Press, 1959.

2. Adrienne Kertzer specifically notes how Ness's approach to presenting trauma differs from the general trend that characterizes Young Adult literature: while writers of realist historical fiction "focus their narrative energy upon trauma as an individual psychological disorder," Ness differentiates between individual and cultural trauma, and also explores how collective trauma effects a community (12).

3. See, for instance, Leo Marx (34–72), Meredith Skura (69) and Leslie Fiedler (Frei 31).

4. From a certain perspective, what happens on New World peculiarly reverberates the events related in one of the most ancient myths, that of the Minotaur. As Hourihan details, the conflict of the myth may be seen as the political rivalry between the ancient Minoan kingdom and the young city, Athens. The latter is represented by Theseus, while the former is embodied by the Minotaur. However, on a more symbolic level, the hybrid, monstrous Minotaur stands for transgressing natural laws (as he is born from the sexual encounter between a

bull and a human queen). "In killing the Minotaur, Theseus is therefore simultaneously asserting the autonomy of Athens, the dominance of humanity over nature and the power of reason to control irrational passions and fears" (Hourihan 109). The transgression is a female sin in this myth, and the political fight is directed against the matriarchy. In a similar fashion, Mayor Prentiss directs his anger and power against both groups of beings who benefit from the planet's natural environment: the Spackle, who rely on the Noise-germ in their communication, and the women, who threaten patriarchal hegemony due to their partial resistance to the germ. The mayor thus becomes very similar to Theseus, who may not only be seen as a hero but also "an oppressor intent upon destroying the indigenous, female-centered culture of the Minoans" (Hourihan 109). In both cases, the repressed anxiety is linked to the fear of hybridity and what it stands for: an ultimate transgression that threatens human existence.

5. Naseeb Shaheen notes that although there is no English Bible that uses the word "bigger" instead of "greater," the reference is still Biblical, and the change of vocabulary serves the purpose of demonstrating Caliban's primitive language (741–42).

6. As the mayor explains to Todd, "David will learn what real courage looks like…. "He will learn what it's like to act with honor, what it's like to act like a real man. What it's like, in short, to act like you, Todd Hewitt" (Ness, *The Ask* 61–2).

7. The mute Spackle, whose bodies are uncanny versions of the human body, raise associations with the disabled, allowing the reader to interpret the fantastic, imagined Other very directly as otherness present in contemporary society. This linkage becomes especially significant when volume three presents the Sky as a leader who alone understands diversity and the necessity for a harmonious co-existence with those who are different and act wrongly often out of fear and due to the lack of sufficient knowledge.

8. Cf. The mayor's question: "So you agree we're not that different, she and I?" (Ness, *The Ask* 137).

9. Cf. Bettina Bildhauer on the monstrous nature of menstrual blood, noted already by Pliny (Bildhauer 204) and on scribes' practice of writing *monstrum* instead of *menstrum* (205).

10. An important subcategory of these YA novels is formed by those narratives in which "a female protagonist's awakening is catalyzed by her experiences within nature and that these experiences shape nature into a place ideal for claiming her agency" McDonough and Wagner (157). For a detailed discussion of this motif, see McDonough, Megan, and Katherine A. Wagner. "Rebellious Natures: The Role of Nature in Young Adult Dystopian Female Protagonists' Awakenings and Agency." *Female Rebellion in Young Adult Dystopian Fiction*, edited by Sara Kay Day, Miranda A. Green-Barteet and Amy L. Montz. Ashgate, 2014. pp. 157–170.

Chapter 9

1. This book chapter is the completed version of my article that first appeared as Limpár, Ildikó. "GMO New World Garden: The Arena as Monster in Collins's The Hunger Games Trilogy." *TOPOS: Journal of Space and Humanities*, vol. V, no. 1, edited by Éva Bús and Andrea F. Szabó, 2016, pp. 93–103.

2. The original trilogy, comprised of *The Hunger Games*, *Catching Fire*, and *Mockingjay*, was completed by *The Ballad of Songbirds and Snakes*, a prequel published in 2020. In this essay I discuss the original trilogy and hence I use the term trilogy to refer to these novels. I only tangentially make references to the prequel.

3. The vampiric aspects of Snow's image in *The Hunger Games* trilogy correspond to the president's method of governing Panem's people. His smell of blood reveals his bloody dictatorship that demands the consummation of blood, which the annual Hunger Games epitomizes. The cult of fashion, youth, and body perfection in the Capitol links Snow and the Capitol characters to the discourse of artificiality and monstrosity, as they embody the Other for Katniss with their freakish appearance and inhuman(e) behavior. Furthermore, Snow's power to transform humans to his own

monstrous image, and very importantly, the act of manipulation, one significant motif of which is masking the bloody with the pleasant, also support the construction of Panem's president as a vampire in the reader's imagination. All of these aspects of Snow's character are indicated in Katniss's first personal encounter with the dictator, where the most important impression he gives comes via the smell—the smell of blood and roses. For a more detailed study on President's Snow as an alluded vampire monster, see Limpár, Ildikó. "Smell of Roses and Blood: The Vampire Empire of The Hunger Games trilogy." *Monsters and the Monstrous* vol. 4, no. 2, Winter 2014, pp. 15–24.

4. To read more about the various implications and effects of the media broadcasting the Hunger Games, see Limpár, Ildikó. "Arena on the Screen: Heterotopia and Theatricality in The Hunger Games Trilogy." *Displacing the Anxieties of Our World: Spaces of the Imagination*, edited by Ildikó Limpár. Cambridge Scholar Publishing, 2017. 177–199.

5. This phenomenon in contemporary American culture is noted by Stephen T. Asma, who interprets the dehumanizing effect of luxury and consumption as a zombie-like existence (241).

6. Victoria Flanagan emphasizes especially the role of surveillance (also dependent on technology) in this respect (141–142).

7. In the prequel, Collins elaborates the metaphorical connection between Snow and snakes and explains in detail how the president's rise to leadership roots in his experience with snake mutts engineered in the Capitol's experimental laboratory.

8. The apple is important in Katniss's imagination, she compares objects to apples and remembers the apple tree in Peeta's garden, which makes that place a withered, weak image of an Eden, but still an Eden within the poverty-stricken District 12 (Collins, *The Hunger* 28). But Collins also foregrounds the apple when in the private session with the Gamemakers Katniss sends an arrow through an apple that is in a roast pig's mouth to call attention to herself (97). Taking the apple this way challenges the authorities in the Capitol, which is an act reminiscent of Eve's defying God's authority, but here Katniss actually challenges a society of people aligned with the Serpent—President Snow, who has a rich serpent imagery in the trilogy. Later in the Games apples are given an important role again: Katniss manages to blow up the other tributes' food supplies by freeing a bag of apples to start a series of explosion (210). The apple is a recurrent image connected to the fight to survive, a metaphor connected to death and life questions; and in the end the bag of apple brings destruction to the camp that Cato and his allies build at the cost of other tributes' death. Metaphorically speaking, *The Hunger Games* accentuates that those who actually bite into the apple grown on the Tree of Knowledge in Panem—those who accept the Serpent's temptation—will be expelled from Paradise for good and die a real or a moral death.

Chapter 10

1. Cf. Judith Halberstam's claim that *Frankenstein* "presents itself not as the making of a monster but as the making of a human. In what ways does the monster construct Frankenstein, in other words? Who actually builds whom and who destroys whom?" (32).

2. The City upon a Hill is a phrase derived from Jesus' parable of Salt and Light (Matthew 5:14), cited by John Winthrop to the first Massachusetts Bay colonists before their departure to the New World, and often used in modern U.S. politics to indicate the United States of America's moral firmness and her role in the world to provide hope and help for others.

3. The information on the structure of the tower comes from Kim Renfro's article.

4. The amusement park provides access to a fantasy that is promised by western movies, most notably by TNT (Turner Network Television) westerns, which "reinforce traditional, western conceptions of masculinity by offering viewers fictional, male-dominated worlds where men can be men" (Pierson 59) and where the male and female characters are assigned "mythically well-defined gender roles" (60).

5. This experience evokes a well-designed theatrical performance with clearly defined roles; it is no wonder that "in *Westworld*, the world-as-stage metaphor is pushed, by means of science fiction technology, to an entirely new level. The series literally envisions life as a play and the world as a theatre" (Winckler 175).

6. See also Asma's comment "Films like *American Psycho* and *Donnie Darko* (2001) [that] explore the idea that American culture itself is the source of horror," presenting American individualism "like a form of selfish infantilism" (241). *Westworld* presents a similarly horrifying place, in which infantilism does not exclude but, in fact, manifests in utter violence and perversion.

7. Cf. what Ray White writes about B western movies: "these movies seem to suggest that Americans believe that under the right conditions it is acceptable to violate the law to achieve justice" (149).

8. In the tower, the same abjecting function is assigned to the nudity of the androids. Even when the work related to the host in the labs does not demand its nudity, the host is deprived of its clothing to remind the employees in Delos that they work with machines and not humans. The androids' naked bodies on the tables are reminiscent of dead bodies on the morgue's slab. Bareness objectifies the hosts, and it poses, at the same time, a psychological test to the workers: whoever is bothered by—or excited by—the spectacle of the naked android body is not suitable for the job. This working condition indicates that it is not the clothes that provide the difference between the two groups of employees; the real difference between humans and androids is consciousness—a quality invisible on the outside.

9. A curious anomaly concerning the reflections on the mirrors when Bernard questions a host may be either an error on the part of the producers or a message using a moving reflection when Bernard practically makes no movement. If this was done on purpose, the reflections on the glass may hint at the fact that it is Arnold talking to the host, and not Bernard (mjb22 in youtubehead).

10. On the interpretation of dream in *Westworld* in this context, see Kelly Bulkeley's brief, but to the point article "Dreaming in 'Westworld.'"

11. This ontological dilemma is dissected in an analysis on one of the fundamental science fiction texts of this kind, Philip K. Dick's *Do Androids Dream of Electric Sheep?* by Tamás Bényei (219–20).

Works Cited

Abbott, Stacey. *Undead Apocalypse: Vampires and Zombies in the Twenty-first Century*. Edinburgh University Press, 2016.

Agamben, Giorgio. *Homor Sacer: Sovereign Power and Bare Life*. Translated by Daniel Heller-Roazen. Meridian: Crossing Aesthetics. Stanford University Press, 1998.

———. *State of Exception*, translated by Kevin Attell. Chicago University Press, 2005.

Aldiss, Brian W. *The Detached Retina: Aspects of SF and Fantasy*. Liverpool Science Fiction Texts & Studies. Liverpool University Press, 1995.

"Amends." *Buffy the Vampire Slayer: The Complete Third Season on DVD*, season 3, Episode 4, written and directed by Joss Whedon, Twentieth Century Fox Home Entertainment, 2002.

Ames, Melissa. "Engaging "Apolitical" Adolescents: Analyzing the Popularity and Educational Potential of Dystopian Literature Post-9/11." *The High School Journal*, vol. 97, no. 1, 2013, pp. 3–20.

Anatol, Giselle Lisa, editor. *Bringing Light to Twilight: Perspectives on a Pop Culture*. Palgrave Macmillan US, 2011.

Anders, Charlie Jane. "Holy Crap, *The Girl With All the Gifts* Will Blow Your Mind." *i09*. Gizmodo, July 1, 2014.

Asma, Stephen T. *On Monsters: An Unnatural History of Our Worst Fears*. Oxford University Press, 2011.

Attebery, Brian. Introduction. *Stories about Stories: Fantasy and the Remaking of Myth*. Oxford University Press, 2014.

Auerbach, Nina. *Our Vampires, Ourselves*. University of Chicago Press, 1995.

Babaee, Ruzbeh, Sue Yen Lee, and Siamak Babaee. "Ecocritical Survival through Psychological Defense Mechanisms in M.R. Carey's *The Girl with All the Gifts*." *MOSF Science Fiction Journal*, vol.1, no.2, 2016, pp. 47–55.

Baker, Carissa Ann. 'Outside the Steam: The Construction of Relationship to Panem's Nature." Garriott, Jones and Tyler, pp. 198–219.

Basford, Kathleen. *The Green Man*. Boydell and Brewer, 1998.

Battey, Chris. "Review: Down Among the Sticks and Bones by Seanan McGuire." *Pyrlogos*, June 25, 2018. Blog.

"Beauty and the Beasts." *Buffy the Vampire Slayer: The Complete Third Season on DVD*, season 3, Episode 4, written by Marti Noxon, directed by James Whitmore, Jr., Twentieth Century Fox Home Entertainment, 2002.

Becher, Dominik. "Neil Gaiman's Ghost Children." *Ghosts—or the (Nearly) Invisible: Spectral Phenomena in Literature and the Media*, edited by Maria Fleischhack and Elmar Schenkel, Peter Lang, 2016, pp. 91–105.

Benczik, Vera. "The City in Ruins: Post-9/11 Representations of Cataclysmic New York on Film." *Utopian Horizons: Ideology, Politics, Literature*, edited by Zsolt Cziganyik. CEU Press, 2017, pp. 199–216.

Bentley, Christopher. "The Monster in the Bedroom: Sexual Symbolism in Bram Stoker's *Dracula*.' *Dracula: The Vampire and the Critics*. Studies in Speculative Fiction 19, edited by Margaret L. Carter. UMI Research Press, 1988, pp. 25–34.

Bényei, Tamás. "Az utolsó krimi." [The Ultimate Crime Story.] Philip K. Dick:

Álmodnak-e az androidok elektronikus bárányokkal?. [*Do Androids Dream of Electric Sheep?*] Agave könyvek, 2015. 207–25.

Bernstein, Susan David. *Confessional Subjects: Revelations of Gender and Power in Victorian Literature and Culture*. Political Science 62. University of North Carolina Press, 1997.

Berresford Ellis, Peter. *Dictionary of Celtic Mythology*. ABC-CLIO, 1992.

Bildhauer, Bettina. "Blood, Jews and Monsters in Medieval Culture." Weinstock pp. 192–210.

Bishop, Kyle William. *The Rise and Fall (and Rise) of the Walking Dead in Popular Culture*. McFarland, 2010.

———. "Teaching Zombies, Developing Students: Pedagogical Success in *The Girl with All the Gifts*." *The Written Dead: Essays on the Literary Zombie*, Bishop and Tenga, pp. 167–82.

Bishop, Kyle William, and Angela Tenga, editors. *The Written Dead: Essays on the Literary Zombie*, McFarland, 2017.

Boon, Kevin Alexander. "And the Dead Shall Rise." (Part Introduction). *Better Off Dead: The Evolution of the Zombie as Post-Human*, edited by Deborah Christie and Sarah Juliet Lauro. Fordham University Press, 2011, pp. 5–8.

———. "Ontological Anxiety Made Flesh: The Zombie in Literature, Film and Culture." Niall Scott, pp. 33–43.

Boorstin, Daniel. 1972. *The Americans: The Democratic Experience*, Kindle ed., Rosetta Books, 2002.

Borderlands History Team. "Westworld and the Frontier Imaginary." *Borderlands History*. December 8, 2016.

Bradford, Clare, Kerry Mallan, John Stephens, and Robyn McCallum. *New World Orders in Contemporary Children's Literature: Utopian Transformations*. Palgrave Macmillan, 2008.

Braidotti, Rosi. *The Posthuman*. Polity, 2013.

Branagh, Kenneth. Dir. *Marry Shelley's Frankenstein*. TriStar Pictures, 1994.

The British Critic. [Review of Frankenstein.] *The British Critic*, N.S., 9 (April 1818): 432–38; also rpt. In *The Port Folio* [Philadelphia] 6 (September 1818): 200–07. *Romantic Circles*. (The Mary Wollstonecraft Shelley Chronology & Resource Site. Reviews.)

Buckley, Chloe. "Gothic and the Child Reader, 1850–Present." *The Gothic World*, edited by Glennis Byron and Dale Townshend. Routledge, 2014.

Bulkeley, Kelly. "Dreaming in 'Westworld.'" *Huffpost*. March 22, 2017.

Burke, Brianna. "The Great American Love Affair: Indians in the *Twilight* Saga." *Anatol*, pp. 207–19.

Burnham, Karen. "Review: *Raising Stony Mayhall* by Daryl Gregory." *SF Signal*. July 12, 2011.

Butler, Judith. *Bodies That Matter: On Discursive Limits of "Sex."* Routledge, 1993.

———. *Gender Trouble*. Routledge, 1990.

Carey, M.R. *The Girl with All the Gifts*. Orbit, 2014.

Carlin, Nathan. "A Psychoanalytic Reading of *A Monster Calls*: Biblical Congruencies and Theological Implications." *Pastoral Psychology* vol. 66, no. 6, June 2017, pp. 1–19.

Carroll, Noël. "The Nature of Horror." *The Journal of Aesthetics and Art Criticism*, vol. 46, no. (Autumn, 1987), pp. 51–59.

Cavanagh, Natali. "Toxicity in Themes of Control: An Analysis of the Anglo-Western Cancer Rhetoric in *A Monster Calls*." *Digital Literature Review*, vol. 4, 2017, pp. 1–13.

Chemers, Michael M. *Staging Stigma: A Critical Examination of the American Freak Show*. Palgrave MacMillan, 2008.

"Chestnut." *Westworld*, season 1, episode 2. HBO Entertainment, October 7, 2016.

Claridge, Laura P. "Parent-Child relationship in Frankenstein: A Search for Communion." *Studies in the Novel*, vol. 17, no. 1, spring 1985, pp. 14–26.

Clute, John. "Otherworld." *The Encyclopedia of Fantasy*, Digital Version, edited by John Clute and John Grant. 1997.

———. "Portals." *The Encyclopedia of Fantasy*, Digital Version, edited by John Clute and John Grant. 1997.

Coatney, Dereck. "Why Does Katniss Fail at Everything She Fakes?: Being versus Seeming to Be in the Hunger Games Trilogy." Dunn and Michaud, pp.178–192.

Coats, Karen. "Between Horror, Humor, and Hope: Neil Gaiman and the Psychic Work of the Gothic." *The Gothic in Children's Literature: Haunting the Borders*, edited by Anna Jackson, Karen Coats, and Roderick McGillis, Routledge, 2009, pp. 77–92.

———. *Looking Glasses and Neverlands: Lacan, Desire, and Subjectivity in Children's Literature*. University of Iowa Press, 2007.

Coats, Karen, and Farran Norris Sands. "Growing Up Frankenstein: Adaptations for Young Readers." *The Cambridge Companion to Frankenstein*, edited by Andrew Smith. Cambridge University Press, 2016. pp. 241–255.

Cochran, Tany R., and Jason A. Edwards. "*Buffy the Vampire Slayer* and the Quest Story: Revising the Hero, Reshaping the Myth." *Sith, Slayers, Stargates & Cyborgs: Modern Mythology in the New Millennium*, edited by John R. Perlich and David Whitt. Peter Lang, 2008, pp. 145–69.

Cohen, Jeffrey Jerome. "Monster Culture (Seven Theses)." *Monster Theory: Reading Culture*, edited by Jeffrey Jerome Cohen, University of Minnesota Press, 1996, pp. 3–25.

———. "Undead (A Zombie Oriented Ontology)." *Journal of the Fantastic in the Arts*, vol. 23, no. 3 [86], 2012, pp. 397–412.

Coker, Catherine. "That Girl: Bella, Buffy, and the Feminist Ethics of Choice in *Twilight* and in *Buffy the Vampire Slayer*." *Slayage* vol. 8, no.4 [32], Winter 2011.

Collins, Suzanne. *The Ballad of Songbirds and Snakes*. Scholastic Press, 2020.

———. *Catching Fire*. Scholastic Press, 2009.

———. *The Hunger Games*. Scholastic Press, 2008.

———. *Mockingjay*. Scholastic Press, 2010.

Creed, Barbara. "Horror and the Monstrous-Feminine: An Imaginary Abjection. *Screen*, vol. 27, No. 1, January/February 1986, pp. 44–71.

———. *The Monstrous-Feminine: Film, Feminism, Psychoanalysis*. Popular Fictions Series. Routledge, 2015.

Crenshaw, Kimberle. "Demarginalizing the Intersection of Race and Sex: A Black Feminist Critique of Antidiscrimination Doctrine, Feminist Theory and Antiracist Politics." *The University of Chicago Legal Forum*, iss. 1, art. 8, 1989, pp. 139–167.

Croft, Janet Brennan. "'What if I'm still there? What if I never left that clinic?': Faërian Drama in Buffy's 'Normal Again.'" *Slayage: The Journal of Whedon Studies*, 16.2 [48], Summer/Fall 2018. 29–51.

Davies, H. "Can Mary Shelley's Frankenstein Be Read as an Early Research Ethics Text?" *Medical Humanities*, vol. 30, no.1, 2004, 32–35.

Davies, Helen. *Neo-Victorian Freakery: The Cultural Afterlife of the Victorian Freak Show*. Palgrave Macmillan, 2015.

Davis, Lennard J. "Constructing Normalcy: The Bell Curve, the Novel, and the Invention of the Disabled Body in the Nineteenth Century." *The Disability Studies Reader*, Second Edition, edited by Lennard J. Davis. Routledge, 2006, pp. 3–16.

———. *Enforcing Normalcy: Disability, Deafness and the Body*. Verso, 1995.

Davis, Roger. "Why Should It Be Us Who Die for You?." *Handmaids, Tributes, and Carers: Dystopian Females' Roles and Goals*, edited by Myrna Santos, Cambridge Scholars Publishing, 2018, pp. 18–35.

Day, Giskin. "Good Grief: Bereavement Literature for Young Adults and *A Monster Calls*." *Medical Humanities*, vol. 38, no. 2, pp. 115–19.

Dean, John, and M.A. "The Uses of Wilderness in American Science Fiction" (Représentations de la nature sauvage dansla S-F américaine). *Science Fiction Studies*, vol. 9, no. 1, March 1982, pp. 68–81.

de Bruin-Molé, Megen. *Gothic Remixed: Monster Mashups and Frankenfictions in 21st-Century Culture*. Bloomsbury Academic, 2019.

Dendle, Peter. "The Zombie as Barometer of Cultural Anxiety." Niall Scott, pp. 45–57.

———. *The Zombie Movie Encyclopedia*. McFarland, 2001.

Dickinson, Emily. "One need not be a Chamber—to be Haunted—." (No. 670.) *The Complete Poems of Emily Dickinson*, edited by Thomas H. Johnson, Faber & Faber, 1975. p. 333.

Diehm, Jan, and Amber Thomas. "Someone Clever Once Said Women Were Not Allowed Pockets." (study.) *pudding.cool*. August 2018.

Doll, Mary Aswell. "Chapter 10: The Monster in Children's Dreams: Its Metaphoric Awe." *To the Lighthouse and Back: Writings on Teaching and Living*,

Counterpoints Vol. 19, Peter Lang, 1995, pp. 99–110.

Dunn, George A., and Nicolas Michaud, editors. *The Hunger Games and Philosophy: A Critique of Pure Treason.* Wiley, 2012.

Faircloth, Kelly. "Why Daryl Gregory Created a Zombie Messiah for Raising Stony Mayhall." *i09. Gizmodo.* July 19, 2011.

Farnia, Fatemeh, and Farideh Pourgiv. "Empowerment in *A Monster Calls* by Patrick Ness." *Linguistic and Literary Broad Research and Innovation*, vol. 6, no. 2, 2017, pp. 41–49.

Fetters, Ashley. "At Its Core, the 'Twilight' Saga Is a Story About." *The Atlantic* (Culture) November 15, 2012.

Fiedler, Leslie A. "The New World Savage as Stranger; or, 'Tis New to Thee.'" *The Stranger in Shakespeare.* Stein, 1972. 199–253.

Flanagan, Victoria. *Technology and Identity in Young Adult Fiction: The Posthuman Subject.* Palgrave Macmillan, 2014.

"Fool for Love." *Buffy the Vampire Slayer: The Complete Fifth Season on DVD*, season 5, episode 7, written by Douglas Petrie, directed by Nick Marck, Twentieth Century Fox Home Entertainment, 2003.

Foucault, Michel. *Abnormal: Lectures at the College de France 1974–1975*, edited by Valerio Marchetti and Antonella Salomoni, translated by Graham Burchell. Verso, 2003.

_____. *The History of Sexuality, Volume 1: An Introduction.* Translated by Robert Hurley, Vintage Books, 1990.

_____. "Of Other Spaces." Translated by Jay Miskowiecz, *Diacritics* vol. 16, no.1, Spring 1986, pp. 22–27.

Freud, Sigmund. *The Interpretation of Dreams. The Complete and Definitive text*, edited and translated by James Strachey. Basic Books, 2010.

_____. "The 'Uncanny.'" *The Standard Edition of the Complete Psychological Works of Sigmund Freud*, Volume XVII (1917–1919): *An Infantile Neurosis and Other Works*, edited by James Strachey, The Hogarth Press and the Institute of Psychoanalysis, pp. 217–256.

Gaiman, Neil. *Coraline.* Illustrated by Chris Riddell. HarperCollins, 2012.

_____. *The Graveyard Book.* Illustrated by Dave McKean. HarperCollins, 2008.

_____. "A Midsummer Night's Dream." *The Sandman* 19. D.C. Comics, 1990.

_____. *Neverwhere.* William Morrow Paperbacks, 2016.

Garriott, Evans Deidre Ann, Whitney Elaine Jones, and Julie Elizabeth Tyler, editors. *Space and Place in The Hunger Games: New Readings of the Novels.* McFarland, 2014.

Gelder, Ken. *Reading the Vampire.* Routledge, 1994.

George, Sam. "Spirited Away: Dream Work, the Outsider, and the Representation of Transylvania in the Pied Piper and Dracula Myth in Britain and Germany." *Dracula: An International Perspective*, edited by Marius-Mircea Crişan. Palgrave Gothic. Palgrave Macmillan, 2017, pp. 69–93.

Ghoshal, Nishan, and Paul O. Wilkinson. "Narrative Matters: A Monster Calls—A Portrayal of Dissociation in Childhood Bereavement." *Child and Adolescent Mental Health* June 8, 2018. pp. 1–2.

Giroux, Henry A. *Channel Surfing: Race Talk and the Destruction of Today's Youth.* Macmillan, 1997.

Glasglow, Jacqueline N. "Teaching Social Justice through Young Adult Literature." *The English Journal*, vol. 90, no .6, 2001, pp. 54–61.

Goebel. "'Embraced' by Consumption: *Twilight* and the Modern Construction of Gender." Anatol, pp. 169–78.

Goodfriend, Wind. "Relationship Violence in 'Twilight': How 'Twilight' teaches teens to love abusive relationships." *Psychology Today*, Nov 09, 2011.

Gooding, Richard. "'Something Very Old and Very Slow': Coraline, Uncanniness, and Narrative Form." *Children's Literature Association Quarterly*, vol. 33, no. 4, 2008, pp. 390–407.

Gordon, Charlotte. Introduction. *Frankenstein: The 1818 Text*, edited by Charlotte Gordon. Penguin, 2018.

Goss, Theodora. *European Travel for the Monstrous Gentlewoman.* The Extraordinary Adventures of the Athena Club Book 2. Saga Press, 2018.

_____. *The Sinister Mystery of the Mesmerizing Girl.* The Extraordinary Adventures of the Athena Club Book 3. Saga Press, 2019.

_____. *The Strange Case of the Alchemist's Daughter.* The Extraordinary

Adventures of the Athena Club Book 1. Saga Press, 2017.

Grant, Charles. "Development Tale: *The Girl with All the Gifts.*" *Sight & Sound*, October 2016, pp. 16–17.

Green, Miranda. *Symbol and Image in Celtic Religious Art*. Routledge, 2004.

Gregory, Daryl. *Raising Stony Mayhall*. Del Rey, 2011.

Griffin, Sarah Maria. *Spare and Found Parts*. Titan Books, 2018.

Grossberg, Lawrence. *We Gotta Get Out of This Place*. Routledge, 1992.

Grubbs, Jefferson. "Who's In The Photo With Ford & Arnold On 'Westworld'? This Mystery Has Already Been Solved." *Bustle*. December 2, 2016.

Gunn, Giles. "The Myth of the American Adam." *Handbook of American Folklore*, edited by. Richard M. Dorson and Inta Gale Carpenter. Indiana University Press, 1983. 79–85.

Halberstam, Jack. "Parasites and Perverts: An Introduction to Gothic Monstrosity." *The Monster Theory Reader*, edited by Jeffrey Andrew Weinstock, University of Minnesota Press, 2020, pp. 148–169.

Halberstam, Judith. *Skin Shows: Gothic Horror and the Technology of Monsters*. Duke University Press, 1995.

"Halloween." *Buffy the Vampire Slayer: The Complete Second Season on DVD*, season 2, episode 6, written by Carl Ellsworth, directed by Bruce Seth Green, Twentieth Century Fox Home Entertainment, 2002.

Hanlon, Tina L. "Coal Dust and Ballads: Appalachia and District 12." Pharr and Clark, pp. 49–58.

Haraway, Donna. "The Promises of Monsters: A Regenerative Politics of Inappropriate/d Others." Weinstock 459–521.

Hartcher, Peter. 'Is the Right-Wing Populist Monster Dying?' *The Sydney Morning Herald*. 27 May 2017.

Hayles, N. Katherine. *How We Became Posthtuman: Virtual Bodies in Cybernetics, Literarture, and Informatics*. University of Chicago Press, 1999.

Heaton, Sarah. "Re-dressing Revenants: Anxieties of the Body, the Self, and Desire When the Undead Make a Stylish Return." *The Supernatural Revamped: From Timeworn Legends to Twenty-First Century Chic*, edited by Barbara Brodman and James E. Dohan, Fairleigh University Press, 2016, pp. 145–59.

"Helpess." *Buffy the Vampire Slayer: The Complete Third Season on DVD*, season 3, Episode 12, written by David Fury, directed by James A. Contner. Twentieth Century Fox Home Entertainment, 2002.

Hesiod. *Works and Days*. Translated by Hugh G. Evelyn-White. [1914]. *Internet Sacred Text Archive*.

Hoggett, Reuben. "1880—Steam Man 'Frankenstein'—Hornburg (Australian)." *cyborneticzoo*. October 6, 2009.

"Homecoming." *Buffy the Vampire Slayer: The Complete Third Season on DVD*, season 3, Episode 5, written and directed by David Greenwalt. Twentieth Century Fox Home Entertainment, 2002.

Hourihan, Margery. *Deconstructing the Hero: Literary Theory and Children's Literature*. Routledge, 2005.

Housel, Rebecca. "The Real Danger: Fact vs. Fiction for the Girl Audience." Housel and Wisnewski, pp. 177–190.

Housel, Rebecca, and J. Jeremy Wisnewski, editors. *Twilight and Philosophy: Vampires, Vegetarianism, and the Pursuit of Immortality*. John Wiley & Sons, 2009.

Howarth, Michael. *Under the Bed, Creeping: Psychoanalyzing the Gothic in Children's Literature*. McFarland, 2014.

"Into the Woods." *Buffy the Vampire Slayer: The Complete Fifth Season on DVD*, season 5, episode 10, written and directed by Marti Noxon, Twentieth Century Fox Home Entertainment, 2003.

Jackson, Debra. "Throwing Like a Slayer: A Phenomenology of Gender Hybridity and Female Resilience in *Buffy the Vampire Slayer.*" *Slayage: The Journal of Whedon Studies*, vol. 14, no.1 [43], Winter 2016.

Jacobs, Joseph. "The Beauty and the Beast." Folktales of Aarne-Thompson-Uther type 425C translated and/or edited by D.L. Asliman. University of Pittsburgh.

Jenkinson-Brown, L. "Why Every Classicist Needs to Read: M R Carey's *The Girl with All the Gifts*." A Medium Corporation. *Teaching Classics*. August 27, 2016.

Jones, Ernest. *On the Nightmare*. 1931. Liveright Publishing Corporation, 1951.

Jung, C.G. *The Archetypes and the Collective Unconscious. The Collected Works of C.G. Jung* Complete digital ed., edited by Gerhard Adler, translated by R.F.C. Hull, vol 9. Part I., Bollinger Series XX, Princeton University Press, 1980.

Kar3ning. "What do you see in him again?" *Captain's log.* LiveJournal, 02:15 am November 22, 2009.

Kearney, Richard. *Strangers, Gods and Monsters: Interpreting Otherness.* Routledge, 2003.

Kennedy, John F. "The New Frontier." Democratic National Convention Nomination Acceptance Address, July 15, 1960. *American Rhetoric.*

Kennon, Patricia. "Monsters of Men: Masculinity and the Other in Patrick Ness's Chaos Walking Series." *Psychoanalytic Inquiry*, vol. 37, no. 1, 2017. pp. 25–34.

Kérchy, Anna. "Dilemmák a társadalmi nemek tudománya és a fogyatékosságtudomány metszéspontjain." *A felelet kérdései között: Fogyatékosságtudomány Magyarországon.* (FOTRI digitális könyvek 1.), edited by Ilona Hernádi and György Könczei. Eötvös Loránd Tudományegyetem Bárczi Gusztáv Gyógypedagógiai Kar, 2015, pp. 32–47.

Kérchy, Anna, and Andrea Zittlau. Introduction. *Exploring the Cultural History of Continental European Freak Shows and 'Enfreakment,'* edited by Anna Kérchy and Andrea Zittlau. Cambridge Scholars Publishing, 2012, pp. 1–19.

Kertzer, Adrienne. "Pathways' End: The Space of Trauma in Patrick Ness's Chaos Walking." *Bookbird: A Journal of International Children's Literature*, Vol. 50, No. 1, 2012, pp. 10–19.

Kim, Joo Ok, and Giselle Liza Anatol. "Trailing in Jonathan Harker's Shadow: Bella as Modern-Day Ethnographer in Meyer's *Twilight* Novels." Anatol, pp. 191–206.

King, Sharon D. "(Im)Mutable Natures: Animal, Human and Hybrid Horror." Pharr and Clark, pp. 108–117.

Klapcsik, Sandor. "The Double-edged Nature of Neil Gaiman's Ironical Perspectives and Liminal Fantasies." *Journal of the Fantastic in Arts*, vol 20, no. 2, 2000, pp. 193–209.

Kokotz, Daniel. "Frankenstein's Failure." *Frankenstein and Philosophy: The Shocking Truth*, Kindle ed., edited by Nicolas Michaud. Popular Culture and Philosophy, vol. 79. Open Court, 2013.

Komsta, Marta. "'Men are Noisy Creachers': Dystopian Consciousness in Patrick Ness's *Chaos Walking* Trilogy." *Explorations of Consciousness in Contemporary Fiction*, edited by Grzegorz Maziarczyk and Joanna Klara Teske, Brill Rodopi, 2017. pp. 38–55.

Kotanko, Alexandra. "A Daughter's Sacrifice: Saving the 'Good-Enough Mother' from the Good Mother Fantasy." *Mothers in Children's and Young Adult Literature: From the Eighteenth Century to Postfeminism.* Children's Literature Association Series, edited by Lisa Rowe Fraustino and Karen Coats, University Press of Mississippi, 2016, pp. 170–181.

Kristeva, Julia. "Approaching Abjection." *The Powers of Horror: An Essay on Abjection.* Translated by Leon. S. Roudiez. Columbia University Press, 1982, pp. 1–31.

Kushner, Tony. "Foreword: Notes Toward a Theater of the Fabulous." *Staging Lives: An Anthology of Contemporary Gay Theater*, edited by John M. Clum. Westview Press, 1996, pp. vii–ix.

Lauro, Sarah Juliet. Introduction. Lauro, *Zombie Theory*, pp. vii-xxiii.

Lauro, Sarah Juliet, editor. *Zombie Theory: A Reader*, University of Minnesota Press, 2017.

_____. *The Transatlantic Zombie: Slavery, Rebellion, and the Living Dead.* Rutgers University Le Fanu, J.S. *Uncle Silas: A Tale of Bartram-Haugh.* 1899. Project Gutenberg, 2005.

Le Guin, Ursula K. *The Language of the Night: Essays on Fantasy and Science Fiction.* HarperPerennial, 1989.

Lenz, Wylie. "Toward a Genealogy of the American Zombie Novel: From Jack London to Colson Whitehead." Bishop and Tenga, pp. 98–119.

Levina, Marina, and Diem-My T. Bui. "Introduction: Toward a Comprehensive Monster Theory in the 21st Century." *Monster Culture in the 21st Century: A Reader*, edited by Marina Levina and Diem-My T. Bui. London, Bloomsbury, 2013, pp. 1–13.

Lewis, R.W.B. *The American Adam: Innocence, Tragedy, and Tradition in the Nineteenth Century.* University of Chicago Press, 1959.

Liebelt, Claudia, Sarah Böllinger, and Ulf

Works Cited

Vierke, editors. *Beauty and the Norm: Debating Standardization in Bodily Appearance.* Palgrave Macmillan, 2019.

Limpár, Ildikó. "Arena on the Screen: Heterotopia and Theatricality in The Hunger Games Trilogy." *Displacing the Anxieties of Our World: Spaces of the Imagination,* edited by Ildikó Limpár. Cambridge Scholar Publishing, 2017, 177–199.

———. "GMO New World Garden: The Arena as Monster in Collins's The Hunger Games Trilogy." *TOPOS: Journal of Space and Humanities,* vol. V, no.1, edited by Éva Bús and Andrea F. Szabó, 2016, pp. 93–103.

———. "Masculinity, Visibility and the Vampire Literary Tradition in *What We Do in the Shadows.*" *Journal for the Fantastic in the Arts* vol. 29. no. 2, 2018, pp. 266–288.

———. "Smell of Roses and Blood: The Vampire Empire of The Hunger Games trilogy." *Monsters and the Monstrous,* vol. 4, no. 2, Winter 2014, pp. 15–24Logan, Peter Melville. "On Culture: Matthew Arnold's *Culture and Anarchy,* 1869." *BRANCH: Britain, Representation and Nineteenth-Century History,* edited by Dino Franco Felluga, Extension of *Romanticism and Victorianism on the Net.*

Lorrah, Jean. "Dracula Meets the New Woman." *The Blood Is the Life: Vampires in Literature,* edited by Leonard G. Heldreth and Mary Pharr. Popular Press, 1999, pp. 31–42.

Lower, Claire. "Confirmed: The Pockets on Women's Pants Are Indeed Bullshit." *lifehacker.* August 16, 2018.

Luckhurst, Roger. *Zombies: A Cultural History.* Reaktion Books Ltd., 2015.

Mann, Bonnie. "Vampire Love: The Second Sex Negotiates the Twenty-First Century." Housel and Wisnewski, pp. 131–145.

Marchbanks, Paul. "A Space, a Place: Visions of a Disabled Community in Mary Shelley's Frankenstein and The Last Man." *Body and Mind: Essays on Disability in Gothic Literature,* edited by Ruth Bienstock Anolik. McFarland, 2010, pp. 23–34.

Margolis, Rick. "The Last Battle: With 'Mockingjay' On Its Way, Suzanne Collins Weighs In On Katniss and the Capitol." (Interview with Susan Collins.) *School Library Journal.* August 1, 2010.

Martin, B. 2014. Political Muttation: "Real or Not Real?." Garriott, Jones and Tyler, pp. 220–242.

Marx, Leo. *The Machine in the Garden: Technology and the Pastoral Ideal in America.* 1964. Oxford University Press, 2000.

McClelland, Bruce A. *Slayers and Their Vampires: A Cultural History of Killing the Dead.* University of Michigan Press, 2006.

McCormack, Patricia. "Posthuman Teratology." Weinstock, pp. 522–39.

McCulloch, Sandra. "Star in *Twilight* vampire movies poor role model for girls says Victoria professor." *Times Colonist.* November 11, 2009.

McDonald, Brian. "'The Final Word on Entertainment': Mimetic and Monstrous Art in the Hunger Games." Dunn and Michaud, pp. 8–25.

McDonough, Megan, and Katherine A. Wagner. "Rebellious Natures: The Role of Nature in Young Adult Dystopian Female Protagonists' Awakenings and Agency." *Female Rebellion in Young Adult Dystopian Fiction,* edited by Sara Kay Day, Miranda A. Green-Barteet and Amy L. Montz. Ashgate, 2014. pp. 157–170.

McGuire, Seanan. *Beneath the Sugar Sky.* Wayward Children 3. Tor.com, 2018.

———. *Down Among the Sticks and Bones.* Wayward Children 2. Tor.com, 2017.

———. *Every Heart a Doorway.* Wayward Children 1., Tor.com, 2016.

McNally, David. *Monsters of the Market: Zombies, Vampires and Global Capitalism.* Haymarket Books, 2012.

McRuer, Robert. "Compulsory Able-Bodiedness and Queer/Disabled Existence." *The Disability Studies Reader,* Second Edition, edited by Lennard J. Davis. Routledge, 2006, pp. 301–8.

Mebane, John S. *Renaissance Magic and the Return of the Golden Age: The Occult Tradition and Marlowe, Johnson, and Shakespeare.* University of Nebraska, 1989.

Mendlesohn, Farah. *Rhetorics of Fantasy.* Wesleyan University Press, 2008.

Meyer, Robinson. "No Old Maps Actually Say 'Here Be Dragons.' But an Ancient Globe Does." *The Atlantic.* Technology. December 12, 2013.

Millard, Kenneth. *Coming of Age in Contemporary American Fiction.* Edinburgh University Press, 2007.

Mitchell, Jennifer. "A Mom-Shaped Hole." *Mothers in Children's and Young Adult Literature From the Eighteenth Century to Postfeminism*, edited by Lisa Rowe Fraustino and Karen Coats. University Press of Mississippi, 2016.

Monaghan, Patricia. *The Encyclopedia of Celtic Mythology and Folklore*. Facts on File, 2004.

Motoko, Rich. "The Graveyard Book Wins Newbery Medal." *The New York Times*. January 26, 2009.

Müller, Vivienne. "Same old 'Other' mother'?: Neil Gaiman's *Coraline*. *Outskirts Online Journal*, vol. 26, May 2012.

National Cancer Institute. "A Story of Discovery: Natural Compound Helps Treat Breast and Ovarian Cancers." *National Cancer Institute: Research*. March 31, 2015.

Ness, Patrick. *The Ask and the Answer*. Candlewick Press, 2010.

———. *The Knife of Never Letting Go*. Candlewick Press, 2009.

———. *A Monster Calls*. (From an original idea by Siobhan Dowd.) Walker Books, 2015.

———. *Monsters of Men*, Kindle edition, Candlewick Press, 2010.

Nicol, Rhonda. "'When you kiss me, I want to die': Arrested Feminism in *Buffy the Vampire Slayer* and the *Twilight* Series." Anatol, pp. 113–23.

"Nightmares" (1.10) *Buffy the Vampire Slayer: The Complete First Season on DVD*, season 1, episode 10, written by Joss Whedon and David Greenwalt, directed by Bruce Seth Green, Twentieth Century Fox Home Entertainment, 2002.

Nikolajeva, Maria. *Reading for Learning: Cognitive Approaches to Children's Literature*. John Benjamins Publishing Company, 2014.

Nodelman, Perry. *The Hidden Adult: Defining Children's Literature*. The Johns Hopkins University Press, 2008.

Nord, Glynda Joy. *Official State Flowers and Trees: Their Unique Stories*. Trafford Publishing, 2014.

"Normal Again." *Buffy the Vampire Slayer: The Complete Sixth Season on DVD*, season 6, episode 17, written by Diego Gutierrez, directed by Rick Rosenthal, Twentieth Century Fox Home Entertainment, 2004.

Olsson, Craig A., Lyndal Bond, Jane M. Burns, Dianne A. Vella-Brodrick, and Susan M. Sawyer. "Adolescent Resilience: A Concept Analysis." *Journal of Adolescence*, vol. 26, no. 1, 2003, pp. 1–11.

Ovid. (P. Ovidius Naso). *Metamorphoses*, edited and translated by Brookes More, Cornhill Publishing Co., 1922, Perseus Digital Library.

Oziewicz, Marek. "Growing Up with (Ir) Replaceable Parents: Neil Gaiman's *The Day I Swapped My Dad for Two Goldfish*, *Coraline*, and *The Graveyard Book*." *Bohemica litteraria*, vol. 18, no. 2, 2015, pp. 83–98.

Palatinus, Dávid Levente. "Humans, Machines and the Screen of the Athropocene." *Americana: E-Journal of American Studies in Hungary*, vol. XIII, no. 2, Fall 2017.

Panka, Daniel. "Transparent Subjects: Digital identity in Mary Shelley's *Frankenstein* and Charlie Brooker's '"Be Right Back."' *Science Fiction Studies*, v. 45, no. 2, 2018, pp. 308–324.

Parsons, Elizabeth, Naarah Sawers, and Kate McInally. "The Other Mother: Neil Gaiman's Postfeminist Fairytales." *Children's Literature Association Quarterly*, vol. 33, no. 4, 2008, pp. 371–389.

Pavlik, Anthony. "Absolute Power Games." Pharr and Clark, pp. 30–38.

Perkin, Joan. *Women and Marriage in Nineteenth-Century England*. 1989. Routledge, 2003.

Perry, David M. "The Author Remixing Narraitve Tropes to Improve Representation in Sci-Fi and Fantasy." *PacificStandard*, June 15, 2017.

Pharr, Mary F., and Leisa A. Clark, editors. *Of Bread, Blood and The Hunger Games: Critical Essays on the Suzanne Collins Trilogy*. Critical Explorations in Science Fiction and Fantasy 35. McFarland, 2012.

"Phases." *Buffy the Vampire Slayer: The Complete Second Season on DVD*, season 2, episode 15, written by Rob Des Hotel & Dean Batali, directed by Bruce Seth Green, Twentieth Century Fox Home Entertainment, 2002.

Pierson, David. "Turner Network Television's Made-for-TV Western Films and the Social Construction of Authenticity." *Film & History*, vol. 33, no. 2, 2003, pp. 55–64.

Prideaux, William Francis. *Mother Goose's Melodies*. A.H. Bullen, 1907. The Internet Archive.

"Primeval." *Buffy the Vampire Slayer: The Complete Fourth Season on DVD*, season 4, episode 21, written by David Fury, directed by James A. Contner, Twentieth Century Fox Home Entertainment, 2002.

"Prophecy Girl." *Buffy the Vampire Slayer: The Complete First Season on DVD*, season 1, episode 12, written and directed by Joss Whedon, Twentieth Century Fox Home Entertainment, 2002.

Renfro, Kim. "HBO made a secret map of the 'Westworld' offices and it shows how the park is run." *Insider* (Culture). Oct 14, 2016.

Renner, Karen J. *Evil Children in the Popular Imagination*. Palgrave Macmillan, 2016.

Renner, Karen J., editor. *The Evil Child in Literature, Film and Popular Culture*. Routledge, 2013.

"Reptile Boy." *Buffy the Vampire Slayer: The Complete Second Season on DVD*, season 2, episode 15, written by Rob Des Hotel and Dean Batali, directed by Bruce Seth Green, Twentieth Century Fox Home Entertainment, 2002.

Rhodes, Deborah L. *The Beauty Bias: The Injustice of Appearance in Life and Law*. Oxford University Press, 2010.

Risko, Guy Andre. "Katniss Everdeen's Liminal Choices and the Foundations of Revolutionary Ethics." Pharr and Clark, pp. 80–88.

Rocha, Lauren. "Wife, Mother, Vampire: The Female Role in the *Twilight* Series." *Journal of International Women's Studies*, vol. 15, no. 2, July 2014, pp. 286–298.

Ross, Sharon. "'Tough Enough': Female Friendship and Heroism in Xena and Buffy." *Action Chicks: New Images of Tough Women in Popular Culture*, edited by Sherrie A. Inness, Palgrave Macmillan, 2004.

Rubery, Jill. "Is equal pay actually possible?" *BBC News*. Business. February 22, 2019.

Rudd, David. "An Eye for an I: Neil Gaiman's *Coraline* and Questions of Identity." *Children's Literature in Education*, no. 39, 2008, pp. 159–68.

Ruland, Richard, and Malcolm Bradbury. *From Puritanism to Postmodernism: A History of American Literature*. Penguin Books, 1992.

Rusvai, Mónika. "Szörnyeteg apaszerepben. (Neil Gaiman: A temető könyve.)" [Monster in the role of the father. (Neil Gaiman: The Graveyard Book.)] *Szkholion* 2017/2. 95–102.

Rutherford, Jennifer. *Zombies*. (Shortcuts.) Routledge, 2013.

Ryle, Robin. "Book Review: Raising Stony Mayhall." *You Think Too Much* Blog, February 10, 2012.

Salovey, Peter, Alexander J. Rothman, Jerisha B. Detweiler, and Wayne T. Steward. "Emotional States and Physical Health." *American Psychologist*, vol. 55, no. 1, 2000, pp. 110–121.

Sambell, Kay. "Carnivalizing the Future: A New Approach to Theorizing Childhood and Adulthood in Science Fiction for Young Readers." *The Lion and the Unicorn*, vol. 28, no. 2, 2004, pp. 247–267.

———. "Presenting the Case for Social Change: The Creative Dilemma of Dystopian Writing for Children." *Utopian and Dystopian Writing for Children and Young Adults*, edited by Carrie Hintz and Elaine Ostry, Routledge, 2003, pp. 163–78.

Saravia Vargas, José Roberto, and Juan Carlos Saravia Vargas. "A Girl in the Dark with Monsters: The Convergence of Gothic Elements and Children's Literature in Neil Gaiman's Coraline." *Revista de Lenguas Modernas*, no. 21, 2014, pp. 77–94.

Schmid, David. "The Limits of Zombies: Monsters for a Neoliberal Age." *Zombie Talk: Culture, History, Politics*, written by David R. Castillo, David Schmid, David A. Reilly, and John Edgar Browning. Palgrave MacMillan, 2016, pp. 92–107.

"School Hard." *Buffy the Vampire Slayer: The Complete Second Season on DVD*, season 2, episode 3, written by Joss Whedon and David Greenwalt, directed by John T. Kretchmer, Twentieth Century Fox Home Entertainment, 2002.

Scott, Niall, editor. *Monsters and the Monstrous: Myths and Metaphors of Enduring Evil*. At the Interface series. Rodopi, 2007.

Scott, Walter. [Review of Frankenstein.] *Blackwood's Edinburgh Magazine* 2 (March 1818): 613–20.

Seelinger Trites, Roberta. *Disturbing the Universe: Power and Depression in Adolescent Literature*. University of Iowa Press, 2000.

———. "Theories and Possibilities of Adolescent Literature." *Children's Association Quarterly*, vol. 21, no. 1, Spring 1996, pp. 2–3.

Shaffel, Andre. "The Joy of Watching Others Suffer: Schadenfreude and the Hunger Games." Dunn and Michaud, pp. 75–89.

Shaheen, Naseeb. *Biblical References in Shakespeare's Plays*. University of Delaware Press, 1999.

Shakespeare, William. *Hamlet*, edited by Ann Thompson and Neil Taylor. Arden Shakespeare Third Series, Bloomsbury, 2006.

———. *Macbeth*, edited by Sandra Clark and Pamela Mason, The Arden Shakespeare Third Series, Bloomsbury, 2015.

———. *Romeo and Juliet*, edited by and Reneì Weis. The Arden Shakespeare Third Series, Bloomsbury, 2012.

———. *The Tempest*, edited by Frank Kermode. The Arden Shakespeare. Thomas Nelson and Sons, 1998.

Simon, Erika. "Satyr-plays on Vases in the time of Aeschylos." *The Eye of Greece: Studies in the Art of Athens*, edited by Donna Kurtz and Brian Sparkes. Cambridge University Press, 1982. 123–148.

Sincero, Sarah Mae. "Stress and Coping Mechanisms." *Explorable*, November 13, 2012.

Skovron, Jon. *Man Made Boy*. Speak, 2013.

Skura, Meredith Ann. "Discourse and the Individual: The Case of Colonialism and *The Tempest*." *Shakespeare Quaterly*, no. 40, 1989, pp. 42–69.

Stevenson, John Allen. "A Vampire in the Mirror: The Sexuality of Dracula." *PMLA* vol. 103, no. 2, 1988, pp. 139–49.

TalkTim. "Interview: Novelist Daryl Gregory on *Raising Stony Mayhall*." Blogcritics.org. July 12, 2011.

Tallerico, Brian. "A Simple Guide to *Westworld*'s Multiple Timelines." *Vulture*. November 30, 2016.

Thacker, Eugene. "Nekros; or, The Poetics of Biopolitics." Lauro, *Zombie Theory*, pp. 361–80.

Thompson, R. Lowe. *The History of the Devil—The Horned God of the West Magic and Worship*. 1929. Kindle ed. Home Farm Books, 2008.

Torkelson, Anne. "Somewhere between Hair Ribbons and Rainbows: How Even the Shortest Song Can Change the World." Dunn and Michaud, pp. 26–40.

"Trace Decay." *Westworld*, season 1, episode 8. HBO Entertainment, November 20, 2016.

Van Dyke, Christina. "Discipline and the Docile Body: Regulating Hungers in the Capitol." Dunn and Michaud, pp. 250–264.

Varner, Gary R. *The Mythic Forest, the Green Man and the Spirit of Nature: The Re-emergence of the Spirit of Nature from Ancient Times Into Modern Society*. Algora Publishing, 2006.

Vonberg, Judith. "'Women must earn less than men,' Polish politician says." *CNN World*. Europe. March 3, 2017.

Waugaman, Elizabeth Pearson. "Names and Identity: The Native American Naming Tradition." *Psychology Today*, July 8, 2011.

Weinstock, Jeffrey Andrew, editor. *The Monster Theory Reader*. University of Minnesota Press, 2020.

Weinstock, Jeffrey Andrew. "Introduction: A Genealogy of Monster Theory." Weinstock pp. 1–36.

"The Well-Tempered Clavier." *Westworld*, season 1, episode 9. HBO Entertainment, November 27, 2016.

White, Ray. "The Good Guys Wore White Hats: The B Western in American Culture." *Wanted Dead or Alive: The American West in Popular Culture*, edited by Richard Aquila, University of Illinois Press, 1996. pp. 135–59.

WHSmith. "Patrick Ness: An Exclusive Interview on A Monster Calls." *WHSmith blog*. December 16, 2016.

Wilcox, Rhonda. *Why Buffy Matters: The Art of Buffy the Vampire Slayer*. I.B. Tauris, 2005.

Williams, Anne. *Art of Darkness: A Poetics of Gothic*. University of Chicago Press, 1995.

Winckler, Reto. "This Great Stage of Androids: *Westworld*, Shakespeare and the World as Stage." *Journal of Adaptation in Film & Performance*, vol. 10, no. 2, July 2017, pp. 169–188.

Wise, Jeff. *Extreme Fear: The Science of Your Mind in Danger*, Kindle ed., MaSci series, St. Martin's Griffin, Reprint edition, 2011.

Wolff, Cynthia Griffin. "The Radcliffean

Gothic Model: A Form for Feminine Sexuality." *The Female Gothic*, edited by Julian Fleenor. Eden Press, 1983, pp. 207–223.

Wolk, Steven. "Reading for a Better World: Teaching Social Responsibility with Young Adult Literature. *Journal of Adolescent & Adult Literacy*, vol. 52, no. 8, 2009, pp. 664–73.

Wright, Alexa. "Monstrous Strangers at the Edge of the World: The Monstrous Races." Weinstock, pp. 173–191.

Young, Susan C. "Bella no match for Sookie at vampire love: Subservient 'Twilight' heroine a terrible model for pre-teen girls." *Today Television*. June 10, 2009.

youtubehead. "OMG. The photo of Arnold is Bernard. If you photoshop Bernard, as clean shaven, and Caucasian, he'll look like Arnold." *Reddit*. November 6, 2016.

Zack, Naomi. "Bella Swan and Sarah Palin: All the Old Myths are NOT True." Housel and Jeremy Wisnewski, pp. 121–129.

"The Zeppo." *Buffy the Vampire Slayer: The Complete Third Season on DVD*, season 3, Episode 13, written by Dan Vebber, directed by James Whitmore, Jr., Twentieth Century Fox Home Entertainment, 2002.

Zizek, Slavoj. "How the Non-Duped Err." *Qui Parle: Literature, Philosophy, Visual Arts, History*, vol. 4, no. 1, 1990, pp. 1–20.

Index

abjection 1, 4, 26, 27, 60, 75–78, 137, 210–211, 226, 234
Adam Iron *see* Iron, Adam
adaptiveness 8, 14, 23, 165, 167, 168, 178
agency 18, 27, 36–37, 54–56, 89, 91, 95–96, 105, 111, 116–117, 119, 134, 137–138, 148, 170, 197, 202, 206, 232
alien 12, 160, 163–166, 169, 173, 175, 178–181, 216
American Adam 12–13, 161, 179, 182–183, 194, 217
American Eve 12–13, 179, 183, 217
android 14, 71, 197–202, 207–210, 212–213, 217, 234; *see also* robot
anthropocentrism 51, 221; *see also* post-anthropocentrism
apocalypse 7–8-9, 19, 36, 40, 43–44, 48, 50–51, 53, 56, 58, 80, 222
archetype 1, 11, 17, 109, 119, 125–126, 139, 144, 146, 230
artificial intelligence 58, 71, 197

Bella Swan *see* Swan, Bella
Bod Owens *see* Owens, Nobody
Buffy Summers *see* Summers, Buffy
Buffy, the Vampire Slayer 5–7, 16, 18–19, 23–24, 28–29, 31–35, 222

Capitol 13, 181–191, 193, 195, 232–233
Chaos Walking 12, 160–162, 166–167, 173, 221
civilization 12–13, 73, 160, 162, 181, 204–206, 210, 217
communication 3, 9, 49, 91, 108, 111, 123, 138, 154–155, 165, 168, 172–173, 176–177, 179, 182, 192, 194, 196, 222, 232
consumerism 7, 21–22, 34–35, 206, 226
coping 6, 18, 20, 26, 70, 72, 86, 89, 118–119, 121, 145, 152, 156, 162, 163, 175, 183, 186–187, 191, 219; coping mechanism 10, 11, 12, 77, 119, 123, 131, 132, 139, 156; maladaptive coping mechanism 132, 156;
Coraline 109–119, 122–123, 144–145, 149, 151, 170–171, 229–230

Coraline 10–11, 62, 100, 109, 113–116, 118, 122–123, 139, 145–146, 150, 155, 170, 222, 229–230
cyborg 9, 62, 73

deviant 10, 63–64, 72, 134, 157, 164; *see also* non-normative
disability 12, 63, 65–67, 73, 80, 154, 227
disprivileged 8, 36, 52, 54, 57, 65, 67, 81–82, 98; *see also* marginalization
Dr. Jekyll 24, 68, 83
Dr. Jekyll and Mr. Hyde 68, 83–84, 89, 95
double 11–12, 42, 92, 102, 115, 143
Dracula 17, 21, 112
Dracula 17, 83, 231
dystopia 8, 12–13, 39, 50–51, 53–55, 58, 61, 72, 80, 160, 166, 171, 178, 184, 191, 193–196, 214, 216, 219–221, 232

Eade, Viola 161, 164, 159, 172–173, 177, 180
Everdeen, Katniss 13, 182–189, 191–195, 232–233

fairness *see* justice
faith 21, 34, 130–132; *see also* religion
femininity 17–18, 23, 37, 92, 112, 146, 148, 226, 231
feminism 27, 61, 82, 87–88, 96–97, 205, 226
film 2, 4, 16, 18, 37, 39, 60, 67, 108, 209, 213, 219–222, 225, 227, 234; *see also* movie; television
Frankenstein 8–9, 58–59, 61, 68–71, 74, 82–83, 86, 94, 98, 143, 188, 190, 208, 222, 228, 233
Frankenstein 8, 58–59, 61–62, 68–69, 71, 77, 79–80, 83, 86, 97–98, 190, 196–197, 222, 227, 233
Frankensteinian 5, 9, 13, 29, 58, 61, 68, 72–74, 76–77, 81, 94, 143, 166, 188, 197
Freud, Sigmund 1, 17, 74, 84, 96, 112, 126–127, 132, 170, 213, 229–230
friendship 6–7, 11, 16, 19, 23–24, 27–33,

247

248   Index

41–44, 64, 66, 77, 94, 102, 104, 107, 152, 167, 176, 205, 226
frontier 12–14, 159–160, 168, 181–183, 198, 200–201, 207, 209, 211, 213, 214; *see also* Wild West

gender 9–10, 24, 64, 77, 81–82, 85, 88–90, 92, 96, 98, 143–146, 148, 151, 154, 157, 162, 174, 222, 226, 229, 231, 233
The Girl with All the Gifts 8, 36, 38, 48, 221
The Graveyard Book 10–11, 100–101, 105–106, 108–109, 113, 116, 118–119, 122, 134, 146, 222, 228

hero 5, 12, 18–19, 24–26, 28–29, 31, 44–45, 51–52, 56, 65, 100, 136, 145, 147, 161, 175, 179, 182–183, 189, 192, 194, 204, 207, 209, 216, 225–226, 232; superhero 34, 39, 43–45, 47, 65, 182
heroine *see* hero
Hewitt, Todd 13, 160–161, 163, 169–173, 175–180, 232
home 5–6, 12, 32, 34, 40, 66, 73, 75, 84, 94–95, 101–102, 107, 109, 116, 118–119, 140–141, 145, 151–157, 162, 171, 222, 229–231
hope 8, 26–28, 39, 50, 52, 55, 57, 82, 126, 129, 134, 137–138, 140–141, 153, 161, 165–166, 170, 173, 178, 194–195, 203, 219–223, 233
hubris 8–9, 68, 70, 73–74, 83, 147, 167, 175, 190
The Hunger Games 182–185, 188–189, 191–192, 196, 232–233
The Hunger Games 13, 53, 181, 183, 185, 187–188, 191, 193, 195–196, 232–233
hybridity 3, 9–10, 16, 20, 73–74, 82, 84–85, 103–104, 107, 111, 124, 147, 163–164, 173, 175, 177–179, 190, 194–195, 210, 221, 227, 231–232

innocence 19, 160–161, 169–170, 181, 194, 206, 219
integrity 13, 18, 47, 53, 56, 67, 77, 80, 119, 127, 129, 150, 153–155, 160, 171, 173, 176, 194–195
invisibility 20, 44, 67, 70, 77–78, 93, 97, 104–106, 109, 134–135, 204, 230, 234; *see also* visibility
Iron, Adam 65–66, 69
isolation 9, 23, 28–29, 32, 36, 62, 65, 72–73, 79–80, 125, 141, 152, 168–169, 176–178, 182, 200, 220

Jack and Jill *see* Wolcott, Jack; Wolcott, Jill
Jack Wolcott *see* Wolcott, Jack
Jill Wolcott *see* Wolcott, Jill
justice 11, 51, 118–119, 128, 207, 220, 234; injustice 63, 65, 68, 129, 189

liminality 3, 20, 32, 38, 56, 82, 84–85, 88–89, 95, 97–98, 101, 135, 149, 157, 228
living dead *see* undead

mad scientist 9, 12, 83, 143, 146–147, 151–152
Man Made Boy 8, 58, 61, 63, 65–68, 71–72, 79–81, 91, 222
marginalization 53, 60, 63–65, 67, 69, 87–89, 92, 95–96, 98, 157, 165–166, 174; *see also* disprivileged
masculinity 18, 24, 78, 92, 204–207, 225–226, 230, 233
Mayhall, Stony 8, 38–54, 56
mental landscape 6, 10–11, 109–110, 118–119, 121, 137, 144–145
Mr. Hyde 24, 68, 71, 83–84
A Monster Calls 10–11, 121, 123, 126, 136, 139, 141, 155–157, 222, 230
movie 42, 207, 233, 234; *see also* film; television

New World 6, 12–13, 41, 50, 73, 125, 160, 161–162, 169–170, 181–182, 194, 213, 217, 232–233
New Word (planet) 160–161, 163–166, 169–170, 173–174, 178, 231
non-normative 60, 65, 75, 171, 222; *see also* deviant
nostalgy 14, 167, 200, 206–207, 211, 216–217

O'Malley, Conor 11, 121–139, 141, 156
oppression 9, 36, 53, 66, 81, 86–88, 91, 93, 97–98, 162, 165, 175, 181, 189, 232
the Other Mother 110–11, 113–114, 116–118, 120, 145, 149, 170–171, 229–230
otherworld 10–11, 101, 111, 113–116, 123, 141, 144–145, 147, 151, 154–155, 229–230
Owens, Nobody 101–108, 110, 113, 116–117, 119, 122, 134

patriarchy 18, 77, 81–82, 85–86, 88, 90–91, 93, 96–97, 170, 232
post-anthropocentrism 178, 180; *see also* anthropocentrism
post-apocalyptic *see* apocalypse
posthuman 17, 37, 73–75, 178, 180
President Snow 13, 181–182, 184, 188, 190, 192, 196, 232–233
psychic landscape *see* mental landscape
psychoanalysis 1, 6, 10, 17, 74, 123, 141, 155, 222, 231; *see also* psychology
psychology 4, 62, 75, 82, 119, 136, 137–139, 144, 152, 170, 198, 226, 229, 231, 234; *see also* psychoanalysis

queerness 11–12, 61, 65–68

Index

raising *see* resurrection
Raising Stony Mayhall 8, 36, 38–39, 50, 221
rebel 4, 8, 12, 53, 58, 74, 85, 115, 145, 192, 194, 216, 232
religion 21, 43, 46, 58, 162, 166; *see also* faith
resurrection 8, 41, 43–48, 71, 76, 79, 125, 146, 153, 226
robot 14, 71, 73–74, 76–80, 166, 197–198, 210, 214; *see also* android
romance 6–7, 9, 16–18, 20, 25–26, 28, 162; *see also* vampire romance

Shelley, Mary 8, 58–60, 62, 68–69, 71, 77, 83, 86, 97–98, 143, 191, 196–197
Shelley, Percy Bysse 227–228
Silas 11, 102–105, 107, 229–230
Spare and Found Parts 9, 58, 61, 72, 79–81, 222
Stevenson, Robert Louis 68, 83
Stony Mayhall *see* Mayhall, Stony
Summers, Buffy 7, 18–19, 23–34, 226
supernatural romance *see* vampire romance
Swan, Bella 7, 19–23, 25–35, 226

technology 9, 13, 37, 58, 61, 64–65, 71–73, 79–80, 162, 163–167, 181, 183, 189–191, 196–198, 200–201, 205, 210, 213–214, 217, 233–234
television 5–6, 13, 18, 28, 113, 197–198, 204–206, 213, 222, 227, 233; *see also* film; movie
Todd Hewitt *see* Hewitt, Todd
transgression 2, 4, 8–10, 16–17, 70, 78, 81, 83–85, 92–97, 103, 115, 149, 150, 187, 197, 206, 208–210, 222, 231–232
trauma 10–12, 68, 70, 82, 93, 95–96, 119, 121–122, 125, 127, 137–138–139, 141, 145, 155, 162, 174, 179, 183, 187, 219, 222, 231
TV *see* television
Twilight 6–7, 16, 18–21, 23, 25, 27, 31, 3–34, 226

uncanny 1, 12, 26, 40, 42, 60, 75, 107, 109–112, 115–119, 151, 197, 226, 229–230, 232
undead 7, 16–17, 20, 36, 37, 38, 40, 42, 44, 51, 53–54, 103, 147–149, 151

vampire 5–7, 11–12, 15–26, 27–28, 30, 32–36, 38, 83, 102–104, 111–112, 144, 146–153, 225–231, 233
vampire romance 5–6, 16–18, 225–226; *see also* romance
Viola Eade *see* Eade, Viola
visibility 13, 16–17, 20, 67, 70, 73, 104–105, 117, 134, 172, 189, 192, 204, 207, 212, 214, 217, 225; *see also* invisibility

Wayward Children 10–11, 139–142, 155, 157, 222
Westworld 201, 203–209, 211, 213–216
Westworld 13–14, 197–198, 201, 203, 208, 211, 214–217, 222, 234
Wild West 13, 198, 200, 204, 207, 209, 211, 213; *see also* frontier
Wolcott, Jack 11–12, 141–148, 150–155
Wolcott, Jill 11–12, 141–155, 231

Zombie 5–8, 36–57, 149, 221, 227, 233